THE *impossible* DAVID LYNCH

FILM AND CULTURE SERIES: JOHN BELTON, GENERAL EDITOR

THE *impossible*
DAVID LYNCH

TODD McGOWAN

COLUMBIA UNIVERSITY PRESS   NEW YORK

Columbia University Press
Publishers Since 1893
New York   Chichester, West Sussex

Library of Congress Cataloging-in-Publication Data
McGowan, Todd.
    The impossible David Lynch / Todd McGowan
        p.   cm. — (Film and culture)
    Includes bibliographical references and index.
    ISBN-13: 978-0-231-13954-0 (cloth : alk. paper)
    ISBN-10: 0-231-13954-3 (cloth : alk. paper)
    — ISBN 0-231-13955-1 (pbk. : alk. paper)
    1. Lynch, David, 1946– —Criticism and
interpretation.   I. Title.   II. Series.

PN1998.3.L96M34 2007
791.43023'3092—dc22
[B]   2006028223

Columbia University Press books are printed on
permanent and durable acid-free paper.

Printed in the United States of America

c 10 9 8 7 6 5 4 3 2 1
p 10 9 8 7 6 5 4 3 2

For Dashiell and Theo Neroni, who allowed me
to understand *Eraserhead*

CONTENTS

ACKNOWLEDGMENTS

Thanks to the University of Texas Press for permitting me to reprint material that first appeared in Cinema Journal. Much of chapter 7 originally appeared as "Finding Ourselves on a Lost Highway: David Lynch's Lesson in Fantasy," *Cinema Journal* 39.2 (Winter 2000): 51–73, and much of chapter 9 appeared as "Lost on *Mulholland Drive*: Navigating David Lynch's Panegyric to Hollywood," *Cinema Journal* 43.2 (Winter 2004): 67–89, copyright © 2000 and 2004 by the University of Texas Press; all rights reserved.

I owe a tremendous debt to Juree Sondker at Columbia University Press for having faith in the book even when this faith seemed misplaced, and to Roy Thomas for his careful work on the manuscript.

Thanks to Dashiell and Theo Neroni, for sitting patiently while I first composed many of the chapters, and for providing relief when I wasn't composing anything.

Many of the ideas in this book were refined over two summer courses, during which the contributions of many students, including those of Cate Racek, Sara Burnett, Carly Marino, and Jonathan Sanborn, were extremely helpful.

Thanks to Elisabeth Bronfen, whose thoughtful comments on the manuscript allowed me to see the overall direction of the argument in a new light.

I would like to thank Ken Reinhard for putting together the Seminar on Experimental Critical Theory in the summer of 2004, which informed the direction of my thoughts on Lynch and allowed me the opportunity to present what ultimately developed into the conclusion of this book.

Slavoj Žižek provided an insightful reading of the manuscript, and his work has remained the starting point and the end point for my approach to Lynch.

My conversations with David Jenemann allowed me to anticipate many of the potential objections to the arguments advanced here.

Anna Kornbluh was instrumental in advancing my thought and helping me to work through many of the issues of the book.

Quentin Martin also helped me to develop my thinking on Lynch.

Thanks to Sarah Nilsen and Jean Wyatt for their conscientious analysis of significant portions of the book and for highlighting its most dogmatic moments.

I owe a huge debt to Phil Foster for reviewing the book in a rough form and for helping me to construct a first intelligible draft.

I appreciate Daniel Norford's careful reading of the manuscript.

Myles Jewell provided a detailed reading that helped highlight all the places where the book wasn't clear.

Thanks to Vinney Cavallo for the subtle suggestions that made this a much more readable and accurate work.

Finally, thanks to Walter Davis, Paul Eisenstein, and Hilary Neroni, who have informed everything I think about Lynch and have acquainted themselves so thoroughly with this book that they have almost written it themselves.

THE *impossible* DAVID LYNCH

INTRODUCTION The Bizarre Nature of Normality

Watching from a Distance

The greatness of a work of art depends on its ability to transform the audience. As Rilke formulates it in his poem "The Archaic Torso of Apollo," the great work of art tells us that we have to change our lives.[1] If one accepts this definition, it immediately throws the idea of a great film into doubt. Though we may project ourselves into filmic narratives through identification with the camera or with characters, the limitations of the medium mean that the film we are watching never sees us and never addresses us directly. Perhaps this is why Orson Welles insists that "no movie that will ever be made is worthy of being discussed in the same breath [with one of Shakespeare's plays]."[2] One doesn't simply watch a play; as an audience member, one is part of the performance—or at least one has the possibility of seeing how the performance takes its audience into account. A play from Shakespeare can address its audience members directly and demand that they change their own lives based on what transpires on the stage. For their part, novels involve their readers by demanding an imaginative act that completes the artwork. But the cinema is predicated on the distance that the viewing situation tends to create between spectators and what they see on the screen.

Spectators watch from a distance; they watch the screen images from a position that ensures their lack of direct involvement in what they see. In contrast with attending a play, watching a film, as numerous film theorists have noted, allows us a high degree of anonymity. Much of the appeal of film spectatorship stems from our ability to watch filmic events without being seen. The unidirectional viewing situation permits the spectator to remain safe within the anonymity of darkness.[3]

The distance between screen and spectator becomes a more significant problem insofar as it so often remains unperceived amid the illusory presence of screen images and events. Through identification with the camera and characters, the spectator attains a sense of proximity and involvement with what transpires on the screen. When watching a film, one often feels oneself in a position internal to the events rather than external. But this proximity is imaginary, proximity from a distance, and the distance allows the spectator to avoid any encounter in the cinema that might challenge or alter the spectator's subjectivity. Any experience of a film's immediacy is a thoroughly mediated one because characters on screen remain seen but never see while the spectator sees without being seen.

From his first feature *Eraserhead* (1977) through each of his subsequent films, the films of David Lynch present a challenge to this viewing situation. The great achievement of his films lies in their ability to break down the distance between spectator and screen. Rather than permitting the imaginary proximity that dominates in mainstream cinema, Lynch's films implicate the spectator in their very structure. The structure of a Lynch film alters the cinematic viewing situation itself and deprives the spectator of the underlying sense of remaining at a safe distance from what takes place on the screen. Lynch includes cinematic moments that force the spectator to become aware of how the film itself takes into account the spectator's desire. His films confront one with sequences that reveal one's own investment in what one sees.

It is in this sense that Lynch is "weird": one cannot watch a Lynch film in the way that one watches a standard Hollywood film nor in the way that one watches most radical films. The structure of a Lynch film challenges the spectator's traditional experience of the cinema just as it engages and challenges the history of film theory. The aim of this book is to take up that challenge and to pursue the theoretical possibilities presented to us in Lynch's films.

Lynch's challenge to spectators departs significantly from the approach that dominates radical cinema, which consists in enhancing the spectator's sense of distance from events on the screen rather than eliminating it. This approach has informed not just how alternative filmmakers construct their films but also how theorists have conceived the possibility of a radical cinema. To understand Lynch's uniqueness as a filmmaker, we must first examine the alternative that his films defy.

Psychoanalytic film theorists in the late 1960s and 1970s such as Christian Metz and Jean-Louis Baudry were attuned to cinema's ability to create spectators who watch at a distance without at the same time having any awareness of this distance. They saw this viewing situation as the primary way in which cinema functioned ideologically to aid in subjecting spectators. While watching a film, as Metz puts it, "it is always the other who is on the screen; as for me, I am there to look at him. I take no part in the perceived, on the contrary, I am *all-perceiving*. All-perceiving as one says all-powerful (this is the famous gift of 'ubiquity' the film gives its spectator); all-perceiving, too, because I am entirely on the side of the perceiving instance."[4] The act of watching a film, according to this way of thinking, is a one-way experience in which the spectator has no involvement in what is visible on the screen. By leaving the spectator in this situation of being "all-perceiving," the cinema allows the spectator to experience the combination of distance from and proximity to the screen events, a combination that permits the spectator to be simultaneously involved and not.

Insofar as it works to sustain spectator distance, the cinema seems fundamentally voyeuristic. As Laura Mulvey notes, "the extreme contrast between the darkness in the auditorium (which also isolated the spectators from one another) and the brilliance of the shifting patterns of light and shade on the screen helps to promote the illusion of voyeuristic separation."[5] Mulvey is careful to note here that the separation or distance inherent in cinematic voyeurism (and in voyeurism as such) is illusory. Why? The thrill of voyeurism depends on a fundamental failure of self-recognition. The voyeur believes that she/he is looking at a scene that simply exists in itself and that has not been constructed for her/his look. Hence, the voyeur can see others in their private world, what exists beneath their public face, and the voyeur's enjoyment derives from seeing this private world. This utterly private moment would be, in the thinking of the voyeur, what others were really like, how they appear when no one is looking.

But when the voyeur looks on this private moment, what she/he misses is its structured nature. Even the most intimate moments in our lives structure themselves around a public look, even when that look is absent. The subject in a private moment continues, albeit most often unconsciously, to act and present her/himself for an imagined look.[6] We perform our intimate activities in ways that confirm a certain idea we have of ourselves, and this self-image implies an external look— what Freud calls an ego ideal—that apprehends it. The implicit on-looker gives meaning and structure to the private activity. Without the implicit onlooker or ego ideal, we would have no sense of how to act in private, no method for organizing our private lives.[7] In short, the scene that the voyeur witnesses is always a scene created for the look of the voyeur, and this is what the voyeur cannot see.

There is something fundamentally disappointing about voyeurism: it never sees what it's looking for but instead sees a moment created for its look. The structured nature of the private moment is most emphati-cally true in the case of cinema: we cannot even imagine a film not or-ganized around the look of a spectator, and yet this is precisely what most films—and, just as importantly, most spectators—attempt to dis-avow. In this sense, the film itself does look back at the spectators inso-far as its very structure takes their desire as spectators into account. There is no film that has been made not to be seen.[8]

While watching a film, especially a typical Hollywood film, the spec-tator does not experience her/himself playing a role in the events. They happen—the film plays—and the spectator simply looks on. What be-comes masked in this situation is the structuring dynamic behind the events: what the spectator sees on the screen is not simply there to be seen, but created specifically with the spectator's look in mind. Every event on the screen anticipates a spectator who completes it through the act of watching. Rather than being uninvolved with and distanced from the events on the screen, the spectator is fully enmeshed.[9]

Not only does the combination of distance and proximity inform the cinematic viewing situation itself, but it also informs the societal atti-tude to the cinema as such. Spectators keep the cinema itself at a dis-tance by consigning it to the realm of fantasy and seeing it as a place of escape from their daily reality. If we try to think through the disturbing or traumatic nature of a film we have seen, we often hear—or even say to ourselves—that "it's just a movie." The common practice of critics calling hit films "great rides," as if the cinema were an amusement park, fits into this pattern of distancing. If we conceive of the cinema solely as an escape, then we dissociate ourselves from what takes place there. One goes to the cinema for fun, for release, but never for an experience that might impact one's real life. Even films that don't promise fun in the traditional sense—like *Monster* (Patty Jenkins, 2003) or *Schindler's List* (Steven Spielberg, 1993)—offer us a glimpse of a foreign world that we tend to see as having no relation to our own.

At the same time that spectators relegate cinema to the status of an escape, they also accept the reality of what they see in the cinema. Spectators distance themselves from the cinema and its effects by acknowledging its purely fantasmatic status, and yet when they go to the cinema, they take the images on the screen seriously. As spectators, we tend to endow film with what Joel Black calls the "reality effect." According to Black, "one of film's key effects has been to provide viewers with a kind of enhanced, X-ray vision that allows them to feel that they can penetrate the veil of superficial appearances and see the hidden structure of reality itself."[10] The ability to "see the hidden structure of reality itself" is, of course, false, but it nonetheless informs the nature of the cinematic experience. As a result, the "escape" from reality—the cinema itself—becomes the privileged site for determining the way in which the subject understands that reality.

Jean-Luc Godard as Alternative

In response to the situation of the cinematic spectator, radical theorists and filmmakers of the 1960s and 1970s called for a cinema that eschewed the imaginary proximity of the typical Hollywood film and forced spectators to recognize their alienation. They adopted an approach to the cinema that mirrored Bertolt Brecht's approach to the theater. In his politicized theater, Brecht wants to produce detached spectators who are aware of their detachment and in no way prone to identification with what happens on stage. As Brecht puts it, "The essential point of the epic theatre is perhaps that it appeals less to the feelings than the spectator's reason. Instead of sharing an experience the spectator must come to grips with things."[11] Brecht's spectator watches from a distance but always remains aware that she/he watches from a distance, which is what distinguishes his spectator from the traditional cinematic spectator. In order to facilitate greater understanding on the spectator's part, Brecht's theater challenges spectators to experience their actual social position without its fantasmatic reprieve.

Transferring Brecht's theoretical innovations from the theater to the cinema, film theorists and filmmakers embraced a filmmaking style that foregrounded spectator distance from the activities on the screen and took up what Brecht calls the "alienation-effect." In the same essay in which she denounces classical Hollywood cinema's use of imaginary proximity, Laura Mulvey champions precisely this type of response:

> The first blow against the monolithic accumulation of traditional film conventions (already undertaken by radical film-makers) is to free the look of the camera into its materiality in time and space and the look of the audience into dialectics, passionate detachment. There is no doubt that this destroys the satisfaction, pleasure and privilege of the "invisible guest," and highlights how film depended on voyeuristic active/passive mechanisms.[12]

Mulvey's goal for radical filmmaking—"passionate detachment"—is a state in which the spectator thinks rather than blindly identifies. Mulvey champions films that privilege the symbolic situatedness of the specta- tor—or, as Christian Metz puts it, films that "attempt to disengage the cinema-object from the imaginary and to win it for the symbolic."[13]

This allusion to psychoanalytic theorist Jacques Lacan's categories of experience—the imaginary and the symbolic—provides another way of understanding the relationship between proximity and distance in the cinema. The symbolic order, for Lacan, is the order of language and society: it provides the structure that organizes our social reality and creates the identities that we inhabit. This order underlies the visible world and thus remains largely invisible, though its laws determine much of what happens in the visible world. It functions through ab- sence, shaping our lives in ways that we remain unaware of. What we see, in contrast, is the imaginary, a world of images that appear to be immediately present. The imaginary deceives us insofar as it hides the underlying symbolic structure that upholds it. For instance, the image of an authority figure as a genuinely caring person, even if it is true, masks the domination that inheres in her/his very symbolic position as an authority figure. She/he appears warm and accessible, but this obscures the symbolic, structural distance between the authority figure and us as ordinary subjects. Exposing the symbolic authority beneath the imaginary guise becomes a political project. Similarly, theorists like Mulvey and Metz want to lay bare the symbolic structure of the cinema by confronting the imaginary mode in which we experience it.

According to these theorists, making spectators aware of their distance from the events on the screen represents the only possibility for an alternative cinema. The attempt to go the other way—to increase the spectator's sense of proximity and eliminate the spectator's symbolic distance—cannot succeed. Distance is, for these theorists, the sine qua non of the cinematic experience, and proximity is always an illusion that attempts to hide this fundamental fact of the cinema. Filmmakers can struggle against the imaginary proximity that the cinema creates, but they can't do anything about the distance that exists between the spectator and the screen which is the result of the facts of film exhibition and even the social order itself. Layers of mediation separate the spectator from the events a film depicts. The economic system that produces the film, the director's vision, the technological apparatus that displays the film—these forces and others mediate what the spectator sees on the screen, and one cannot simply eliminate them.

This is why Constance Penley takes issue with supposed radical filmmakers who attempt to rely solely on radical images to shock spectators into change. Such filmmakers, according to Penley, inevitably contribute to the very cinematic fascination and imaginary blindness that they set out to contest. This is because, according to Penley, "Images have very little analytical power in themselves; their power of identification and fascination is too strong. This is why there must always be a commentary *on* the image simultaneously with the commentary *of* and *with* them."[14] Penley's critique here calls for a filmmaker who would forsake the false immediacy of the cinematic imaginary for a filmmaking style that highlighted the symbolic mediation always at work but unperceived in the cinematic experience. The most prominent filmmaker who embodies this theoretical aspiration is undoubtedly Jean-Luc Godard (though it predominates throughout avant-garde cinema).[15]

Godard's films constantly remind the spectator that she/he is watching a film. By doing this, he aims to break the fascinating power of the cinema over the spectator and create awareness of the process that produces the events on the screen, thereby facilitating a more thoughtful engagement between the spectator and the film—a more dialectical experience. As Pascal Bonitzer notes, "the image, since Godard, has been affirmed as resolutely false."[16] Even as early in his career as *À Bout de souffle* (*Breathless*, 1960), the jump cuts and self-conscious allusions to other films have an alienating effect that highlights the constructed nature of the image. As he develops as a filmmaker, however, this quality becomes more pronounced (in films such as *Vivre sa vie* [*My Life to Live*, 1962], *Les Carabiniers* [*The Riflemen*, 1963], and *Pierrot le fou* [1965]). *Le Mépris* (*Contempt*, 1963), for instance, begins with a long tracking shot of a tracking shot being shot by the actual cameraman for the film while we hear the film's credits read aloud. This beginning confronts the spectator with visual evidence that breaks down any illusion of proximity to the events that will follow. It signals to the spectator that the events are not real and are, in fact, thoroughly mediated.

Later in the 1960s, Godard develops this aesthetic further in *Week End* (1967), where we see shots of text interspersed at points in the film interrupting an extraordinarily long tracking shot. In addition, the second half of the film completely unravels the narrative structure that opens the film, thereby demanding that the spectator recognize the constructed nature of the filmic narrative—and of all filmic narrative. The viewer of *Week End* constantly has her/his immediate relation to the film interrupted by blatant intrusions of mediation. This film, like almost all of Godard's films, aims to eliminate the hallucinatory proximity that seems to inhere in the cinematic situation and to allow the spectator to watch from a distance. In doing so, these films work to strip away the lie of the cinema, to make it a less fantasmatic experience. Godard's subsequent films move even more radically in this direction. His aim remains constant: alienating the spectator into a proper grasp of cinematic distance. Godard wants to create a cinema of mediation as part of a struggle against Hollywood and bourgeois ideology's illusion of immediacy.

The hope underlying this type of cinema is actually a fundamentally anti-cinematic one. It aims to use the cinema to assist the spectator in transcending the cinema's fascination. The ideal spectator for this alternative cinema will escape the seduction of fantasy and thus be able to see the actual structure of the cinema and of society itself. That is, the ideal subject will see the reality of the production process rather than the fascinating commodities that disguise this process. By accomplishing this, the spectator will be on the way to becoming a radical subject ready to change existing social relations because this spectator will no longer be blind to the way things really are. Ideally, such a spectator will overcome commodity fetishism itself, in which, according to Marx's famous formulation, "a definite social relation between men . . . assumes . . . the fantastic form of a relation between things."[7] By exposing the image as constructed, as the product of a "definite social relation," Godard's films attack this form of fascination at a site (the cinema) where it usually predominates. Grasping one's alienation in the cinema would become the key, ultimately, to revolutionizing capitalist society.

The problem with the attempt to create a spectator whom the cinema does not seduce is its tacit assumption: it imagines that the spectator can attain a pure viewing position. The Brechtian aesthetic forgets about the desire of the spectator and fails to see how desire necessarily implicates the spectator in what occurs on the screen. Even though distance is inherent in the cinematic viewing situation itself, no spectator can remain completely distanced, even from a Godard film. Some element of fascination remains at work and continues to involve the spectator in the images on the screen—*or else the spectator would simply walk out of the film*. In other words, a film's alienation-effect has to fail to some extent in order for the film to retain the desire of its spectators. The successfully distanced spectator ceases to be a spectator at all.

The impossibility of the pure spectator condemns the Brechtian aesthetic to an unending pursuit, but doesn't necessarily indicate that the pursuit itself is wrongheaded. The deeper problem with the opposition to cinematic fascination lies in its conception of what motivates political activity and change. This position contends that knowledge itself—seeing how things really are, how the production process really works, etc.—has a radicalizing effect on spectators and subjects in general. According to this view, subjects accept their subjection to an oppressive social order only because they fail to recognize that an element of fascination has duped them into this acceptance. Thus, the thinking goes, if we remove the fascination and expose the relations of production as they actually are, we will produce radical subjects. But knowledge without desire does not inherently create political subjects. Contemporary capitalist society thrives on the participation of subjects who see through the prevailing ideology and yet continue to obey.[18] For instance, we continue to enjoy the gratuitous sex scene in *Wayne's World* (Penelope Spheeris, 1992) even when a subtitle labels it as such, or we continue to support wars even when we see through the deceptive rationale given for them. Subjects adopt a position of cynical distance in which the transparency of the game becomes part of the game itself. In this sense, a cinema that emphasizes distancing the spectator only plays into the hand of contemporary ideology.

The further lacuna in the Brechtian aesthetic is its inability to consider a motivation for political change within fascination itself. Though fascination accommodates subjects to their subjection, it also has the ability to encourage them to challenge that subjection. This is because fantasy as such emerges in order to cover up a real gap within ideology or the symbolic order. Lacan uses the term "real" as a third category of experience (in addition to imaginary and symbolic) to indicate the incompleteness of the symbolic structure, its failure to constitute itself as a coherent whole. Ideology uses fantasy to shore up its point of greatest weakness—the point at which its explanations of social phenomena break down—and this injects a potential radicality into every fantasy that proponents of the Brechtian aesthetic fail to see. In the act of decrying fantasy as an imaginary manipulation, the proponents of a distancing cinema fail to see the real moment within every fantasy. It is this moment that the films of David Lynch emphasize.

The Proximity of David Lynch

David Lynch began making films at the Pennsylvania Academy of Fine Arts in Philadelphia, where he initially went to become a painter. His first film, *Six Figures Getting Sick* (1967), which he made there, lasts one minute and repeats on a continuous loop. After directing a four-minute follow-up film, *The Alphabet* (1968), he moved to Los Angeles, where he attended the American Film Institute and made a 34-minute film entitled *The Grandmother* (1970). Each of these early shorts evinced Lynch's interest in using film as a fantasmatic medium, but it is *The Grandmother* that inaugurated the fundamental aesthetic structure that would dominate Lynch's feature films. In 1972, Lynch received $10,000 from AFI to make *Eraserhead* (1977), which he proposed as another short. After five years of preproduction, shooting, and postproduction, it became Lynch's first feature, beginning a career in the cinema that stands out like no other.

Lynch's distinctiveness stems from his ability to exist within mainstream cinema and independent cinema simultaneously. His films often show at the local multiplex, and he has received three Academy Award nominations for Best Director (for *The Elephant Man* [1980], *Blue Velvet* [1986], and *Mulholland Drive* [2001]). He is not simply a director celebrated at Cannes and ignored in Los Angeles. But his films also challenge viewers in ways that few other widely distributed films do. They contain disturbing images (like the sexual assault of Lula [Laura Dern] in *Wild at Heart* [1990]), narrative confusion (like the transformation of the main character into someone else in the middle of *Lost Highway* [1997]), and unusual shot sequences (like the opening montage in *Blue Velvet*). Lynch's films do not always receive a welcome reception among critics or the public, but the bare fact that films such as his gain widespread attention at all is startling.

This book is an attempt to come to terms with the incongruity of Lynch's position within contemporary cinema and to link this incongruity with the aesthetic that Lynch develops in his films. Lynch's work has occasioned some important works of criticism, including Michel Chion's *David Lynch* (BFI, 1995) and Slavoj Žižek's *The Ridiculous Sublime: On David Lynch's "Lost Highway"* (University of Washington Press, 2000), but only one book-length study dealing with Lynch's films from a sustained theoretical perspective—Martha Nochimson's *The Passion of David Lynch: Wild at Heart in Hollywood* (University of Texas Press, 1997).[19] For Nochimson, Lynch is the poet of the creative power of the subconscious. His films encourage us to let go of our fantasies of controlling others and access, via our empathy, the real connections between people. According to this theory, Lynch is a realist, antifantasmatic filmmaker, a filmmaker opposed to standard Hollywood practice. His films don't strike us as realistic because we are so enmeshed in an ideologically driven fantasy underwritten by Hollywood. As Nochimson puts it, "Lynch seeks to avoid the Hollywood trap of creating substitutes for life."[20] What Nochimson's thesis leaves unexplained is the predominance of "substitutes for life"—Hollywood fantasies—within Lynch's films.

As a filmmaker who privileges fantasy and what it can accomplish, David Lynch turns Godard's program on its head. Though both share the aim of altering the spectator's relationship to the given social reality, they go about accomplishing this in opposite ways. Whereas Godard (like many alternative filmmakers) works to alienate spectators and force them to recognize their distance from the images on the screen, Lynch tries to close this distance to an even greater extent than typical Hollywood films. If Godard is a filmmaker of distance, Lynch is a filmmaker of proximity.

But Lynch does not create proximity in the way we might expect—by deconstructing the binary opposition between fantasy and daily reality, between the outside world and the cinema. Unlike traditional alternative filmmakers, Lynch has no interest in deconstruction because deconstruction involves sustaining oneself at a distance from the opposition that one is deconstructing.[21] Rather than complicate or even undo binary oppositions, Lynch revels in them. Not only that: he pushes binary oppositions to an extreme. In his films we see stark oppositions in character, in mise-en-scène, in editing style, and in narrative structure. This is apparent, for instance, in the opposition between the two worlds of John Merrick (John Hurt) in *The Elephant Man*: the propriety of Merrick's daytime existence at the hospital contrasts absolutely with the perversity and ugliness of his nights there. During the day, Treves (Anthony Hopkins) and Merrick's visitors treat Merrick with kindness and respect, whereas at night, the night porter (Michael Elphick) and the visitors he brings to see Merrick treat him as a freak, returning Merrick emotionally to his days in the carnival under the vicious control of Bytes (Freddie Jones). Some such opposition structures all of Lynch's films, and in each case Lynch sustains the opposition throughout the film, contributing to the bizarre quality of his work.

Ironically, the films seem bizarre to us precisely because of the excessiveness of their normality—another twist in the separation between a filmmaker such as Jean-Luc Godard and Lynch. Whereas Godard aims at offering an alternative to bourgeois cinema and bourgeois life, Lynch wants to embody it fully. He is, in a word, bizarrely normal. This is what separates Lynch from so many of the other filmmakers existing on the outskirts and outside of Hollywood. By taking up mainstream filmmaking wholeheartedly, he reveals the radicality and perversity of the mainstream itself. He is *too* mainstream for the mainstream.

Through the act of taking normality to its logical extreme, Lynch reveals how the bizarre is not opposed to the normal but inherent within it. To this end, his personal idiosyncrasies function as an extension of this fundamental idea informing his films. Through the way that Lynch engages in them, behaviors central to American mythology take on an alien appearance. This leads Paul Woods to label Lynch "an All-American Martian Boy."[22] Lynch's childhood in small-town Missoula, Montana, his success in the Boy Scouts (becoming an Eagle Scout), his daily trips to the local Big Boy restaurant, and his delivering the *Wall Street Journal* to finance *Eraserhead* all evince his embodiment of the norm in a way that causes it to seem irregular or strange.

But it is Lynch's mode of dress that best reveals his relation to normality. During the 1970s, fashion dictated that the shirts of stylish men should be unbuttoned enough to reveal their chest. This style, popularized by, among others, John Travolta in *Saturday Night Fever* (John Badham, 1977) signified rebelliousness against the office dress code that demanded a coat and tie. One opened one's shirt and felt one's radicality. The more buttons unbuttoned, the more radical. The conservative option involved leaving just the top button undone. Lynch took—and still takes—this conservative position one step further and buttoned his shirt all the way. Without an accompanying tie, the shirt fully buttoned takes on an odd appearance, especially at a time when fashion dictates an unbuttoned look. One looks at Lynch with the fully buttoned shirt, and one sees something strange—perhaps even radical—but not something outside the mainstream. His attire brings to light the oddity of the mainstream itself.

Lynch's style of dress is important only insofar as it follows from and illuminates his filmic project. His films are excessively normal in precisely the same way. They create a division between the realm of desire and the realm of fantasy, between the exigencies of social reality and our psychic respite from those exigencies.[23] This near-absolute division in Lynch's films plays a major part in the quality of the bizarre that we find in them, and yet this type of separation between social reality and fantasy represents the very definition of normality.

We tend to think of normality as culturally relative and thus as bereft of theoretical significance: the norm in one culture is abnormal in another; gay partners holding hands in public is normal in New York City and unacceptable in rural Kansas. But by tracing how the desiring subject comes into being, a more theoretically significant conception of normality can become visible. The desiring subject emerges when an individual encounters social demands—demands for socially accept-able behavior—from parents or some other social authority. In Lacan's idiom, this figure who embodies the social order and its regulations is the Other. The subject enters the social order confronted with the Oth-er's articulated demand, but this demand conceals unarticulateable de-sire. We hear a demand from an authority figure—"Clean up your room!" or "Do as you're told!"—but we don't know exactly what the authority really desires from us. On one level, of course, the authority just wants us to obey, but no authority wants strict obedience. The un-imaginative child or student who follows every rule to the letter inevi-tably disappoints the parent or teacher even more than the rebel. Fol-lowing every rule to the letter indicates that one has not seen the desire beneath the demand.

The subject receives demands from the Other, but no words can tell the subject what the Other desires. When we confront a demand, we can ask the Other what she/he *really* wants from us, but the Other can only answer in words, which will produce another question as to what desire those words are hiding. When, in *Blue Velvet*, Jeffrey Beau-mont (Kyle MacLachlan) confronts the demand of Detective Williams (George Dickerson) that he put an end to any interest in the case sur-rounding the detached ear that he found, it is not at all clear what De-tective Williams really desires. His demand is unambiguous, but one can also surmise that he appreciates Jeffrey's interest in the intricacies of police investigation. When Jeffrey defies Detective Williams' explicit demand and pursues his own investigation, he is following—or believes that he is following—the desire that lies beneath this demand. The point is not that Detective Williams makes a hypocritical demand but that all demands conceal some desire. The depthlessness of signifiers—as Joan Copjec insists, *"signifiers are not transparent"*[24]—inevitably cre-ates a sense of mystery concerning the desire that might lie beneath. The subject's desire arises out of the encounter with the indecipherable desire of the Other, and in this sense, as Lacan often repeats, one's desire is the desire of the Other. The problem of this desire is that it is always elsewhere; we can never pin it down, just like we can never pin down the moment that is "now." For the subject within language (for every subject), it is an impossible object.

As desiring subjects, we live in a world of antagonism. Desire offers us two antagonistic possibilities—having the object as it ceases to be *the* object, or not having the object—and neither of these possibilities are satisfying. But antagonism is not simply a negative category. It constitutes our sense of reality: the external world appears real to us because of the absence of the desire of the Other, the absence of the object that would offer the subject the ultimate enjoyment. But this also means that this social reality leaves us never fully satisfied as subjects.

Fantasy provides a way for the subject to bear the dissatisfaction of the social reality. In this sense, it supplements the functioning of ideology and keeps subjects relatively content with an imaginary satisfaction. Through fantasy, we do the impossible, accessing the impossible desire of the Other and glimpsing the enjoyment that it promises. The Other's desire becomes a secret that one might uncover, not a constitutively impossible object that exists only in its absence. We don't necessarily fantasize obtaining this impossible object and enjoying the possession of it. Instead, fantasy constructs a narrative that explains the loss of the object and/or points toward its recovery. This narrative gives meaning to the loss of the object and transforms the impossible object into a possible one. For instance, the fantasy of humanity's expulsion from the Garden of Eden allows us to believe that paradise is a possibility, even though it is lost. Such an idea offers us a feeling of hope amidst the generalized dissatisfaction that characterizes our experience of the object as an impossibility.

But fantasy is not just a private compensation for public dissatisfaction. It silently informs our everyday experience of the social reality itself and has the effect of taking some of its dissatisfaction away. Fantasy's transformation of the Other's desire allows the subject to experience a reality where the ultimate enjoyment is a possibility residing just beneath the surface of things. Fantasy bleeds into our experience of the external world and gives us our sense of the fullness of reality.

But the normal subject, in psychoanalytic terms, maintains an absolute divide between social reality and fantasy—what Freud calls the external and the internal—and knows how to distinguish them. For the normal subject, as Freud puts it, "what is unreal, merely a presentation and subjective, is only internal; what is real is also there *outside*."[25] *Normal* thus means no confusion of external and internal, social reality and fantasy. This idea of normality is not just a Freudian one: most psychologists—and even most of the population at large—accept the idea that normal subjects are those with the ability to distinguish what really happens in the world from what they fantasize. Such normality, however, is impossible a priori: no one experiences reality without some fantasmatic investment. Which is to say that what we fantasize that we will see informs what we do see.[26]

Nonetheless, according to the strict psychoanalytic definition, normality allows no such confusion, which is why psychoanalysis also recognizes that we never encounter a normal subject. There is always some slippage between normality on the one hand and neurosis and psychosis on the other. Unlike the "normal" subject, neurotics and psychotics don't experience things so clearly. The psychotic confuses reality and fantasy and experiences them as equivalent, while the neurotic seeks in fantasy a substitute satisfaction for what she or he did not find in reality. Hence, for the psychotic every experience, even a fantasmatic one, seems real, and for the neurotic every experience, even a real one, has at least a hint of fantasy. There is, in both cases, a blurring of the lines.[27]

This blurring of the lines occurs in most films as well. Narrative films typically revolve around the intermixing and interaction of desire and fantasy. Desire fuels the movement of narrative because it is the search for answers, a process of questioning, an opening to possibility. Fantasy, in contrast, provides an answer to this questioning, a solution to the enigma of desire (albeit an imaginary one), a resolution of uncertainties. In our experience of most films—films that have an evident narrative coherence—the relationship between desire and fantasy appears seamless: we can't readily delineate the precise moment at which we pass from desire to fantasy, nor do they appear as separate realms. Instead, fantasy is constantly there, clearing up desire's ambiguities. We don't know exactly what will happen next, but we do feel secure in a reality replete with meaning—a reality in which events fundamentally make sense. It is the task of fantasy to provide us with this sense of inhabiting a truly meaningful reality, a reality in which meaning itself is not up for grabs.[28]

The relation between desire and fantasy in film may become clearer in light of a film that offers little fantasmatic resolution—Christopher Nolan's *Memento* (2000). Though one quickly adjusts to the (generally) backwards movement of the film's narration, one cannot construct an unambiguous account of the events that the film suggests have happened. No matter how many times a spectator views the film, she/he could not discover the truth of the film's central event: how the wife of Leonard Shelby (Guy Pearce) died, and who was responsible for her death. This event motivates the action in the film, and the narrative moves in the direction of this mystery. But it remains completely enigmatic. The film prompts spectator desire for a solution but does not provide the fantasmatic scenario that would allow the solution to appear. The impossible object remains impossible even at the end of the film. Rather than providing a (fantasmatic) solution to the crime, the ending shows us only Leonard's willful self-deception that puts him on the track of someone he doesn't think is responsible. *Memento* sticks out because it provides a world of desire in a relatively pure form, not blending it with fantasy.[29]

In the very common films that blur the line between desire and fantasy, we never have an initial experience of desire in its purity prior to the onset of fantasy, just as we don't initially experience a question apart from some idea of an answer, or doubt without some kind of certainty. Fantasy, in other words, exists alongside desire from the beginning, structuring its very path; it isn't something added on to desire after the fact. In this sense, films that blur the line between desire and fantasy best approximate our quotidian experience of the world, in which fantasy saves us from having to endure the inherently traumatic desire of the Other unprepared. Fantasy is the set of blinders that obscures the traumatic (unanswerable) question that this desire asks of us.

We can see this clearly in the case of film noir. In the figure of the femme fatale, desire and fantasy operate simultaneously: on the one hand, she is a traumatic figure for the spectator and the noir hero—we confront her traumatic desire and are thereby reduced to the position of the desiring subject—but on the other, she fits neatly into our fantasy frame precisely insofar as she is a femme fatale, a representative of transgressive pleasure. For instance, when Phyllis Dietrichson (Barbara Stanwyck) makes her famous appearance at the top of the stairs wearing only a towel in *Double Indemnity* (Billy Wilder, 1944), Walter Neff (Fred MacMurray) and the spectator see her through the lens of fantasy—as the licentious femme fatale. When we see her as femme fatale, we have an initial fantasmatic frame through which to make sense of her and her desire. In other words, from the beginning we know that she means trouble. All the indiscernibility of her desire that follows in the film—up to her inability to shoot Walter near the film's end—emerge against the background of this initial fantasmatic frame. Our relationship to Phyllis and her desire doesn't exist apart from the fantasmatic image of her as femme fatale. In *Double Indemnity*—as in most films and as in our everyday experience—the worlds of desire and fantasy overlap and commingle. Lynch's films, however, attempt to hold these worlds separate.[30]

This separation marks the beginning of Lynch's impossible cinema. The idea of a pure desire, a desire unmediated by fantasy, is itself the ultimate fantasy; desire does not exist prior to fantasy but emerges out of it. Fantasy does not simply provide an answer for the question posed by desire; instead, desire poses the question for the answer that fantasy provides. Or, as Slavoj Žižek puts it, "It is only through fantasy that the subject is constituted as desiring: *through fantasy, we learn how to desire*."[31] Hence, Lynch's depiction of the world of desire prior to fantasy would be unthinkable outside the fantasmatic medium of film itself. He uses filmic fantasy to present desire in its immediacy and thereby allows us to see precisely how desire and fantasy interrelate.

Lynch's films present the distinct worlds of desire and fantasy through radical differences in form within each film. The model for his films is *The Wizard of Oz* (Victor Fleming, 1939), which creates a division between the social reality of Kansas and the dream world of Oz. Fleming uses black-and-white photography to depict the dissatisfaction Dorothy (Judy Garland) feels in Kansas and color to indicate the enjoyment that the Oz fantasy brings. The first part of the film follows the logic of desire insofar as Dorothy seeks a satisfaction that seems constitutively denied to her. No one pays attention to her on the family ranch, and her only friend, her dog Toto, faces execution for his unruly behavior. In Kansas, she can long for an impossible object that exists "somewhere over the rainbow," but it is clear that she cannot attain it. The turn to the world of Oz changes Dorothy's fortune completely. She becomes the center of attention, the source of hope for others, and a hero for having killed the Wicked Witch of the East. Even the difficulties that she encounters bring an excitement and enjoyment that were impossible in Kansas. The fantasmatic land of Oz solves the dilemmas that the Kansas section of the film, the world of desire, presents as insoluble. The emergence of color photography is at once the emergence of new possibility.

Though Lynch never uses this precise way of creating an opposition between social reality and fantasy, the idea of the separation itself informs each of his films.[32] In a film like *Mulholland Drive* (2001), the differences between the drab social reality in which Diane (Naomi Watts) exists and the colorful fantasmatic alternative where she becomes Betty (also Naomi Watts) become almost as conspicuous as Fleming's splitting through the use of different film stock. Lynch claims that *The Wizard of Oz* "must've got inside me when I first saw it, like it did a million other people."[33] He learns from it an aesthetic structure that allows him to separate two filmic worlds and then link together what has been separated, though he ultimately uses this structure to far different ends than Fleming, whose film uses the dream of Oz to reconcile spectators to the monotony of their Kansas.

Taking *The Wizard of Oz* as his point of departure, Lynch depicts worlds of desire by emphasizing the absence of the object. These worlds are typically sparse and bland, if not bleak and desolate. The dark lighting, stilted acting, minimal décor, and an absence of movement within shots in the first part of *Lost Highway*, for example, contribute to the mise-en-scène that is meant to spur spectator desire. In *Eraserhead*, we see characters constitutively deprived of any enjoyment—that is, stuck in the dissatisfaction and lack that is desire—but even more, we as spectators experience our own sense of lack when confronted with an image that is largely dark and empty. These worlds of desire bombard the spectator with displays of absence.

The worlds of fantasy in Lynch's films mark a definitive contrast. Here, the excess and heightened presence of the filmic image that we associate with cinema as such bursts forth. Rather than enduring the absence of the impossible object-cause of desire, the spectator finds indications of this object everywhere, either in specific characters like Frank Booth (Dennis Hopper) populating the underworld in *Blue Velvet* or in the bright and colorful setting we see when Laura Palmer (Sheryl Lee) first appears in *Twin Peaks: Fire Walk with Me* (1992). Through their excessiveness, the fantasy worlds unleash enjoyment on both the characters within them and the spectator watching. As a result, they are as difficult to experience as the worlds of desire, though for the opposite reason. While watching the worlds of fantasy unfold in a Lynch film, one sees too much of the object and enjoys too much. But this alternating experience of absence and excessive presence is normality itself. By separating the realms of desire and fantasy, Lynch's films provide an unsettling insight into normality that everyday life militates against.

One effect of this separation is to make clear the way in which fantasy acts as a compensation for what the social reality—the world in which we can only desire—doesn't provide. Unlike the social reality, fantasy provides the illusion of delivering the goods; it offers a form of enjoyment for subjects that social reality cannot—like, for instance, the enjoyment that comes from watching a filmic narrative unfold. This becomes clearly visible in Lynch's films, however, only because Lynch maintains a separation between the world of social reality and that of fantasy, a separation as disconcerting as it is revealing.

The separation between the world of desire and the world of fantasy becomes increasingly pronounced as Lynch's career develops. It is far more visible in later films such as *Lost Highway* or *Mulholland Drive* than earlier films like *Eraserhead* and *The Elephant Man*. Looking at the films chronologically, we can see Lynch constantly changing the way he creates opposing worlds, adding nuance as his career develops, but the opposition itself remains constant. Each interpretation that follows will stress how each film extends and qualifies the insights of the earlier films. We will not see a straight line of progress but a path of aesthetic exploration and increasing complexity. Furthermore, in order to examine how Lynch operates differently within the same medium (which always provides similar possibilities), I will restrict the focus in this book to his nine feature films, leaving aside his short films and his television work (including *Twin Peaks*). The difficulty of the films themselves suffices without the further complications introduced by the questions of medium specificity and collaboration.

The difficulty of Lynch's films does not lie so much in how subversive or radical they are, but in the fact that they offer a far more normal perspective than mainstream Hollywood film. They create an absolute division between social reality and fantasy, and this is a normality that we aren't used to seeing, either in Hollywood or in our everyday lives. As Freud points out, even the most normal subject we encounter is to some degree a neurotic; that is, she or he allows fantasy to shape her or his experience of reality.[34] Lynch's films disconcert us precisely because they confront us with normality—and normality seems completely foreign. But in the divide between desire and fantasy Lynch allows us to experience the cinema in a way that challenges its typical relationship with ideology.

The Impossible David Lynch

When cinema exists simply as an escape for spectators—i.e., when films deploy fantasy without fully investing themselves in it—it can effectively play the role of a fantasmatic ideological supplement. That is, it can provide subjects with a mode of enjoyment that compensates for the dissatisfactions of their daily reality. If, for instance, subjects experience class antagonism in their lives, they can enjoy the transcendence of this antagonism while watching the romance between the upper-class Rose (Kate Winslet) and the lower-class Jack (Leonardo DiCaprio) in *Titanic* (James Cameron, 1997) and thereby continue a contented existence within the world of class antagonism. The brief elimination of class antagonism in the cinema provides a salve so that subjects don't suffer from it quite so much. But the fantasmatic effect succeeds only as long as spectators experience cinematic fantasies from a distance and fail to take them seriously.

Because Lynch's films create a separation between the realms of desire and fantasy, they have the ability to immerse us as spectators more completely in the fantasmatic world. Films that blend the realms of desire and fantasy allow spectators to remain removed from the fantasy that they depict. They preserve a degree of desire even in their depiction of a fantasmatic resolution, and this permits the spectator to resist wholly committing her/himself to the fantasy. In other words, this type of film—the typical Hollywood film—doesn't fascinate the spectator too much; it fails to fascinate the spectator enough. It offers the spectator just a taste of the fantasmatic resolution with the implicit promise that the enjoyment it provides will extend ad infinitum. But this promise is never—and can never be—redeemed. We never see completely the ramifications of fantasy itself—its costs, its rewards, its effects, and so on. The ramifications remain always on the horizon, yet to be discovered, which allows the spectator to retain some desire and avoid fully committing to the fantasy. Lynch's films compensate for this absence in other films by providing us with a total experience of fantasy. In the typical Lynch film, one follows the logic of fantasy to its end point and in this way experiences both the enjoyment that fantasy brings and its psychic—and often material—costs.

We might imagine a Lynch version of a television program like *Extreme Makeover*, a reality show depicting the complete transformation of a person's appearance through the aid of plastic surgeons, beauticians, and other experts. Each episode ends with the realization of a dream: the once unattractive person meets family and friends in a changed form, and everyone celebrates the improvement, usually with tears and hugs. One need not be a psychoanalytic or Marxist theorist to see how the realization of the fantasy here functions ideologically, not just by curing the participant of her dissatisfaction but by convincing spectators that a potential cure for their own dissatisfaction exists with the proper commodities. The show does nothing to arrest the beauty aesthetic that causes the suffering in the first place but works instead to increase spectator investment in it. The limitation of this critique is that it sees only the ideological function of fantasy where the hypothetical Lynch version of the show would reveal something further.

The pleasure that spectators derive from *Extreme Makeover* depends on the point at which it stops. The show depicts the participant showing off the new look, but it never shows us the new life in its entirety. The Lynch version would continue past the initial meeting and show the new life that the makeover created—perhaps following the participant for the next year. It would invest itself more fully in the fantasy than the actual *Extreme Makeover* rather than deconstructing it. We would see the participant discover the surpassed old life return in the new one, which would traumatize both the participant and the spectator. The underlying identity of the exciting alternative and the old tedious reality would become visible, depriving us of the idea of another life where things would be different. This is a radical insight that we cannot arrive at through simply denouncing fantasy; one must fully play it out.

But Lynch's films do not depict fantasy in this unadulterated way in order to display the dangers of fascination. The total experience of fantasy that the Lynch film creates aims to trigger a spectator response of identification with the traumatic moment enacted within the fantasy. Lynch offers the fantasmatic experience in order to facilitate this identification with what seems most distant from and foreign to us as spectators.

Of course, not every cinematic spectator is the same, and film theory has spent many years focused on the nuances of spectator difference. But such discussions have as their foundation an empirical conception of the spectator: they imply that the spectator is external to the film and thus don't focus on the way that films internally posit their own spectators. Every film demands a certain response. It is the task of interpretation to locate this demand, and it is the task of the actual spectator in the theater to be adequate to it.[35] This is especially imperative in the case of Lynch because of his approach to fantasy. In Lynch's films, the fantasies that the cinema enacts for us are not simply a nice diversion, but rather they house the truth of our being as spectators.

Lynch's cinematic fantasies contain the truth of our being insofar as they reveal where we direct our desire. Our everyday experience allows our own desire to remain unconscious: we don't see how our desire shapes what we see; we believe that we simply see what appears in the world to be seen. By presenting us with an alternate fantasmatic world vastly different from our everyday experience, Lynch creates a situation where the distorting power of our desire becomes visible to us. Our very investment in the fantasies that his films offer reveals our unconscious: we experience a familiarity in what is completely unfamiliar.[36]

In this way, Lynch's filmmaking testifies to its kinship with Hegelian philosophy. He is the Hegel of filmmakers, one of the few directors to use cinema to enact a process on the spectator that Hegel can only describe.[37] Philosophical thinking, in Hegel's mind, involves "*pure* self-recognition in absolute otherness," a recognition that one's identity exists outside oneself in the object that appears most other to oneself.[38] This is the recognition of what Hegel calls speculative identity: in the act of speculative identity, the subject grasps its connection with what it cannot encompass.

Hegel begins the *Phenomenology of Spirit* with the complete opposition of subject and substance in order to be able to show the identity of what our thinking formulates as most opposed. The initial division is necessary, for Hegel as for Lynch, in order to make clear that the connection moves through absolute otherness rather than just eliminating it. This leaves the subject no room for respite, no difference into which it might escape. Hegel's most powerful example of speculative identity derives from the—discredited, even during Hegel's time—pseudoscience of phrenology. By linking personality and intelligence to the size and shape of the skull, phrenology allows us to see the fundamental dependence of spirit on its stupid materiality. For all its transcendence—and Hegel thinks this transcendence is nonetheless real, which is why he isn't a phrenologist—spirit cannot escape its inorganic origins.

Even our most profound speculative thoughts remain dependent on our material being, though this speculation believes that it leaves the material world far behind. As Hegel puts it, "the *actuality and existence of man is his skull-bone*."[39] Ultimately, phrenology is not, for Hegel, the last word on spirit. But this is only because it does not yet represent the most extreme form of speculative identity. The position of the absolute, which is where Hegelian philosophy always ends up, involves the subject seeing what it can't see—what Hegel calls "the negative of itself, or its limit."[40] The subject recognizes that the limitation on its understanding is in fact integral to its very ability to understand. This is a recognition mirroring that of the patient at the end of psychoanalysis who sees that "I am that": I identify myself with the traumatic object, and in doing so, I become who I always was.

It is the principal virtue of Lynch's films to insist on speculative identity, this "self-recognition in absolute otherness." In the experience of a Lynch film, one can no longer sustain a sense of distance between oneself as spectator and the events on the screen because his films reveal the underlying identity of every opposition. To return to the example of *The Elephant Man*, we see the identity of Treves, the one who treats Merrick with kindness, and Bytes, the one who exploits him mercilessly. As spectators we gladly identify ourselves with the heroism of Treves and detest the cruelty of Bytes, but the film forces us to see how the actions of Treves mirror those of Bytes, thereby implicating us in the exploitation of Merrick. There is no safe opposition for the spectator in Lynch's cinema.

Lynch's films demand that the spectator revaluate her/his relationship to the cinema. The cinema is no longer an escape without any connection to the outside world, nor is it a reality unto itself. Instead, it is the reverse side of that outside world—the fantasmatic underside that holds the truth of the latter. If we escape at all in Lynch's cinema, we escape into the trauma that remains hidden but nonetheless structures the outside world.

Despite the great variety in their subject matter, Lynch's films always end the same way—with an impossible act that fundamentally alters the very structure of the filmic world.[41] It is the separation of the worlds of desire and fantasy that renders this act visible. In *Eraserhead*, we see Henry attain the Radiator Lady, his fantasy object; in *Elephant Man*, we see John Merrick become a normal person; in *Dune* (1984), we see Paul create rain on a desert planet; and so on. Each of these instances involves a character fulfilling a fantasy and thereby breaking down the distance between the fantasy world and the world of desire (with its constitutive dissatisfaction). To return to Freud's terms, these are cases where the internal successfully becomes the external. These are cases when the impossible becomes possible.

For Lacan, a link exists between impossibility and what he calls the real. Within every symbolic order, the real occupies the place of what cannot be thought or imagined—the position of the impossible. The real is not reality but the failure of the symbolic order to explain everything. When seen in this light, the impossible is not materially impossible but rather logically impossible as long as we remain within the current social structure. In *Seminar XVII*, Lacan claims that "the real is the impossible. Not on account of a simple stumbling block against which we bang our heads, but because of the logical stumbling block of what announces itself as impossible in the symbolic. It is from there that the real arises."[42] What is impossible in the symbolic order is, in the real, perfectly achievable. It is in this sense of the term *impossible* that Lynch's films allow us to experience it actually taking place. They thus provide a fundamental challenge to the ruling symbolic structure, forcing us to see possibilities where we are used to seeing impossibilities.

The events depicted within Lynch's films reflect the relationship with the spectator that these films construct. Just as the characters in Lynch's films must endure the realization of their fantasies without respite, so must the spectator of these films. To watch a David Lynch film properly is always to touch the screen, to find oneself bereft of the safe distance that the very architecture of the cinema seems to promise.[43]

ONE Sacrificing One's Head for an Eraser

The Loss of the Life Substance

Eraserhead (1977) began as a 42-minute student film that Lynch proposed to the American Film Institute in Los Angeles while he was enrolled there. It grew into a 100-minute feature during the five years that it took Lynch to complete it. But not only the length of the film's production stands out: Lynch made much of the film clandestinely in abandoned buildings on AFI property, where he constructed his own miniature studio. Funding was never constant, and shooting stopped many times during the five years when the money dried up. It is the only Lynch film made in this independent way. Subsequently, he would have money—sometimes too much, sometimes less than he would like, but always enough to continue shooting. In order to realize the idea of *Eraserhead*, however, the absence of money was not a barrier to success; it was integral.

Lynch's films explore the psyche to such an extent that they never seem to touch the ground, to engage the economic and political realities that shape our everyday lives. If there has been one sustained theme of criticism of Lynch's work, it has followed these lines: he creates filmic worlds that show little sign of the material world—of class inequality, marginalized people, or economic struggle. In this sense, Lynch is very much a Hollywood filmmaker, unconcerned with the socioeconomic realities of late capitalist life and committed to delivering fantasies to his audiences, even if these fantasies do themselves deviate from the Hollywood norm. On a literal level, there is some truth to this criticism. Lynch's filmic explorations of the psyche tend to remain on that level and leave the link between the psychic and the social implicit. But in his first feature, *Eraserhead*, he demonstrates explicitly the link between the intrapsychic struggles of Henry Spencer (Jack Nance) and his situation as a capitalist subject.

As in Lynch's later films, the structure of *Eraserhead* separates into two disparate worlds of desire and fantasy—the social reality and the escape from that reality. Throughout most of the film, we see Henry existing in a desolate postindustrial landscape where he continually experiences nothing but dissatisfaction. These experiences contrast with his brief moments of ecstasy, which occur when he fantasizes about a small woman (Laurel Near) who sings and dances on a stage hidden in his radiator. The brightness of the scenes with the Radiator Lady parallels the enjoyment that they depict and contrasts with the darkness of the rest of the film. In *Eraserhead*, Lynch employs this separation in order to reveal the relationship between the psychic dissatisfaction of the subject and the functioning of capitalist society. As the film makes clear, this functioning depends on a continual act of sacrifice on the part of the subject—the sacrifice of the subject's kernel of enjoyment for the sake of productivity. The same sacrifice that leads to the chronic dissatisfaction of the subject fuels the social mechanisms of production. When the subject refuses this sacrifice, the mechanisms of production break down. At the end of the film, Henry arrives at the point where he can embrace rather than sacrifice his enjoyment. This becomes possible because he becomes aware of the production process through fantasy.

Rather than being solely a veil that hides the process of production and the subject's role in this process, fantasy in *Eraserhead* works to expose how the subject's castration—the loss that one experiences when entering into society—serves the production process. By showing fantasy functioning in this way, the film challenges traditional ideas about fantasy's relationship to production. For early psychoanalytic film theory, the fantasmatic dimension of cinema represents its greatest ideological danger because fantasy always hides production. In fact, according to this view, fantasy emerges directly out of the attempt to obscure the role that production and labor play in the construction of the social order.

Christian Metz locates this problem in the cinema's privileging of story (what happens on the screen) at the expense of discourse (the act of relating the events on the screen). He notes, "the basic characteristic of [cinematic] discourse, and the very principle of its effectiveness as discourse, is precisely that it obliterates all traces of the enunciation, and masquerades as story."[1] While watching the typical Hollywood film, we invest ourselves in a series of images that take pains to obscure the productive apparatus and the labor that produces them. Building on the analysis of Metz and others, Daniel Dayan adds, "the film-discourse presents itself as a product without a producer, a discourse without an origin. It speaks. Who speaks? Things speak for themselves and, of course, they tell the truth. Classical cinema establishes itself as the ventriloquist of ideology."[2] The filmic fantasy, at least in its traditional manifestation in Hollywood cinema, supplements a specifically capitalist ideology. This ideology depends on hiding the labor that produces every commodity in order to facilitate the "free" exchange of commodities.

In *Eraserhead*, Lynch challenges this traditional conception of fantasy (and thus of film) as an ideological supplement. Fantasy (as played out in Henry's dream) becomes the means through which the subject's sacrifice of enjoyment for the sake of social productivity becomes visible. Though fantasy does obscure the mechanisms of production, at the same time it makes visible the genesis of productivity itself—the moment of the subject's insertion into the social order. Every fantasy is in some sense a fantasy of origins: fantasy emerges in order to provide a scenario that explicates the origin of the subject and the origin of the social order, which is what ideology itself remains constitutively unable to explain.

The origin is the site of a gap within ideological explanations: ideology can only explain the emergence of the present social order retroactively, in terms of its result, which means that ideology lacks the proper terminology that a genuine explanation would require. Because ideology works to justify the existing social order, it reduces what is prior to this order to the level of the order itself. In short, ideology's very ability to explain everything leaves it paradoxically unable to explain origin. The question of origin becomes a blank spot within ideology, a moment of contingency within the ideological world of necessity. Any attempt to explain an origin runs into the problem that Kant diagnoses in the dynamical antinomies of *The Critique of Pure Reason*, where he probes the question of whether the world itself had a beginning or not. What Kant finds is that no explanation of origin can ever be definitive because we can always seek the origin of this supposed origin. The search for an origin leads to an infinite regress.[3] Just as reason cannot locate the origin of the world, ideology cannot locate the origin of the social order. But fantasy, because it uses narrative rather than straightforward explanation, can fill in this gap and offer us a way of understanding origin.

Fantasy does this on a social as well as a subjective level. For the individual subject, the fantasy of the primal scene (which is one of the fundamental forms that fantasy takes) transforms the utterly contingent fact of the subject's birth—why *this* individual and not another—into a narrative that renders this birth meaningful. In this fantasy, parental coitus becomes not just an arbitrary act but one full of a definite intention. It has as its specific design creating the individual subject who fantasizes this event. A similar process occurs in fantasies constructed for an entire social order, which take the form of myth. Virgil's creation of the myth in which Aeneas founds the city of Rome strips the founding of contingency and allows Romans to see themselves as the products of a specific destiny. In both these cases, the origin ceases to be a disturbing point and becomes the foundation that solidifies a sense of identity.

Fantasy's orientation toward the origin allows it to play a part in obscuring a gap within ideology. But fantasy can also make this gap visible; it can show us what we otherwise would be unable to see. We require fantasy in order to see our initial sacrifice of enjoyment because this act of sacrifice has no empirical existence. That is to say, as members of society, we have always already sacrificed our enjoyment—our membership in society is defined by this sacrifice—making it impossible to isolate the moment of the sacrifice itself. Not only does the sacrifice have no empirical existence, but the subject in no way *has* any enjoyment prior to its sacrifice. The social order demands that the subject give up what it doesn't have, and it is this sacrifice of nothing—the pure act of sacrifice itself—that constitutes the subject as such.

Fantasy distorts the subject's initial act of sacrifice by making it seem as if we have sacrificed something substantial rather than nothing. But this distortion is at the same time a revelation of the sacrifice that would remain undetected without the fantasmatic distortion. If we understand fantasy in this way, we can revaluate attempts by avant-garde filmmakers to expose the productive process behind their films: while such efforts may in fact expose filmic fantasy as a construct, they also have the effect of detracting from fantasy's power to expose the origins of the social order and the subject. In attempting to deconstruct the ideological power of filmic fantasy, one simultaneously undermines its revolutionary power as well.

Henry Spencer's complete immersion in fantasy demonstrates the power of fantasy to expose the initial sacrifice of enjoyment that makes possible the process of production, even as it obscures that process itself. That is to say, fantasy initially obscures the process of production by seducing us with a series of images, but its attempt to narrate an origin has the subsequent effect of exposing this process. The film enacts the dynamic played out in Henry with the spectator on the level of form. Just as Henry becomes aware of his own sacrifice of enjoyment and its connection to the process of production through his fantasy, the spectator becomes aware of the same thing through the filmic fantasy that is *Eraserhead* itself.

Production and Sacrifice

The film begins with the direct link between Henry's experience of the loss of enjoyment and the onset of industrial production. The opening is completely surreal: we see the upper part of Henry's body floating in space while lying on its side. Lynch superimposes the image of Henry on that of a planet. When Henry disappears from the frame, the camera moves closer to the planet. After a cut to what seems to be the planet's surface, the camera enters a cabin where a man sits by a window with three levers in front of him. The film cuts back to the image of Henry whose expression changes from one of dull anxiety to terror. After a quick shot that returns to the man in the cabin as he suddenly jerks, we see Henry's mouth open and a spermlike substance seems to emerge from it (though the creature is superimposed on the image of Henry). Lynch cuts back to the man in the cabin, who pulls one of the levers, which seems to have the effect—which we see in the subsequent shot—of sending the spermlike substance shooting out of the frame. The man in the cabin pulls a second and third lever, and we see the substance splashing into a pool of water. The camera goes into the puddle and moves forward in the puddle into a bright white light that completely consumes the frame. This white light ends the film's seven-minute opening sequence.

Through the crosscutting of Henry expelling the spermlike substance from his mouth and the man in the cabin pulling the three levers, the film emphasizes the link between these two seemingly disparate events. This allows us to see the role that Henry's sacrifice of enjoyment plays in the production process. The spermlike substance is a piece of Henry that detaches itself. It is what Henry loses as he becomes a determinate, sexed being within society. Prior to losing this piece of himself, Henry floats in air, existing in an indeterminate state. But the loss of the spermlike substance triggers his emergence as a determinate subject.[4] In order to become a subject, the film makes clear, one must lose this essential piece of oneself—what Lacan calls the "lamella"—which is the pure life substance subtracted from the subject as it enters into language and the social order.

Lacan's description of the lamella from *Seminar XI* (known as the *Four Fundamental Concepts of Psycho-Analysis*) bears an uncanny resemblance to the spermlike substance that issues from Henry's mouth in the opening of the film. Lacan describes it as follows: "The lamella is something extra-flat, which moves like the amoeba. It is just a little more complicated. But it goes everywhere. And as it is something . . . that is related to what the sexed being loses in sexuality, it is, like the amoeba in relation to sexed beings, immortal—because it survives any division, any scissiparous intervention. And it can run around."[5] The lamella is the organ of the libido—the life substance itself. It is the little bit of aliveness that I give up as a sexed being and constantly seek to rediscover in sexual encounters. According to Lacan, "It is precisely what is subtracted from the living being by virtue of the fact that it is subject to the cycle of sexed reproduction."[6] One must lose the lamella if one is to become a sexed being because sexed reproduction requires a mortal, lacking subject. The subject only turns toward the Other on the basis of its own experience of lacking this life substance. If the subject were complete or completely alive, it would not have the ability to desire.

Because the loss of the life substance or little bit of aliveness is linked to sexual reproduction, subjects often see it existing in their offspring, which explains the ambivalence that parents feel toward their children.

On the one hand, the parent enjoys this life substance through the child and identifies with the aliveness that the child has (and that the parent her/himself lacks). On the other hand, the parent envies the child's aliveness or enjoyment, viewing it as an enjoyment properly belonging to the parent her/himself. Both the doting parent and the abusive parent are in one sense responses to the initial loss of the lamella or aliveness that constitutes them as subjects who reproduce sexually.

Henry's loss of the lamella inaugurates his existence as a desiring subject, but the lamella doesn't simply disappear: *Eraserhead* confirms Lacan's conclusion that "it can run around." Henry encounters this little piece of himself—or a portion of it—at subsequent points in the film, and each time it appears, it suggests the enjoyment that Henry now lacks. The lamella appears most conspicuously in the middle of Henry's first fantasy of the Radiator Lady. As the Radiator Lady dances across her small stage in the radiator, pieces of the lamella drop from above and land on the stage floor. In this way, the film indicates how fantasy derives out of—and harkens back to—the sexed subject's initial loss of the life substance. The subject fantasizes because it cannot entirely escape this substance; it always comes back to haunt the subject who exists in the world of desire produced out of its sacrifice.

The loss of the lamella produces a world in which the subject constantly experiences its own lack, and the object that would fill this lack remains perpetually out of reach. The loss of the lamella and the onset of mechanical production unleash a world of desire. But this world is not, as Heidegger might put it, our initial mode of being-in-the-world. As subjects, we create the world of desire through our experience of loss. According to the logic developed by the film, our determinate being-in-the-world is not primordial but the result of an initial, pre-ontological act that gives structure to the world. Though we can only access this act through the vehicle of fantasy, an understanding of it is nonetheless crucial for our ability to see the relationship between the subject and capitalist society.

The Malaise of the Desiring Subject

Lynch suggests causality by locating the unfolding of the world of desire just after the opening depiction of Henry's sacrifice of enjoyment in the film. It seems as if this dissatisfaction results from Henry's sacrifice of his enjoyment to the machine of capitalist production. This part of the film begins with a close-up of Henry looking backward over his shoulder at what he is in the process of walking away from. Though we see this shot of Henry looking and a puzzled or anxious look on his face, we do not see a reverse shot of what Henry sees (which we might typically expect in this situation). In this world, the object is missing. Lynch expresses this absence through the film's form—or through the absence of the expected form, the reverse shot.

The film follows the missing reverse shot with a mise-en-scène that further stresses absence rather than presence. This is especially the case in the way that Lynch lights the film—or rather in the way that he doesn't light the film. Lynch's desire for a dark mise-en-scène even informed the way in which the negatives were processed. While having the film developed, Lynch insisted on the darkest feasible look to the prints. The extreme darkness produces a sense of absence within almost every shot of the film.

The distribution of the light emphasizes the experience of absence. Lynch almost never lights a scene evenly; instead, he stresses the contrast between light and darkness. As Michel Chion notes, "Lynch dared to use light which illuminates only in pools, so that parts of the set remained in shadows or in complete darkness."[7] Much of the sense of emptiness that *Eraserhead* creates stems from this use of light. We can never look at a scene and experience the overpresence that we are used to seeing in a film. The gaps in the lighting create a world that entices desire by highlighting what cannot be seen or known.[8]

Even the world moves slowly, structured around a circuitous path to the object of desire. The slowness becomes evident when Henry enters the elevator in his apartment building for the first time. We see a long shot of Henry as he enters the elevator and turns to press the button for his floor, while Lynch sustains the shot until the elevator doors close. In itself, this is not necessarily unusual. But what is distinctive is how much time passes between Henry's pushing the button and the elevator doors closing. The typical film compresses the time that elevator doors take to close; Lynch elongates it: the doors take a full seventeen seconds to close, during which time the camera does not move. Henry himself doesn't move either, which means that we as spectators must endure seventeen seconds of film in which nothing at all happens. This nothing—this temporal absence within the narrative structure of the film—helps to signify that this is a world of desire. Desire revolves around absence and depends on the continual failure of its object to become present.

Jack Nance plays Henry as a character who never moves quickly nor responds quickly to other characters. When we first see Henry, he is slowly walking home with a sack of groceries. And Lynch makes his pace seem even slower by shooting long takes of this walk. When Henry interacts with his neighbor (Judith Anna Roberts) just after arriving home, his slowness becomes even more apparent. The neighbor tells him that his girlfriend Mary (Charlotte Stewart) has called and invited him to dinner, and Henry waits for a prolonged period of time before simply thanking her for the message. This delay creates a sense of awkwardness, as if something is missing in their conversation, and it underlines the absence of any fantasmatic structure in this part of the film. Fantasy serves to fill in awkward lacunas just like this one, to speed up our interactions (and the pace of our lives) so that we don't see the absences. But absences characterize our bare social reality without a fantasmatic supplement.

Henry constantly seems to be missing something. He desires something that remains absent or at least concealed, but he does not even know enough about this object to know what he desires. Lynch himself describes Henry in terms of the attitude of desiring subjectivity: "Henry is very sure that something is happening, but he doesn't understand it at all. He watches things very, very carefully, because he's trying to figure them out. . . . Everything is new. It might not be frightening to him, but it could be a key to something. Everything should be looked at. There could be clues in it."[9] In this first part of the film, Henry's desire does not have the coordinates that might direct it toward an object. It is in this sense that Henry is the pure subject of desire: his desire is unalloyed by fantasy to such an extent that it has no direction at all. Henry privileges no particular object but views the whole world as a mystery that might disclose *the* object; for him, as Lynch himself notes, everything "could be a key."

Both Henry's mode of dress and Jack Nance's way of playing the role make clear his alienation from the world in which he exists. As Paul Woods notes, "His relationship with the world is that of a passive, bemused onlooker—he cannot be said to have any true place in it. His desires are many, but frustrated."[10] Henry is a quintessential desiring subject because he is a complete outsider. He does not dress like someone who fits comfortably within the world that he occupies. Through-out the film, he wears an unfashionable, nondescript suit, pants that are too short, and a pocket protector filled with multiple pens and pencils. As Henry, Nance always moves mechanically in the film. While he walks, he seems to place each foot on the ground with deliberation rather than in a natural manner. He seldom speaks, and when he does, he speaks without much emotion, even in situations where we might expect an emotional display (as when Mrs. X [Jeanne Bates] asks him if he's had sexual intercourse with Mary). Nance's portrayal of Henry's movements and speech indicates his alienated—and thus desiring—relationship to the world.

The association of Henry Spencer with desiring subjectivity appears counterintuitive. When we think of a subject who desires, we tend to think of one the opposite of Henry: emotional rather than stolid, viva-cious rather than mechanical, energetic rather than impassive. But such an association forgets that desire is equivalent to lack. The subject of pure desire would be mechanical and impassive because she/he would be an embodiment of lack. Such a subject would have no vitality at all (which is why the subject of pure desire is unthinkable for us). The de-gree of one's alienation as a subject is at once the degree of one's desire because the alienated subject constantly experiences her/his lack. The more one feels alienated, the more one experiences a desire to escape this alienation, even if the escape remains unimagined.

The film perpetuates Henry's alienation on the spectator. Watching the film, one must endure the lack of light, the barrenness of the image, and the long stretches of time in which nothing happens. This alien-ation pushes the spectator, as it does Henry, into the position of the de-siring subject: like Henry, one experiences oneself in the middle of a world that doesn't make sense, and one desires to access its mysteries. One experiences this desire all the more because a hidden enjoyment seems to be lurking everywhere just out of reach.

Enjoyment has been relegated to the margins, outside human subjectivity—even the film's audio track hosts a constant din of factory noises during all of the exterior and many of the interior shots. The sounds indicate activity and vitality, but it is the vitality of machines. As Greg Hainge notes, "The noise permeating *Eraserhead* is an industrial drone which suggests that the viewer is inhabiting a machinic world."[11] Visually, the burnt-out industrial setting connotes an enjoyment that is located elsewhere—in the years past, before the steel barrels, pipes, and chain fences by which Henry walks became the traces of vanished industrial activity.

The process of industrial capitalist production functions through the sacrifice of laborers who work rather than enjoy themselves. Without this perpetual sacrifice, production would come to a standstill. In this sense, capitalist industry feeds off the enjoyment of those who work for it. But the sacrificed enjoyment does not just disappear. The machines of industry themselves manifest the enjoyment that human workers have given up: they run with a vitality that the human worker lacks.[12] The capitalist production process also displays this enjoyment through its by-product—surplus value. According to Marx, the capitalist pays the worker fairly for the value of her/his labor, but what the capitalist appropriates without compensation is the surplus value that the very productivity of labor generates. Surplus value becomes the source of the capitalist's profit, and it conspicuously alludes to what the worker has sacrificed.[13] But the film never allows us to see directly the industrial production that feeds off the sacrifice of enjoyment made by subjects such as Henry. In this world of desire, there are traces of enjoyment, but enjoyment itself is always elsewhere.

The opposition between the absence of enjoyment among human subjects and the location of enjoyment in production and the natural world becomes clear when Henry goes to dinner at Mary's house. The interaction between Henry, Mrs. X, and Mary just after Henry's arrival displays the contrast. In the X living room, we see Henry and Mary sitting on a couch while Mrs. X sits on a nearby chair. Long stretches of silence and misunderstanding punctuate their conversation. Mrs. X asks Henry what he does, and, after a long pause, Henry responds, "I'm on vacation." This response, which clearly misunderstands her question, forces Mrs. X to ask, "What did you do?" The stilted nature of the conversation between Henry and Mrs. X reveals the role that lack plays in this world. Neither of these characters displays any aliveness in the scene, which is what makes the conversation seem so difficult.

The grandmother (Jean Lange) exhibits more conspicuously the lifelessness at the X house. Throughout Henry's entire visit, she sits in the same chair in the kitchen without standing up or saying a word. Her only movement occurs when Mrs. X uses her to prepare the salad. Mrs. X lays the salad bowl in the grandmother's lap and places salad tongs in the grandmother's hands. She stands behind the grandmother, grabs her hands holding the tongs, and tosses the salad by manipulating her hands. This brief sequence highlights the inactivity of the grandmother. She exists here as a lifeless puppet, a status confirmed by what happens subsequently. After using the grandmother to toss the salad, Mrs. X puts a cigarette in the grandmother's mouth and lights it. Puffing on the cigarette is the only activity we see the grandmother do, though we never see her lift her hand to remove the cigarette from her mouth. Lynch draws attention to her utter immobility in order to emphasize the absence of animation not only in the X family but also in Henry's entire world.

Aliveness appears where we wouldn't expect to see it. Throughout the conversation between Henry, Mrs. X, and Mary, we hear in the background the obtruding noise of several puppies suckling their mother. Of course, puppies suckling their mother is not an uncommon occurrence, but what is uncommon is its visibility and audibility. After we see Henry, Mary, and Mrs. X seated in the living room, Lynch cuts to a shot of the floor that graphically shows the puppies and their mother. The sound of the suckling stands out to such an extent that the entire subsequent conversation seems to occur in the background of the suckling puppies. This juxtaposition stresses the extreme opposition between the excess of enjoyment in the animal world and the lack of it in the human world.

A similar opposition becomes apparent during the dinner itself. For dinner, Mr. X (Allen Joseph) prepares what he calls "man-made chicken." But when Henry tries to cut the "chicken," it begins to move spontaneously, and a liquid oozes out of it. After we see a shot of the chicken's movement, the subsequent shot depicts Mrs. X beginning to convulse as her eyes roll to the back of her head. Lynch cuts to a close-up of the moving chicken and then back to a medium shot of Mrs. X moaning with her head tilted back. The sequence of shots here indicates a causal relationship: Mrs. X's convulsions emerge in response to the man-made chicken's display of aliveness—an aliveness that she herself lacks.

Eraserhead depicts a world of absence in order to show what results from the initial sacrifice of enjoyment. In this world, the absence of the object-cause of desire colors every scene. Henry exists here as a dissatisfied, desiring subject. But because the dissatisfaction exists in the very structure of the filmic world itself—in the mise-en-scène, in the editing, in the composition of the shots—it becomes evident that Henry cannot simply rouse himself: the dissatisfaction has a constitutive status for Henry and, the film implies, for the subject as such. The desiring subject necessarily exists in a world of absence where the only satisfaction is elsewhere.

The Cause of Fantasy

Despite what we might think, dissatisfaction and frustration alone do not lead directly to the development of a fantasmatic alternative to the world of desire. Typically, we tend to see fantasizing solely as a response to dissatisfaction within social reality. Freud gives a general description of this process in the Clark Lectures. He says, "The energetic and successful man is one who succeeds by his efforts in turning his wishful phantasies into reality. Where this fails, as a result of the resistances of the external world and of the subject's own weakness, he begins to turn away from reality and withdraws into his more satisfying world of phantasy, the content of which is transformed into symptoms should he fall ill."[14] Here, Freud claims that fantasy provides an internal compensation for what the subject fails to attain in the external world. In *Eraserhead*, Lynch does not so much refute this idea as add a degree of nuance. For Lynch, fantasy remains a response to dissatisfaction with one's social reality, but it doesn't emerge when the subject's desired object is completely absent. It emerges at the moment when the subject encounters a reminder in the Other of the subject's own lack.

Throughout the beginning of the film, Henry endures the dissatisfaction of his existence without recourse to fantasy. When Henry enters his apartment for the first time in the film (after stepping in a puddle while walking home), we see him lie on his bed and stare at the radiator, but at this point he doesn't see the fantasmatic scene that will later appear. He thinks he has lost Mary, and he sits alone in his apartment with nothing to do. In the midst of the complete absence of the object of desire, he does not turn to fantasy, though he does stare at the spot where his fantasy will later take shape. Lynch suggests here that the subject can endure the absence of enjoyment as long as no apparent barrier to this enjoyment is visible. Ironically, it is the barrier to the subject's enjoyment that causes the subject to experience itself as lacking, and the subject turns to fantasy only at the moment when she/he must confront this barrier.[15]

After the dinner scene at the X home, the film cuts to Mary taking care of the baby (a startling, reptilian-like mutant) in Henry's apartment. It is only after we see Mary and the baby at Henry's apartment that Henry begins to have intimations about the enjoyment that he has sacrificed. The baby's constant crying signals to Henry and to the spectator not so much its own enjoyment as Henry's lack of it. The baby embodies a barrier to Henry's enjoyment, even though, as we know, Henry wasn't enjoying himself before the baby's arrival anyway. This contrast becomes evident when Henry checks his mail slot. The first time that Henry checks his mail slot early in the film, its emptiness is indicative of the emptiness of his world—the complete absence of the object. But when Mary and the baby arrive, Henry finds a small object that resembles the spermlike substance from the opening of the film. This object is a piece of the life substance that he sacrificed in the act that gave birth to Henry's social reality. The object harkens back to the original lost enjoyment, and it will energize his fantasies about this original state.

Henry begins to fantasize about the Radiator Lady after he brings this object into his apartment. By locating Henry's fantasy within the radiator, Lynch suggests that a relationship exists between the industrial world and fantasy. On the one hand, Henry turns to fantasy in order to escape this world and the dissatisfaction that it creates; on the other hand, fantasy emerges from a machine that belongs to that same industrial world. Fantasy is an escape into an alternative world, but that new world is the product of the old world that one flees. The world of desire—the social reality—always anchors the world of fantasy. As Lacan puts it in *Seminar X*, "The fantasy is framed," just as the materiality of the radiator provides the frame for the stage on which the Radiator Lady appears.[16]

Even though this world of fantasy emerges from the materiality of the world of desire, Lynch emphasizes its status as otherworldly. The film's form changes when this fantasy occurs, as if to suggest that we are entering an alternate space. We see Henry looking into the radiator, followed by a shot of two metal doors that cover the entire screen and open into complete blackness. Out of the blackness, the camera begins to pan along the foot of a stage as a series of lights come on one by one. After the lighting of the last light, the camera pans to the feet of a woman on the stage. As she starts to dance, the whole body of the woman becomes visible. This scene is unlike any that have come before it: not only is the lighting much brighter than in the rest of the film, but the entire cheery atmosphere of the scene stands in stark contrast to the somber tone of all the scenes up till now.

In the fantasy of the Radiator Lady, Henry experiences what he misses in the world of desire. Here, the object of desire becomes a present object that one can see, if not actually touch. As Michel Chion notes, "The Lady in the Radiator is related to perfect love and the dream of incestuous fusion. When Henry comes on to the stage of his fantasy and touches her with his fingertips, a blinding flash and a burst of sound are used to convey the unbearable intensity of this moment."[17] This kind of intensity is entirely lacking in the world of desire that the rest of the film depicts. It serves as a harbinger of the film's conclusion, in which Henry's turn to fantasy becomes complete. But Henry's fantasy at this point is not confined to the encounter with the Radiator Lady; it also reveals the truth of his situation within the system of production.

During the fantasy sequence, Henry imagines himself on the stage with the Radiator Lady, who holds her hands in front of her face inviting him toward her. But when Henry touches her hands, the screen becomes completely white with light—a light so bright that it forces the spectators to look away, especially after one has become accustomed to looking at such a sparsely lighted film. This whiteness suggests the ultimate enjoyment embodied in the fantasy object, but just after the experience of it, the Radiator Lady disappears.

Capitalist Production and Human Reproduction

In this fantasy scene, Henry comes close to the enjoyment of his fantasy object but finally cannot reach it. His failure exposes his castration, which is the lack of full enjoyment that every subject has as a result of being subjected to the restrictions of the social order. In psychoanalytic terms, castration is not a literal event but a metaphorical process that produces the desiring subject. It is the mythical sacrifice of life substance that occurs at the beginning of *Eraserhead*. Just as we see castration unfold at the beginning of the film, Henry sees it occur during the fantasy sequence that begins with the Radiator Lady.

After the disappearance of the Radiator Lady, the fantasy continues as some kind of protuberance emerges from Henry's body and displaces his head, knocking it to the ground. The head of the baby then rises out of Henry's body and assumes the place of his head. The source of Henry's castration is not, as we might expect from the standard psychoanalytic account, a demand by the social law that Henry give up his privileged love object. Instead, it is Henry's own baby whose head emerges out of Henry's torso and thereby pops Henry's own head off. This striking image suggests that the misshapen baby is itself the source of Henry's castration. The link between the baby and the subject's lack derives from the reproductive process. In the act of reproduction, the subject attests to its status as lacking—as a sexed being. If the subject were complete in itself, it would have no need or even ability to reproduce itself. When sexed reproduction occurs, the child emerges as a replacement for the parents and embodies the life substance that they have sacrificed.[18] Thus, as Hegel puts it, when parents give birth to a child, "they generate their own death."[19] In Henry's fantasy sequence, he is able to witness this process at work in a way that remains veiled in the ordinary experience of reality. That is to say, subjects typically don't see directly the role that their children play in objectifying or signifying their castration. But because fantasy brings the subject back to the nonexistent moment of originary loss, it allows the subject to see the impossible.

By allowing the subject this view of the impossible, the fantasy lies. It narrates or temporalizes an experience of loss that has no temporal existence. Loss constitutes the subject as a subject; to narrate this loss is to imagine a subject prior to loss—or a subject existing prior to becoming a subject. In doing so, fantasy creates a sense of paranoia in the subject: rather than seeing its loss as constitutive, the subject identifies an agent responsible for the loss—in Henry's case, the baby. Clearly, Henry lived in a desolate world barren of enjoyment before the arrival of the baby, but the fantasy locates the theft of Henry's enjoyment in this figure. In one sense, the fantasy deceives Henry concerning the real source of his dissatisfaction, but in another sense it provides him with a unique glance at what his everyday life obscures. Fantasy's lie acts as a vehicle through which it can reveal a fundamental truth about subjectivity.

The insight of Henry's fantasy sequence stems from the relationship that it envisions between the loss that occurs in sexed reproduction (in sexuation as such) and the loss that occurs for the laborer under capitalism. This is a vexed question for psychoanalysis, and it often causes historicist thinkers to dismiss the psychoanalytic account of castration.

This account, so the critique goes, conceives a structural process at work when the process is actually historically rooted.[20] That is to say, for its detractors the psychoanalytic narrative of castration fails to accommodate historical variegations—specifically, the form of loss that capitalism produces in the subject.

But Lynch makes clear the connection between the loss that accompanies sexed reproduction and the loss necessitated by capitalist production when the film depicts the role that Henry's head plays in the productive process. After the dream sequence depicts Henry's head falling to the ground, we see a puddle of blood form around it, and eventually the head surreally drops through this puddle onto the ground outside Henry's apartment building. Through this seemingly impossible sequence of events, the dream logic connects Henry's private psychic drama to the functioning of society as a whole. Lynch's film emphasizes here the interconnection of these two realms despite their seeming incongruity.

After Henry's head falls to the ground outside, a young boy runs and picks it up. He brings Henry's head to a pencil factory where he tries to sell it. The factory buys the head from the boy after a technician tests its usefulness by drilling into it and extracting material to insert into a machine that produces pencil erasers. After the machine produces an eraser with the material from Henry's head, the technician tests the eraser to confirm that it works properly. We see Henry's castration directly providing the material for the production of a commodity.[21]

But not just any commodity. Henry fantasizes his head becoming material for an eraser because it allows him to imagine himself playing a part in the elimination of the materiality of the signifier. Not only is Henry subjected to the signifier like all of us, but he also works as a printer: his labor involves the production of signifiers. The eraser undoes this labor and renders it useless. The fantasy thus provides an avenue through which Henry can negate the source of his dissatisfaction. But the by-product of this process is an insight into the violence of the productive apparatus.

Clearly, no one makes erasers from human heads. But what Lynch's film suggests here is the ability of capitalist production to capitalize on the loss that occurs in castration. Every social order demands castration—that is, it demands a sacrifice of enjoyment by its subjects. What makes capitalism distinct, according to the dream sequence of

Eraserhead, is what it does with the sacrifice. It uses the sacrificed enjoyment to feed its ever-expanding production process. There is a direct link between individual acts of sacrificing enjoyment and the growth of capitalism. This is what Marx is getting at in the 1844 *Manuscripts* when he claims,

> The less you eat, drink and buy books; the less you go to the theater, the dance hall, the public house; the less you think, love, theorize, sing, paint, fence, etc., the more you *save*—the *greater* becomes your treasure which neither moths nor dust will devour—your *capital*. The less you *are*, the less you express your own life, the greater is your *alienated* life, the more you *have*, the greater is your store of estranged being.[22]

Capitalism requires an ever-increasing quantity of sacrifice—the ceding of enjoyment for what Marx calls "estranged being"—since the acts of sacrifice feed the growth that capitalism must have.

To our contemporary ears, Marx's idea that capitalism demands that we eat, drink, and buy less seems absurd. Consumer capitalism not only tolerates excessive eating, drinking, and buying, but it actually demands these activities, just as it discourages saving. But to dismiss Marx's claim as anachronistic in our current version of capitalism would miss the importance of the contrast he draws. A capitalist economy demands that we place an emphasis on having rather than being, and it prompts us to think of all our experiences in terms of what we can have. Even in consumer capitalism, the logic of having predominates. One wants literally to have a good time, not to allow oneself to enjoy.[23] The more we want to have, the more we support the machinery of capitalist production.

But the subject under capitalism is not simply a hopeless victim of this production process. As Lynch indicates through this dream sequence, a way out exists through fantasy. Fantasy has a radical potential because it can render visible the subject's castration and the role that this castration plays in the functioning of capitalist society. It stages Henry's castration for him through the way that it presents the impossible object. As long as Henry exists as a subject in the world of desire, he experiences a vague sense of lack, but he never grasps exactly what bars his access to the privileged object. In this world, the object is simply absent. But in the fantasmatic fiction, the object becomes present and seemingly accessible. The illusion of the object's accessibility allows Henry to see his castration as the barrier preventing him from attaining it and to see the role that his castration plays in mechanical production. The vision provided by fantasmatic experience enables him to struggle against the perennial dissatisfaction that had hitherto defined his existence.

The Proximity of the Enjoying Other

After Henry awakens from the dream, the film indicates that he experiences a changed reality. The first shot after the dream sequence shows him waking up in his bed in his apartment. What is instantly striking in this shot is the lack of the noise that we usually hear in the apartment—the baby crying. This absence provides the first clue that something has changed, which Henry's subsequent glance out the window confirms. This look out the window is shocking in the first instance simply because Henry can see outdoors. Though prior to the dream a brick wall was flush against the window, eliminating any possible view, now the wall no longer exists. Looking through the window, Henry sees someone violently assaulting another person. Like the very existence of the window, this incident tells us a great deal about the transformation that Henry has undergone in his dream.

Whereas before the dream Henry lives in a world of absence and little enjoyment, the postdream world forces Henry to experience the enjoyment that occurs around him. Because the dream fantasy allows Henry to witness his own castration, he now feels his own failure to enjoy—and the ubiquitous enjoyment of the Other—all the more tangibly. The unavoidable dissatisfaction of the bricked-over window gives way to an image of violent enjoyment and thus presents a turn from absence to presence. Henry can now see what lay hidden in the empty spaces and absences of the world of desire, and this changes the way that he exists as a desiring subject.

The visibility of enjoyment becomes most apparent in Henry's relationship with his neighbor. When she appears in the first part of the film, the neighbor exudes a sense of mystery, but Henry never learns anything about her. In the dream sequence, Henry fantasizes about the neighbor having sex with him in his bed. After the dream, however, the status of the neighbor changes dramatically. When he hears a noise in the hall, Henry opens his door and sees the neighbor with another man.

From Henry's perspective, we see the man groping the neighbor as she is opening the door to her apartment. Then we see the neighbor looking directly at Henry with a puzzled expression. A reverse shot shows the head of the baby on Henry's shoulders in the place of his own head. This sequence reveals the presence of enjoyment surrounding Henry, but it also depicts his own sense of castration (and the visibility of that castration). Henry quickly shuts the door after this encounter and stares through the keyhole as the door to the neighbor's apartment shuts behind the couple. After this encounter with the enjoying other and with the foregrounding of his own castration, Henry lashes out violently against the baby.

Cutting away the baby's bandages—an act signifying Henry's refusal to accept the restrictions that the social order places on one's enjoyment—has two related effects, and both indicate an attempt to unleash enjoyment. The most obvious effect is the death of the baby itself. Henry's fantasy has shown him the part that the baby plays in his castration, and here Henry responds by destroying the baby, thereby rejecting that castration and its attendant loss of enjoyment. The second effect is metaphorical: Henry allows the insides of the baby to burst forth. The act of stabbing these insides with his scissors, though it kills the baby, releases a huge quantity of foamy substance from within the baby. The film depicts this substance oozing out and completely covering its body. Here, we see unleashing of bodily enjoyment after the social restrictions have been cut away. This unleashing of enjoyment destroys the baby, disrupts the mechanisms of production, and even creates a hole in the world. But it frees Henry from his castration and makes it possible for him to experience the direct contact with his fantasy object that was previously impossible.

By detailing Henry's violent destruction of the helpless baby, Lynch begins to elaborate the price that one pays for the realization of one's fantasy. The grotesque form of the baby doesn't necessarily lessen the horror of the act. But nonetheless, the film depicts it as a triumph for Henry. The conclusion that this act brings about provides its implicit justification.

Lynch's point here is not that we must kill our children if we are to enjoy ourselves. It is rather that the realization of fantasy, while fully possible, is always violent. In the act of realizing one's fantasy, one necessarily destroys some barrier to enjoyment that fantasy posits. *Eraser-*

head implicates the spectator directly in Henry's act of destruction because it invests the spectator in the realization of Henry's fantasy.

At this early point in his filmmaking career, Lynch is at his most ambivalent about remaining true to one's fantasy. Though he depicts Henry's reality as oppressive and restricting, he emphasizes the destructiveness of Henry's embrace of the fantasmatic alternative. In the last instance, *Eraserhead* endorses Henry's act as a political gesture that unleashes the enjoyment that he has sacrificed to capitalist production. The film conceives of allegiance to fantasy as a mode of combating capitalism. But this endorsement does not come without a caveat.

Having It All

Eraserhead ends in the way that every David Lynch film ends: the protagonist realizes her/his fantasy and achieves a moment of complete satisfaction. This would seem to locate *Eraserhead*, despite its bizarre structure, within the orbit of traditional Hollywood film. In the typical Hollywood film, the subject also realizes its fantasy—as, for instance, at the conclusion of *Pretty Woman* (Garry Marshall, 1990) when the wealthy Edward (Richard Gere) arrives in a limousine to ask the prostitute Vivian (Julia Roberts) to marry him. In terms of its narrative trajectory, the conclusion of *Eraserhead* is every bit, if not more, fantasmatic: Henry manages to embrace the wholly fantasmatic—and hitherto out of reach—Radiator Lady, and we see their embrace bathed in an ethereal white light. The difference between these two conclusions lies in their exploration of the full consequences that attend fantasmatic fulfillment.

In the case of *Pretty Woman* (or any typical Hollywood film), the culminating fantasy has the power to solve antagonisms—that is, sexual or class antagonisms—that the narrative has previously explored. But the film never shows us the cost of this solution. The resolution has no effect on the structure of the social order, on the desire of the characters involved, or on the structure of the narrative itself. It is precisely this lacuna that locates *Pretty Woman* within the orbit of the traditional Hollywood film. In this sense, unlike *Pretty Woman*, *Eraserhead* refuses to employ fantasy and hold it at a distance simultaneously. It evinces a full commitment to fantasy in its denouement, and this full commitment exposes both fantasy's liberating possibilities and its steep costs.

After Henry destroys the baby, the film's form changes in order to convey the unleashing of enjoyment. The lights in Henry's apartment begin to flicker. At an electrical outlet where a lamp is plugged in, sparks fly out. A background hum grows louder and louder. Then Lynch includes a series of alternating shots of Henry's head and the baby's head in rapid succession. This sequence concludes with a close-up of the light, which finally burns out into a total darkness that covers the screen. Next, the film cuts to a shot of the planet (from the opening sequence) breaking open. The dust from this explosion sparkles behind Henry's head in a shot that places Henry in front of a black background. After this famous image of Henry, the camera returns to the planet and moves forward into the hole that has broken open. The subsequent shot of the man in the cabin indicates the effect that Henry's choice of refusal of castration has on the mechanical production process. We see him striving to hold the final lever in place, but he cannot. The film fades to white, and the Radiator Lady appears. She walks forward and hugs Henry, as he attains the hitherto inaccessible fantasy object.

With this concluding embrace of the Radiator Lady, Henry finally escapes the dissatisfaction that has haunted him throughout the film. He discovers the enjoyment that derives from embracing one's private fantasy. Through the act of opting for his fantasy, Henry attains enjoyment but shatters his world and destroys his baby. Of course, this world is bleak industrialized wasteland, and his baby is inhuman. In this sense, Henry's act at the end of the film seems perfectly justified and even appropriate. However, even if the final turn toward fantasy is liberating, Lynch never allows us to forget that it necessitates destruction as well. One has a choice, the same choice that every subject has as it enters the social order: either dissatisfaction within a consistent social reality or enjoyment without it. By returning to this choice and reversing his earlier decision, Henry frees himself from his own sacrifice, just as the film suggests that we can.[24]

The embrace of fantasy destroys the consistency of our social reality because its consistency depends on the shared sacrifice of enjoyment. If even one subject abandons this sacrifice, such an act creates a disturbance in our social reality. The political implications of embracing one's fantasy stem from its link to the refusal of sacrifice. The subject who refuses to sacrifice at the same time refuses the capitalist production process and does violence to the world sustained by this process.

In *Eraserhead*, Lynch reveals how the capitalist system of production capitalizes on the sacrifice of enjoyment that the subject makes in the act of becoming a sexed being. This sacrifice produces dissatisfaction for the subject, but it also produces the surplus enjoyment that moves the gears of capitalist production. By accepting our dissatisfaction, we sustain this movement. The film thus compels us to see our individual complicity in the furtherance of this production process. However, the attempt to escape this state of dissatisfaction cannot occur without violence. As *Eraserhead* shows, we can get what we want—we can accomplish the impossible—and escape the chronic dissatisfaction of the capitalist world, but we can't do so without the destruction of the world itself.

This is a barrier that few, even the most radical subjects, are able to cross. Our investment in the capitalist world derives from the stable grounding that it provides for our identity. In *Seminar XX*, Lacan points out that a secure and constant "meaning is provided by the sense each of us has of being part of his world."[25] Our world is not just a place we inhabit; it is a fictional center to which we can always appeal. Specifically addressing the leftists in his audience, Lacan tells them, "you are more attached to it than you care to know and would do well to sound the depths of your attachment."[26] *Eraserhead* offers subjects—leftists and all others—an opportunity to "sound the depths" of their attachment to the dissatisfactions of the capitalist world. By presenting the destruction of this world and the meaning it provides as the price for escaping its chains, Lynch demands that we confront the ultimate barrier to political acts—our investment in the very structure that our acts would contest.

TWO The Integration of the Impossible Object

in *The Elephant Man*

A Doubly Divided Film

Eraserhead (1977) established Lynch as a significant new voice in independent cinema, but not many people saw the film. It screened primarily at midnight showings in New York City, which allowed it to attract a cult following. Respected directors like John Waters and Stanley Kubrick noticed and appreciated the film, but it was Mel Brooks and his love of the film that transformed Lynch's filmmaking career. After watching a private screening of the film, Brooks offered Lynch the chance to direct a project that he was producing for Paramount. This project became *The Elephant Man* (1980), the film that brought Lynch an exponential increase in public and critical recognition. Whereas *Eraserhead* toiled away as a midnight movie, *The Elephant Man* earned Academy Award nominations for Best Picture, Best Director, Best Screenplay, and Best Actor (John Hurt). It changed Lynch's life.[1]

The turn from *Eraserhead* to *The Elephant Man* is a turn from independent and experimental filmmaking to Hollywood cinema. But Lynch's fundamental concerns as a filmmaker nonetheless remain constant. *The Elephant Man* develops and radicalizes the distinction that *Eraserhead* draws between the world of desire and the world of fantasy. Here, the world of fantasy loses the dreamlike quality that it has in

Eraserhead and becomes another mode of reality itself. That is, *The Elephant Man* depicts two versions of reality—one structured through desire and the other through fantasy. In the same way as *Eraserhead*, the film uses this division in order to reveal what results when one fully realizes one's fantasy. Through the turn away from desire, both the spectator and the central characters are able to realize their fantasies, but this realization comes at a visible cost. Fantasy allows the subject to accomplish the impossible but does so by destroying the subject itself. Whereas *Eraserhead* shows how the realization of the fantasy necessitates an act of violent destruction, *The Elephant Man* reveals that the violence must also be done to oneself. In this sense, Lynch suggests that the subject retains its subjective identity by sustaining distance from its fundamental fantasy. *The Elephant Man* erases this distance when it turns from the depiction of a world of desire to immerse us fully in a world of fantasy.

Most critics have noticed the radical division that exists in the reality that *The Elephant Man* presents. For instance, Martha Nochimson notes that "the doppelganger effect of model Victorian life and its shadow is, as in *Blue Velvet*, rendered with a clear division between the two, offering an elementary Lynchian depiction of the carnivalesque relationship between social order and social disorder."[2] For Nochimson, the primary division in the film exists between the kindness shown for John Merrick (John Hurt) during the day and the exploitation of him at night. Merrick's doctor Frederick Treves (Anthony Hopkins) is the representative figure of the first realm, and the night porter (Michael Elphick) is the representative figure of the second. But this division between the daytime kindness of Treves and the nighttime exploitation of the night porter is not a division between a world of desire and its fantasmatic underside. It represents two different modes of fantasmatic experience—one positive and one negative—and it serves to obscure the more radical split between the world of desire and the world of fantasy that Lynch establishes in the film.

Lynch creates the distinction between experience structured through desire and experience structured through fantasy in the way that he deploys the grotesque body of John Merrick. The most controversial decision that Lynch made as the young director of *The Elephant Man* was his refusal to show Merrick's body for the first thirty minutes of the film. But the decision is essential to the structure of the film: Merrick's body initially functions as a present absence in the film, producing a world of desire in which the object-cause of desire—Merrick's body itself—remains an absence that attracts and structures our desire.

Lacan distinguishes between the actual object of desire and the object-cause of desire, which he calls the *objet petit a*. Unlike objects of desire, which we access all the time, the *objet petit a* remains fundamentally inaccessible. It has no actual existence but nonetheless serves to trigger the desire of the subject. It is the inflection that transforms the everyday object into an object of desire, thereby eroticizing the visual field. The subject doesn't see the *objet petit a*, but its absence from the visual field is what makes the subject desire to look. The repulsiveness of Merrick's actual body in no way disqualifies it from playing the role of the *objet petit a* because this object is constitutively absent and cannot become present.

Fantasy envisions access to this impossible object, allowing us to see what otherwise remains invisible. It provides enjoyment for the subject precisely because it changes the impossible object into a possible one. When Lynch exposes Merrick's body after the first thirty minutes of the film, we enter a world of fantasy in which a fantasmatic scenario allows us a mode of access to the impossible object. In this way, *The Elephant Man* operates around the same split that animates all of Lynch's films.

The Inaccessibility of the Horrible Object

After an initial montage sequence that attempts to convey the traumatic elephant attack that allegedly produced the disfigurement of John Merrick, *The Elephant Man* begins with an emphasis on the intense enjoyment that accompanies the experience of seeing Merrick. We see Treves at a carnival freak show on a quest to glimpse the Elephant Man. This scene begins with a close-up of blasts of fire at the carnival, and then the film cuts to a tracking shot of Treves as he walks through a bustling throng of people. This shot stresses the frenetic activity of this crowd, and eventually the camera even loses sight of Treves amidst this activity. After we lose sight of Treves, Lynch cuts to a sign that says "FREAKS" and to a close-up of a door that says "No Entry" above it.[3] These two shots establish the idea of an enjoyment ("FREAKS") that is off-limits ("No Entry"). On his way to sees the freaks, Treves passes through another door that says "No Entry" and walks through labyrinthine narrow corridors. We even see a woman being led in tears out of the exhibit, which suggests the trauma associated with seeing Merrick.

The signifiers that appear in this scene—"FREAKS" and "No Entry"—indicate in similar ways the presence of enjoyment. Enjoyment derives from an encounter with a symbolic limit and thus requires the limit.[4] The freak show allows the subject attending it to transgress the dictates of their own conscience that tells them of its inhumanity and barbarity. One enjoys a freak show not in spite of one's moral revulsion at the idea but because of it. The spectacle allows the subject to enjoy violating its internal superegoic command. The sign that says "No Entry" performs a similar function in relation to the external law. It provides the subject with a signifier of law that the subject can enjoy transgressing. Here we see the most fundamental function of the superego and the law: they act as vehicles for our enjoyment through the limits that they establish.[5]

When Treves finally traverses all the barriers to the Elephant Man exhibit and is on the verge of seeing Merrick for the first time, a police official closes the exhibit. The official tells Bytes (Freddie Jones), Merrick's "manager," that the very grotesqueness of Merrick precludes his public display. The exchange between the official and Bytes helps to create a sense of the extreme nature of Merrick's deformity and thus also the incredible enjoyment that would come from looking at him:

POLICE OFFICIAL: The exhibit degrades everybody who sees it, as well as the poor creature himself.

BYTES: He is a freak. How else will he live?

POLICE OFFICIAL: Freaks are one thing. We have no objection to freaks. But this is entirely different. This is monstrous. It shall not be allowed.

Through this dialogue, the film establishes the absolute prohibition on seeing Merrick and further locates him as an object-cause desire. After the police official's harangue against Bytes, the police usher all the spectators, including Treves, out of the building that houses Merrick. In a final shot, the film shows Bytes saying to the unseen Merrick, "Time to move again, my treasure."

Lynch begins the film with this failed encounter with the Elephant Man in order to locate him beyond the field of representation. The interdiction of the object works both within the film and in the film's relation to the spectator. The spectator experiences the impossibility and prohibition of the object just as Treves and the other characters in the film do. By stressing the impossibility of the object on both levels, Lynch allows the spectator to experience the desire that structures the filmic world he presents.

On the level of narrative, the opening sequence is unnecessary. Lynch might have begun the film with Treves's next attempt to see Merrick, which is successful, but he chooses to begin with the initial failed encounter in order to place the spectator in the position of the desiring subject. When one goes to see a film like *The Elephant Man*, one is to a certain extent prepared for the grotesque. However, by thwarting our encounter with the grotesque and by surrounding the Elephant Man with the aura of impossibility, Lynch suggests that Merrick's grotesqueness will transcend whatever expectations we might have.[6]

The subsequent scenes in the first thirty minutes of the film allow us closer access to the figure of Merrick, but they leave him beyond the field of representation. It is as if the prohibition disappears—the police no longer deny Treves and the spectator access to Merrick—but the impossibility of the object remains. On his next visit to see the Elephant Man, Treves succeeds in seeing him, but we as spectators do not. Lynch shoots this scene in such a way that it further establishes Merrick's status as the *objet petit a* or object-cause of desire insofar as it sustains him as a constitutive absence in the visual field which eroticizes that field.

We see Treves walk through a dilapidated slum in order to arrive at the site where Bytes is now keeping Merrick. Bytes initially refuses to allow Treves to see Merrick. However, when Treves offers to pay for a look, Bytes opens a door to an image of total darkness as a low tone begins to sound in the background. Bytes then leads Treves down a hallway to the room where he has Merrick. In this room, Bytes gives his standard speech recounting the tragic history of the Elephant Man—how his disfigurement results from an elephant attack on his mother during her pregnancy—and then the boy who works for him pulls back the curtain to reveal the Elephant Man. But instead of seeing Merrick himself, we see a reaction shot of Treves, who looks shocked, followed by close-ups of Bytes and the boy. Finally, the film shows Merrick himself in the subsequent shot, though only the outline of his figure is visible because of the extreme darkness of the shot. The scene continues with another reaction shot of Treves, and as the camera moves forward to a close-up of his face, he begins to cry. In the concluding shot of this scene, Treves moves forward to examine Merrick, but just when he begins to remove Merrick's hat and mask, the film fades to black. At every point in this scene, Lynch builds the spectator's desire to see Merrick and subsequently frustrates that desire, placing the figure of Merrick at the center of the spectator's desire.

This world of desire continues even after Treves brings Merrick to the hospital. In fact, Lynch goes to extreme cinematic lengths to sustain Merrick as an impossible object during Treves's lecture to his colleagues concerning Merrick's case. During this lecture, Treves displays Merrick publicly in order to illustrate the case while he lectures on it. Lynch begins with a long shot of Treves lecturing with Merrick positioned next to him behind a curtain. During the lecture, we see a shot of assistants beginning to pull back the curtain in order to expose Merrick's body. But just as they pull the curtain back, Lynch cuts 180 degrees to a shot looking at Merrick from behind through another curtain. As a result, we see Merrick in a silhouette shot rather than in the direct shot that we would have had if Lynch had kept the camera in front of Merrick. The assistants use pointers to refer to the different deformities on Merrick's body while Treves speaks about them, but even this is visible only in silhouette. Finally, when Treves concludes his lecture, Lynch returns to the frontal view of Merrick just as the assistants close the curtains. The dramatic editing in this scene serves to accentuate the impossibility of Merrick's body, its inability to exist within the field of representation.

The Elephant Man begins with a series of failures, but these failures represent the very way in which desire itself succeeds. The first half hour of *The Elephant Man* reveals, as Lacan says in *Seminar XI*, that "what one looks at is what cannot be seen."[7] By denying the spectator access to the impossible object, Lynch here makes clear what all his films emphasize: the missing of the object is at once the way in which desire sustains itself. When one retreats from the absence of the object and fantasizes its presence, one leaves the domain of desire. Neither Treves, Merrick, nor the film itself can remain within the world of desire. Each follows a logic that leads inexorably to a fantasmatic resolution in which the impossible object emerges as a possibility.

The Traumatic Turn to Fantasy

After the first thirty minutes of *The Elephant Man* openly hides Merrick's disfigured body from the spectator's vision, the rest of the film displays this body just as openly. If the first part of the film emphasizes Merrick's status as the impossible object, the second part of the film manages to discover a way of accessing this object. The turn from the one to the other is the turn from a world of perpetually dissatisfied desire to a world of fantasmatic enjoyment. By chronicling this turn into a world of fantasy, the film forces us to recognize the price that accompanies fantasmatic fulfillment.

Initially, the presence of the impossible object emerges as a disturbance in the functioning of the world of desire. Its presence has the status of a trauma because when one perceives it, one perceives something at precisely the point where one expects to perceive nothing—a presence at the site where one has hitherto experienced an absence. While viewing *The Elephant Man*, the spectator experiences this moment along with a young nurse in the hospital who is bringing food to Merrick. The film stresses the naïveté and fear of this woman as she approaches Merrick's room. Lynch shoots this approach with a high-angle shot that makes her stature seem even smaller than it actually is. As she walks, we begin to hear a deep pulsing sound that portends danger. We see her open the door to Merrick's room, and then the film cuts to the first direct image of Merrick's body: he is sitting up on his bed without a shirt on. The film quickly cuts back to a shot of the nurse, who screams as she drops the bowl of food that she has been carrying. The camera quickly tracks forward to a close-up of the horrified look on her face. The quick movement of the camera registers the disturbance that the appearance of Merrick has caused in the field of representation. At the moment when Merrick's body becomes a possible presence in the film, the field of representation undergoes a radical change. We leave a world of desire organized around the impossibility of the object-cause of desire and enter into a world of fantasy organized around accessing this object.

Because Lynch establishes Merrick's body as a form of the *objet petit a* during the first half hour of the film, its appearance within the frame accomplishes the impossible. The *objet a* functions only as an absence, motivating the subject's desire through its inaccessibility. One cannot have a present *objet a*, and yet this is what occurs when Merrick's body initially becomes visible. The moment of seeing the *objet a* directly would be akin to seeing oneself looking; one would see how one's own desire distorts the visual field from within the distorted perspective (which is logically impossible). When Lynch reveals Merrick's body, he forces the spectator to become aware of her/himself as looking and as desiring. In our reaction to this revelation, we ourselves become visible as spectators: the disturbance that Merrick's body causes for our look renders that look—and the desire informing it—evident for the first time. At this point, we can no longer believe that we are neutral observers looking on a preexisting series of images; instead, we are desiring subjects looking on a visual field created specifically for our desire.[8]

Merrick's body does not disturb the visual field because it is grotesque or horrifying. It performs this function insofar as Lynch places it in the structural position of the *objet petit a* through his construction of the beginning of the film. The *objet petit a* or object-cause of desire has the status that it has by virtue of the place that it occupies rather than any positive content. Any object can play this role, especially in a film, provided that one constructs the film around its constitutive absence.

Though the initial appearance of Merrick's body disrupts the world of desire created in the opening of *The Elephant Man*, the film subsequently integrates the presence of this disturbing object into its field of representation.[9] In the rest of the film, Merrick ceases to be an absence that haunts the frame and appears present within the frame like the other characters. In fact, Merrick's body appears so frequently in the film that it completely loses its ability to disturb the spectator. We do not, contrary to what some interpreters of the film contend, experience "the pleasure derived from seeing the private and forbidden."[10] The film shows how even a figure as disturbing as the Elephant Man can be smoothly integrated into society and into the field of representation. This capacity for integration testifies to the power of fantasy and the role that it plays in the functioning of the social order.

The fantasy that the film plays out after Merrick's body appears is one of the complete integration of the impossible object. It is as if our blind spot as spectators, the point from which we are looking, could be rendered visible and become part of the film's narrative structure. Within this fantasy, the camera treats Merrick, despite his appearance, as just another character: he fits seamlessly into the visual field. This radical change in status—from impossible object that resists represen-tation to object fully represented—testifies to the power of fantasy to access the inaccessible. Just as the film turns to fantasy for the spectator, the terrain also shifts for the characters within the film.

Through the efforts of Treves and actress Madge Kendal (Anne Bancroft), Merrick becomes not only a part of Victorian society but a highly regarded element within this society. He gains the acceptance by society that he never had any hope of discovering while he labored in the carnival sideshow. In this sense, the second part of the film provides a fantasy scenario for Merrick and for the spectator who witnesses his entrance into society. The film shows Merrick accomplishing the im-possible with the aid of Treves and Kendal.

After rescuing Merrick from Bytes and finding him a room in the hospital, Treves takes the additional step of having Merrick into his home for tea. There, Merrick meets Anne (Hannah Gordon), Treves's wife, who treats Merrick like an honored guest in her home, even though the film makes clear her discomfort when she initially sees Mer-rick. Anne's treatment of Merrick moves him to tears. As he takes her hand, he begins to cry and says, "I'm not used to being treated so well by a beautiful woman." Merrick's tears here indicate the extent to which he is living out a fantasy scenario. From the perspective in which he ex-ists at the beginning of the film, utterly degraded and dehumanized by Bytes and the carnival goers, this scene with Anne is completely un-imaginable, which is why it moves him to the extent that it does. But the filmic fantasy allows Merrick to accomplish the impossible, which is what makes this such a moving scene.

Though Treves begins the integration of Merrick into polite society, it is Madge Kendal who completes the process. After learning of Merrick's intelligence and his acquaintance with culture, Treves publicizes Mer-rick's case and attracts the attention of Kendal, a famous actress on the London stage. Kendal visits Merrick and reads a scene from *Romeo and Juliet* with him. Afterwards, she tells him, "Mr. Merrick, you're not an elephant man at all—you're Romeo." This kind of acceptance and even adoration allows Merrick to have a taste of the normal life that he has de-sired but never been able to attain. It fantasmatically provides him with a sense of the ultimate enjoyment that he associates with normality. Though he never directly states it, Merrick's desire for normality be-comes apparent in his reaction to each normalizing event: he evinces great joy whenever he experiences the everyday activities of a normal life (drinking tea, reading, going to the theater, and so on). But it is Merrick's final act—lying down to sleep like everyone else, even though he knows it will kill him—that fully reveals the extent of his desire for normality. He wants it so much that he is willing to die for it.

Near the end of the film, Kendal invites Merrick to be her guest at the theater, and after the performance, she appears on the stage and dedicates the performance to Merrick. At this point, the entire audience stands and applauds Merrick. This standing ovation at the theater underlines the acceptance of Merrick and the high point of his fantasy scenario. Even if Merrick is "really" living out this event in the film, he experiences it—and we as spectators experience it—as a fantasy simply because it solves completely the problem of desire with which the film began. We experience the successful integration of the impossible object into our everyday world, and Merrick himself experiences what was for him the impossible normal life. Merrick's existence now seems meaningful: he no longer endures the senseless abjection of the carnival; he has a purpose. But this purpose is wholly fantasmatic because it involves the attainment of the impossible.

Obviously the turn to fantasy for the spectator and for characters within the film is not the same. Films can deploy fantasies for the spectator while depicting characters within their social reality and can leave spectators desiring without a fantasmatic escape while showing characters ensconced in a fantasy world. But in *The Elephant Man* Lynch aligns the spectator's experience with that of the characters: when we turn from an experience of a world of desire to a world of fantasy, Merrick and Treves do as well. This parallel structure that Lynch often employs has the effect of breaking down the opposition between what occurs in the act of screening the film and what occurs within the film itself. The spectator finds her/himself in precisely the same position relative to fantasy as the characters themselves.

Though *The Elephant Man* follows the logic of fantasy, it does not break from the conventions of realism in the way that *Eraserhead* does. It does not signal to us as spectators in a clear fashion that we have moved onto the terrain of fantasy. This marks a further refinement of Lynch's idea of the role that fantasy plays for the subject. With *The Elephant Man*, he begins to see how fantasy is not simply an escape from the social reality, an alternative to our everyday drudgery, but the support of our sense of reality. Fantasy becomes a mode of reality.

The Other Side of Fantasy

In one sense, *The Elephant Man* is a celebration of fantasy and what it is able to provide. When Merrick cries after Anne Treves shows him kindness, when Madge Kendal compares Merrick to Romeo, and when the theater audience gives Merrick a standing ovation, we as spectators share in Merrick's enjoyment. The fantasy scenario that informs these moments produces an enjoyment that stems from accomplishing the impossible. By including and emphasizing these moments, Lynch testifies to the power of fantasy and to its ability to deliver enjoyment. Rather than criticizing the turn to fantasy as an escape from an unsatisfying reality, *The Elephant Man* embraces fantasy as a way of structuring one's enjoyment.[11]

But the film does not unequivocally celebrate the turn to fantasy. Lynch does not simply show the fantasy of Merrick finding acceptance in polite Victorian society; he also shows the underside of acceptance: Merrick's immersion into the ugly underside of Victorian society, represented by the figure of the night porter. Not only does Lynch separate the film into distinct worlds of desire and fantasy, but he also splits the fantasmatic portion of the film into a positive and a negative fantasy. During his daytime experience at the hospital, everyone treats Merrick with kindness and welcomes him as a normal, if not privileged, member of society. But Merrick's nighttime experience is altogether different. The night porter organizes a series of visits to Merrick's room in which members of lower-class Victorian society pay for the privilege of being horrified by Merrick's body. Here, the film makes clear that the fantasmatic integration of Merrick into polite Victorian society also has a nightmarish underside—the nighttime visits of drunken revelers that the night porter brings to ogle and torment Merrick. The daytime adoration of Merrick and the nighttime exploitation of him become visible as the two modes through which fantasy works to integrate the impossible object into society.

When he introduces Madge Kendal, Lynch illustrates the parallel between her and the night porter, suggesting that each of them fulfills a similar role in the filmic fantasy. Lynch shows Kendal in her dressing room reading a letter about Merrick in the *London Times*, and he cuts directly from this scene to one of drunken revelers in a bar listening to the night porter reading the same letter. This striking juxtaposition makes clear that despite the class differences between Kendal and the night porter and despite their vastly different ways of treating Merrick, both characters adopt a similar relation to him. They both transform Merrick into an object of curiosity that people are desperate to glimpse. The difference is that Kendal leads high society to see Merrick and that the night porter leads the lower class. The visits of Kendal and her kind produce the positive mode of Merrick's fantasy experience, while the visits of the night porter and his entourage produce the negative mode of that experience.

By cinematically linking Kendal's treatment of Merrick with the night porter's, Lynch indicts the spectator as well as Kendal. No spectator watches *The Elephant Man* and identifies her/his relationship to Merrick with that of the night porter. The film allows us to identify with the gentler position of figures like Kendal and Treves. That is, Lynch does not treat the spectator as one of the exploiters of Merrick but as one of those who succor him. However, because he hints at the speculative identity of Kendal and the night porter, Lynch does not leave us in this position. As we recognize Kendal's complicity in Merrick's exploitation, we simultaneously must recognize our own as spectators. Our very decision to go to a film like *The Elephant Man*, like the bare fact of Kendal's interest in Merrick, attests to our investment in the idea of Merrick as an oddity, even if all we feel is compassion or friendship for him.

Not only does Lynch cinematically stress the parallel between Kendal and the night porter, he also shows us how the relationship with Kendal and with fashionable society renders the nightly abuse more horrific for Merrick. After Merrick receives a dressing case as a gift, we see a crosscutting sequence that juxtaposes Merrick trying out his new items and the night porter preparing another group to visit him. Lynch shows a close-up of Merrick sampling different colognes followed by a shot of the bar where the night porter rounds up clients for his sadistic tour. Lynch then cuts back to a long shot of Merrick brushing his hair with his new brush, after which he shows the approaching group. We return again to Merrick, who now pretends to address Kendal, but when he turns in the midst of doing so, the film cuts to a shot of the night porter, now present in Merrick's room. The subsequent scene involves the torture of Merrick: a man forces a woman to kiss him in front of the group, the crowd pours alcohol down his throat, the porter forces him to look in the mirror, and after the torture ends, Bytes, hidden among the crowd, steals Merrick away from the hospital.

This scene is perhaps the most traumatic in the film not just because it depicts the abuse done to Merrick but because it links this abuse, through crosscutting, to those who treat Merrick with kindness and compassion. The cut from Merrick preparing to address Kendal to the image of the night porter there in her stead reveals the truth of her position. Her compassion—and ours as spectators—becomes visible as part of the mistreatment of Merrick, not an alternative to it. Lynch's crosscutting establishes the speculative identity of compassion and cruelty. Watching the film, we are constantly reminded of our link to this negative side of fantasy.[12]

Both compassion and cruelty treat the object of their concern with condescension. These attitudes allow the subject to ensure its own elevated status as the one giving compassion or administering cruelty. Furthermore, compassion requires a certain amount of cruelty in order to exist. Without the cruelty committed by others there would be no need for my compassion. Even Merrick's disfigurement would require no compassion if we did not live in a cruel world that brutalizes those who have a distorted appearance. In order to sustain oneself as compassionate, one must not act to change the cruel world that creates opportunities where one can display compassion.[13] Which is not to say that compassion and cruelty are equivalent, that there is no difference between Kendal and the night porter, but simply to insist on the inextricable link, the speculative identity, between them.

Like Merrick's fantasmatic integration into society, every fantasy scenario has both a positive and negative mode. In *The Elephant Man* more than in any of Lynch's other films, the link between the positive and the negative fantasy is apparent. Merrick's acceptance into polite Victorian society is dependent on the nighttime visits of the night porter and his entourage. As the film suggests, one cannot simply opt for a positive fantasy and avoid its dark underside. Without its underside, the positive fantasy would cease to provide the enjoyment that it provides because it would no longer provide any indication of the traumatic nature of the impossible object. Both Merrick and the spectator must endure the negative fantasy in order to sustain the positive one.

Fantasy offers the subject enjoyment through a narrative scenario that accesses that impossible object. However, in addition to accessing this object, fantasy must sustain the idea of this object as threatened in order to sustain its desirability. This is where the negative mode of fantasy comes into play. Whereas the positive mode of fantasy allows the subject to access the impossible object, the negative mode of fantasy threatens that access and works to convince the subject that its relationship to the object remains in peril. In this way, the object manages to hold onto its desirability even when it becomes accessible for the subject in the fantasy. The negative mode of fantasy—the horrific visits of the night porter and his customers—allows the positive mode of fantasy to continue to provide the subject with enjoyment.

This allows us to answer the fundamental question raised by the night porter's visits to Merrick's room. Rather than protest, Merrick endures these visits as if they were the price that he must pay for the kindness he receives during the daytime. Given his deep friendship and the trust that exists between them, why doesn't he protest to Treves? Merrick accepts this treatment unquestioningly not because he is a masochist or suffers from some kind of false consciousness but because he understands unconsciously that the enjoyment of his daytime acceptance depends on this nighttime exploitation. The exploitation serves as a constant reminder to Merrick of the threat to his enjoyment. At the same time that this threat imperils Merrick's enjoyment, it sustains his ability to enjoy. Fantasy can allow Merrick to enjoy the impossible object, but it must preserve the object as endangered if it is to remain enjoyable. If the threat to the object disappeared entirely, it would lose its ability to provide enjoyment. This is the role that the night porter's visits play in Merrick's fantasy life and in the film, and this is why these visits are just as crucial for Merrick as the daytime visits of Madge Kendal and the other respected members of society.

The negative side of fantasy is necessary for us as spectators as well. The threat that the night porter represents constantly reminds us of the tenuousness of Merrick's entrance into normal society. The nightly return to the experience of the carnival that the night porter imposes on Merrick indicates the possibility of an actual return to that horrific existence. This threat sustains a normal life for Merrick as a privileged object of desire rather than allowing normality to become mundane and ordinary. On its own, there is nothing inherently desirable about normality, but as an imperiled object, which it is for Merrick, the status of normality changes dramatically. And in fact, the night porter's visits do eventually lead to Merrick's return to the carnival. The inclusion of Bytes's capture of Merrick and Merrick's melodramatic return to Treves—he escapes from Bytes through the aid of other sideshow performers who take pity on him—highlights even more the difficulty, and hence the desirability, of normality for Merrick.

The depiction of the two sides of fantasy in *The Elephant Man* does not transform the film into a condemnation of fantasy. Instead, this duality mirrors the divided attitude that the film takes toward fantasy. On the one hand, fantasy provides an enjoyment that the subject otherwise lacks, but on the other hand, it does so only by adding to the trauma that the subject has faced. As a result, one can render no easy verdict on the role that fantasy plays for society and for the subject. *The Elephant Man* seems to suggest that fantasy is worth the cost. But what the film absolutely insists on is that when we opt for fantasy we must pay this cost for the enjoyment that it provides us.

The Normal and the Abnormal

Lynch shows the spectator the cost that accompanies fantasy: fantasy provides us with the object, but it does so by stripping the object of the very impossibility that makes it an object-cause desire in the first place. Like *Eraserhead*, *The Elephant Man* shows us what results when one fully realizes one's fantasy. The film realizes a fantasy in three different ways: for the spectator, for Treves, and for Merrick himself. The film gives us precisely what we desire as spectators, but it does so in order to show that we don't really desire our desire. That is to say, the appearance of the impossible object within the second part of the film cannot but disappoint the spectator who eagerly longed for its presence while watching the first part. After Merrick's body becomes plainly visible within the film's mise-en-scène, it loses all the potential for enjoyment that it formerly embodied. One watches Merrick in the second part of the film without any sense that one is experiencing a moment that transcends the limits of the order of the possible.

By realizing our desire to see Merrick's body, Lynch forces us to confront the banality of the object, to recognize that it is not the object itself that produces desire but our desire that elevates an ordinary object into an impossible one. As we watch the second part of the film, we see the strangeness of Merrick's body become ordinary. This is what separates *The Elephant Man* (and Lynch's films in general) from the rest of Hollywood. An ordinary Hollywood film would attempt to preserve Merrick as an *objet petit a* even as it allowed us a quick fantasmatic glimpse of this object. It would, in short, blend together the experience of desire and fantasy in order to sustain the power of fantasy over us as subjects. The typical Hollywood film is fantasmatic to the extent that it holds back from a full immersion in fantasy and thus preserves the fantasy's fundamental illusion—that it can really provide access to the impossible object without destroying the object's impossible status. By refusing to turn wholly into the realm of fantasy, film sustains our belief that the ultimate enjoyment is possible. This is precisely what *The Elephant Man* rejects.

Just as the film forces the spectator to realize her/his desire and face the cost of this realization, it does the same for both Treves and Merrick within the film. Treves begins the film desiring to make a name for himself as a doctor by discovering Merrick and presenting his case to the medical world. Not only does Treves realize this desire, but he also succeeds in introducing Merrick into elite Victorian society. He becomes a famous doctor at the same time that he rescues Merrick from the depredations of Bytes and changes Merrick's life unimaginably. Treves realizes his desire by playing out the perfect fantasy scenario. But this scenario does not provide Treves with the satisfaction that he expects. It leaves him despondent because it exposes an aspect of his character that could remain hidden as long as he was only an ambitious young doctor and not the discoverer of the Elephant Man. He becomes aware that ambition and the desire for renown, not the drive for scientific knowledge, was the motivating force behind his actions.

As the trajectory of Treves shows, fantasy lays bare the hidden kernel of the desiring subject to the subject itself, and this is one reason why we resist fully immersing ourselves in fantasy (in the way that *The Elephant Man* demands that we do). After Madge Kendal visits Merrick in the hospital and high society begins to follow her lead, Treves has a moment of self-recognition. He says to Anne, his wife, "I'm beginning to believe that Mr. Bytes and I are very much alike.... What was it all for? Why did I do it? Am I a good man, or am I a bad man?" After Treves utters this final line, the scene ends with a fade to black, and we do not hear Anne respond. Lynch uses the fade-out and the absence of a response to punctuate the questions and make clear that Treves has grasped something essential about his own desire. He couldn't have scripted the narrative any better: he gains notoriety for discovering Merrick, doctors throughout England now know of him, and Merrick feels indebted to Treves for saving his life and giving him a normal existence. But precisely because of the degree of success he enjoys, Treves begins to suffer. The fantasmatic realization of his desire makes evident the similarity between Bytes and himself. Rather than acting for the good of Merrick or for the good of science itself, Treves has acted as he has in order to become a noted scientist, to increase his cultural capital, just as Bytes has acted in order to enrich himself materially.

The complete success of Treves's fantasy leaves him, as it leaves the spectator, with no alternative but to confront his own desire. The seeming purity of Treves's desire initially allows us to experience ourselves as pure spectators. But Treves's recognition about his own desire indicts us as well: we recognize that there is no pure viewing position from which to watch *The Elephant Man*. Whatever is the driving force behind our decision to see the film, it is not just a simple desire to see. The desire to see, Lynch suggests, is connected to an unconscious desire that we do not avow. One is not simply curious to see Merrick's story; one wants to see his disfigurement. *The Elephant Man* forces this latter aspect of desire to become visible. This is what separates the films of David Lynch from other films. By dividing the experience of desire and fantasy, Lynch's films show what results when we immerse ourselves completely in fantasy. This immersion reveals the real of our desire, and such a revelation is necessarily traumatic. The successful fantasy leaves us no possibility for claiming that this is not what we want.

In addition to revealing the hidden kernel of our desire, the full immersion into fantasy also demonstrates the cost that our fantasies exact from us. Through the final gesture of Merrick himself, we see Merrick sacrifice his life in order to complete his fantasy. Throughout the film, Merrick has sustained the fantasy of becoming a normal subject, and when the film ends, he achieves this fantasy as he finally lies down to sleep in the way that everyone else does. Earlier in the film, Merrick tells Treves, "I wish I could sleep like normal people." By lying down to sleep, however, Merrick knowingly cuts off his ability to breathe and suffocates himself.

Lynch shoots this final sequence of the film in a way that emphasizes its fantasmatic quality. We see Merrick sign the model church that he has completed building, and then we see a long shot of Merrick removing the pillows from his bed. Lynch moves the camera slowly toward Merrick as he begins to lie down. Finally, Merrick closes his eyes and lies flat. The camera pans from Merrick's face to the pictures on his desk and to his model church. As the camera moves up through and into a brilliant starry sky, an image of Merrick's mother appears and then fades to white as the film ends. In this scene, Merrick achieves the perfect fantasmatic bliss: he becomes a normal subject, and he reconciles with an image of his beloved mother.

But this success also destroys him. In a scenario in which the subject can achieve the impossible—Merrick can become normal—the subject must disappear. As Lacan insists, "the I as such is precisely excluded in the fantasy."[14] It is the position of the subject that renders the object impossible, and thus fantasy imagines the object without the presence of the subject. The subject's very identity is tied to its status as lacking; if one eliminates this lack, one simultaneously eliminates the subject. This is why every fantasy, not just that of John Merrick, is a fantasy of the subject's disappearance. Most of the time, however, we indulge in fantasy without recognizing what it entails. *The Elephant Man* demands that we become cognizant of the ramifications of fantasy as it concludes with the fantasy-driven death of Merrick. It asks us to see fantasy for what it is and to opt for it, if we do, while embracing the sacrifice that it demands.[15]

The conclusion of the film completes a radical reversal for the spectator. The final image of Merrick sleeping on his back forces the spectator to experience the speculative identity of normality and abnormality, of what is normal and what is most opposed to the normal. Despite his position as an extreme outsider, Merrick wants nothing other than to exist as the normal subject does. According to the logic that the film develops, the normal subject *is* the Elephant Man. We don't just observe, as James Keller contends, that "the misshapen individual is shown to be ... fully human."[16] Instead, Merrick's alienation and abjection highlight that of the normal subject.

Our very ability to invest ourselves in his fantasy of normality and to find his final gesture a compelling act testifies to our own alienated relation to normality. If we simply inhabited normality, if normality provided a seamless identity for us, we would not have the psychic space to take an interest in Lynch's presentation of Merrick's story. Lynch concludes the film as he does in order to force the spectator into a position of speculative identity with Merrick. Recognition of this speculative identity deprives the spectator of any sense of distance from him and his abnormality. One can no longer view him compassionately because compassion always implies the idea of safe distance from the object. One feels compassion for Merrick or for starving children on the other side of the world only as long as they don't come too close. Lynch's film has the virtue of bringing Merrick too close and demanding that we see ourselves in what first appears as his impossible difference. In so doing, we accomplish the impossible ourselves.[17]

If one watches *The Elephant Man* and experiences one's speculative identity with Merrick, one accomplishes an ethical act. It seems silly, of course, to talk about the bare act of watching a film as an ethical act, since watching a film involves disconnecting from the other and experiencing a private interaction with the screen. But watching Lynch's film in the way that it demands to be seen has the effect of facilitating the transformation of one's mode of relating to the other. The film encourages us to see sameness or identity beneath the other's difference.[18] But what the film proffers is not a universal humanism in which all subjects share an essentially human core that they never lose and on the basis of which they can identify with each other. This is what occurs in most monster movies, which aim to affirm the common humanity hidden beneath the monstrosity. According to the logic of *The Elephant Man*, what we have in common is our monstrosity, a kernel of desire that prevents us from ever adopting a position of neutrality and from ever being simply human. Merrick's body is the objective correlative of our monstrosity, and insofar as we see ourselves in its deformity, we become the ethical subjects that the film asks us to become.

THREE *Dune* and the Path to Salvation

A Hollywood Narrative

After the success of *The Elephant Man*(1980), Lynch had numerous opportunities to advance his status as an up-and-coming director in Hollywood, including an offer from George Lucas to direct the third installment of the *Star Wars* trilogy. Believing that this film would allow him little creative freedom, Lynch opted instead for another science fiction project, this one offered by producer Dino de Laurentiis. This project was based on the novel *Dune* by Frank Herbert, and it provided Lynch a budget of $42 million, the largest budget for any film up to that time (and more money—*not* adjusted for inflation—than Lynch obtained for any subsequent film). Because of the popularity of Herbert's novel (and its sequels), a built-in audience existed for the film. With the success of *Star Wars* and the return of the *Star Trek* franchise in the early 1980s, an appetite for science fiction was present as well. Lynch even signed on not just for *Dune* (1984) but also for two sequels. Despite these positive signs, the film became Lynch's greatest failure, making back just $15 million at the domestic box office and bombing among critics and among most Lynch fans.[1]

Dune is not only the most universally reviled of David Lynch's films but also the one most associated with typical Hollywood filmmaking.

This becomes the standard way of excusing its failure. When he makes *Dune*, according to the standard narrative of Lynch's career, Hollywood swallows Lynch, and the result is a Hollywood failure and not an authentic Lynch film. When Erica Sheen, who laments that "almost nothing of interest has been written about it," attempts to fill in this lacuna, she does so with an essay that stresses, in contrast to the other essays collected in *The Cinema of David Lynch*, the economic background of the film rather than the filmic text itself.[2] Sheen's essay focuses on "the production history of *Dune* as a paradigm of Lynch's often difficult and always critical relations with the film industry."[3] For Sheen, the very structure of the film is the site of a power struggle between the type of film that Hollywood at the time demands and the innovation characteristic of Lynch's style of filmmaking. Lynch himself takes every opportunity to support this version of the film's construction. He claims that, in *Dune*, "I never carried anything far enough for it to really be my own."[4] Despite this contention and despite its narrative dissimilarity with Lynch's other films, *Dune* remains a Lynch film. It is not just that Lynch places his stylistic or formal stamp on the film (though he does) but that the film echoes the fundamental thematic preoccupation of Lynch's other films. Like both *Eraserhead* (1977) and *The Elephant Man* before it, *Dune* explores what occurs when we fully immerse ourselves in the world of fantasy.

Though a clear link exists between *Dune* and Lynch's other films, it is nonetheless true that *Dune* deviates less from classical Hollywood narrative structure than the other films. If this is the result of the exigencies of a major studio production, these exigencies help to create one of Lynch's most theoretically complex films. In order to delve fully into the world of fantasy and to reveal fantasy's cost, Lynch constructs a film with a narrative trajectory that seems completely in keeping with David Bordwell's description of the classical Hollywood plot or syuzhet. Bordwell notes, "Usually the classical syuzhet presents a double causal structure: one involving heterosexual romance (boy/girl, husband/wife), the other line involving another sphere—work, war, a mission or a quest, other personal relationships. Each line will possess a goal, obstacles, and a climax."[5] *Dune*, likewise, brings together these two causal structures—romance and adventure—and both conclude in a denouement that tidily wraps up the loose ends in each. Thus, despite the complaints from some quarters about the confusing nature of the plot in

Lynch's version of *Dune*, it is actually more indebted to the classical Hollywood structure than the plots of any of Lynch's other films. But *Dune* does not simply fall quietly into Hollywood's conventions. Rather, it immerses itself in the classical Hollywood structure to such an extent that it pushes this structure to a breaking point and exposes, as few films do, the radical possibilities implicit in the fantasmatic resolution that classical Hollywood structure promises.

In spite of their reliance on the enjoyment that derives from fantasy, most classical Hollywood narratives provide only the hint of a fantasmatic resolution without fully investing themselves in the logic of fantasy. They employ fantasy, and yet at the same time keep fantasy at arm's length, allowing the spectator to remain at a safe distance. The logic of fantasy is one that accomplishes the impossible: it overcomes or at least finds a way around the antagonisms—especially the sexual antagonism—that haunt every social order.[6] The social order as such continues to exist through antagonism: its failure to constitute itself fully is at once what enables it to endure. Its existence depends on its ability to produce desiring subjects because only desiring subjects— lacking subjects—act as productive citizens. A film that fully invests itself in the logic of fantasy would necessarily depict a radical transformation of the social order itself, since the social order is constructed around the impossibility of what fantasy envisions. But this is not what classical Hollywood narrative does. Instead, the narrative offers a partial fantasmatic resolution while embedding that resolution within the continued existence of a world of desire and antagonism.

At the end of John Ford's *Stagecoach* (1939), for instance, we see the Ringo Kid (John Wayne) successfully defend a troubled stagecoach from Apache attacks and win the affections of the rescued prostitute Dallas (Claire Trevor)—precisely the "double causal structure" that Bordwell identifies and that Lynch employs in *Dune*. This conclusion heals both the sexual and social antagonisms and thereby promises an existence free from antagonism—or at least an existence in which we can imagine ourselves free from antagonism. The film suggests that a complete healing is possible, that the threats to social stability are empirical rather than ontological.[7]

Stagecoach deceives us concerning what the Ringo Kid must undergo to accomplish this impossible healing. He simply adopts the position of the hero in order to save the people on the stagecoach and defeat the

Apaches. His underlying identity and that of society itself remain constant. The fantasmatic resolution requires no radical transformation—or radical destruction. It is in this sense that classical Hollywood narrative uses fantasy to accommodate the spectator to existing social relations. These narratives imply that we can attain a fantasmatic enjoyment while remaining within the security of the current social order. We can achieve the impossible without disrupting the world that cannot accommodate such an act.

Dune enacts the same healing of antagonism that plays itself out in *Stagecoach* and numerous other classical Hollywood films. But it does not go about it in the same way. If *Stagecoach* and the classical Hollywood narrative reduce an ontological antagonism to a merely empirical one, *Dune* elevates an empirical antagonism to the status of an ontological one and heals it nonetheless. That is to say, Paul Atreides (Kyle MacLachlan) is not simply a hero who overcomes an oppressive adversary and gets the woman; in order to save the Fremen and have Chani (Sean Young) as his lover, he becomes the Kwisatz Haderach, what another character in the film calls "the universe's super-being."[8] He is able to end oppression as such, heal the sexual antagonism, and even miraculously defy the laws of nature. At the end of *Dune*, Lynch depicts Paul as a subject who has overcome the problem of subjectivity itself.

Though *Dune* employs classical Hollywood narrative structure, what stands out about Lynch's film is its refusal to permit the spectator any escape from its full implications. Fantasy promises the subject the ultimate enjoyment, which *Dune* depicts, but by showing this impossible act, the film exposes the traumatic nature of the ultimate enjoyment. It is enjoyment completely opposed to pleasure: achieving it shatters the stability and security that constitutes our everyday life. In fantasy, one enjoys beyond the signifier and the order of meaning, which is why fully accessing this enjoyment forces one to recognize its identity with the ultimate horror. Usually, our half-hearted approach to fantasy obscures this identity, and we can find a certain pleasure in fantasy by indulging in it but not taking it seriously. *Dune* places us all the way into fantasy's logic and demands that we suffer the enjoyment it produces just as Paul does.

Total immersion in fantasy allows the film to work out fantasy's political consequences. What *Dune* adds to Lynch's exploration of the logic of fantasy in *The Elephant Man* is this specific focus. The playing out of the perfect fantasy scenario not only transforms the subject (Paul) but also leads to a political upheaval, which occurs because fantasy inherently undermines all external positions of authority in order to access the impossible object.

The revolutionary denouement in *Dune* follows from the completely fantasmatic nature of the film's narrative structure. The trajectory that Paul follows in the film is the perfect fantasy scenario: it fits into an Oedipal narrative structure without requiring Paul to be responsible for the death of his father or requiring him to marry his mother. That is, the narrative allows Paul to have the triumphs that Oedipus does without sharing the latter's guilt. Like Oedipus, Paul becomes the liberator of a subjected people with his mother at his side, and after this liberation he avenges the death of his father. By becoming the liberator of the Fremen, he assumes the destiny that his father has predicted for him. Though, unlike Oedipus, Paul does not play any part in the death of his father, this death is nonetheless necessary for his ascension as the savior of Arrakis. It thrusts Paul and his mother into the society of the Fremen, who alert Paul to his destiny. In the process of assuming his destiny, he finds a spouse among the subjected people, and the romance and adventure plots unite in the manner of the classical Hollywood narrative.

In terms of this narrative structure, *Dune* is too much of a classical Hollywood film, following the model too perfectly and thereby exposing the hidden radicality of the model itself. This is what accounts for much of the negative critical reaction to it. In the act of giving us what we want as spectators, Lynch gives us too much, forcing us to see the consequences of our fantasy, to see what happens when we would escape the constraints of antagonism. Lynch's film forces us to confront the fantasy without the distance that this type of filmmaking typically offers.

No Safe Place to Desire

Not only does *Dune* represent a break from *Eraserhead* and *Elephant Man* through its narrative structure, but it also departs from Lynch's earlier work through the way that it deploys desire and fantasy. In both *Eraserhead* and *Elephant Man*, there are two distinct worlds—one characterized by absence and dissatisfaction (a world of desire) and the other characterized by heightened presence and enjoyment (a world of fantasy). As we have seen, Lynch emphasizes the division through changes in mise-en-scène, editing, camera movement, and sound. The distinction in *Dune* is not so extreme, indicating the increased power and extent of the fantasy in *Dune*. Lynch establishes the two worlds of desire and fantasy as actual different worlds—the planets of Caladan and Arrakis, respectively. Arrakis is the center of the fantasy and the site of the ultimate enjoyment, but the film shows this enjoyment proliferating elsewhere. Only Caladan, the home planet of the Atreides family, offers a degree of respite.

Both the interiors and exteriors on Caladan look different than the other sets in *Dune*. On every other planet, we see extremes in décor, costume, character, and atmosphere. But Caladan seems like a normal planet where people act like we expect them to act. There are no characters here like the diseased Baron Harkonnen (Kenneth McMillan) flying around the room or the completely blue-eyed Fremen dressed in suits that recuperate all their bodily waste, nor are there creatures like the malformed Guild navigators or the worms of Arrakis. The mise-en-scène reveals Caladan as a stable place that is largely bereft of overt fantasmatic intrusions.

Lynch establishes Caladan as a world of desire primarily through the place it occupies in the narrative. It marks the starting point of Paul's quest. Every scene on Caladan conveys an attitude of expectation for the future and helps to generate a desire in the spectator to see it. We see Paul training with the mentors that his father, Duke Leto Atreides (Jürgen Prochnow), has assigned to aid in his development. He spars in a knife fight with Gurney Halleck (Patrick Stewart); he demonstrates a new weapon (the weirding module) that will help in the upcoming war; and he submits to a test of pain threshold given by the Bene Gesserit Reverend Mother Gaius Helen Mohiam (Siân Phillips). Each scene is important not in itself but for what it suggests about where the film is headed.

The depiction of Paul's nighttime conference with his father punctuates the attitude of the film's Caladan sequence. As Paul and Leto look out over the beautiful sea with waves crashing into rocks creating a mist around them, Leto defends his decision to leave for Arrakis, a desert planet where it never rains. Lynch shoots the scene in a way that emphasizes Paul's future. In close-up, Leto says, "Without change, something sleeps inside us and seldom awakens." Lynch cuts to a close-up of Paul listening and back to Leto finishing his statement: "The sleeper must awaken." The cut to Paul just after Leto says the word "awaken" and the final command to awaken implicitly directed toward Paul indicate the prospect of him awakening into a new world, a world in which his fantasies become realized.

Before leaving Caladan, Paul has a dream that Lynch depicts through a montage sequence. We see a drop of water falling into a pool that dissolves to a close-up of Feyd-Rautha (Sting), a member of the House Harkonnen (the enemy of the Atreides), saying, "I'll kill you." Another dissolve leads to the image of a moon (as Paul's voice-over says, "the second moon"), and this dissolves back to more drops of water falling into a pool. The final image depicts the Fremen Chani, who says, "Tell me of your home world, Usul." Through this dream montage, Paul foresees the rest of the film: he will become a Fremen with the name Usul, discover vast amounts of water on Arrakis, fight and kill Feyd-Rautha after freeing Arrakis, and fall in love with Chani. But from the perspective of the world of desire, this is only a dream, not yet a reality. The promised enjoyment exists here only in a futural sense.

But enjoyment does penetrate into the world of Caladan in the form of the threatening other. In *Dune*, the world where the impossible object is absent has only a fleeting existence and finds itself under assault from the beginning. Caladan is an island that enjoyment threatens to overrun. When Paul spars with Gurney, Lynch shows them fighting with shields to protect themselves. These translucent force fields cover the entire body and protect each person from the opponent's knife thrusts. But at the end of the fight, both Paul and Gurney penetrate the other's shield and hold each other at knifepoint. This is possible, as they explain, because the shield cannot defend a slow movement of the knife. One has protection from the threat, but one remains vulnerable.

The threat makes its presence more keenly felt when Reverend Mother Gaius Helen Mohiam tests Paul. She forces him to place his hand in a green box that produces pain, and if he removes his hand, she will stab him with a poison dart. As she activates the box, Lynch shows an image of Paul's charred hand with flames superimposed and smoke coming from it. He alternates a series of shots showing increasing damage to Paul's hand with shots showing his agonized face and the Reverend Mother administering the pain. At the end of the successful test, Paul removes his hand from the box, and we see Paul's undamaged hand. He confronts—and we confront—an image of burning, but not actual burning. The world of desire depicted here is a world in which the real threats and the real enjoyment are elsewhere.

Voices Unhinged

Beyond Caladan, the world depicted in *Dune* is completely fantasmatic: enjoyment is present throughout this world. The indications that the film fully immerses us in a world of fantasy are apparent in the nuances of the film's form. The form lacks the stability and distance that we find in social reality; the barriers and limitations that constitute our experience of external reality are absent. This becomes especially evident in the film's voice-over narration. *Dune* begins with the image of a narrator, Princess Irulan, speaking directly into the camera. Rather than provide a sense of narrative stability that would allow us to locate ourselves within the narrative as spectators, this initial direct address and subsequent voice-over has the opposite effect. In this sense, the role of voice-over narration in *Dune* contrasts with the role that it plays in most other films, especially in film noir.

When film noir employs a narrator, he—almost always he—has the effect of providing a guide for our journey into the darkness of the film noir world. In such films, the narrator serves as our Virgil, guiding us and providing us with a sense of stability in a world lacking it. The film noir voice-over works to offset the radicality of the film's exploration of society's underside. It locates the spectator safely within the social order while investigating challenges to it. But the voice-over narration in *Dune* works in almost exactly the opposite way. It serves to destabilize the spectator because of its unusual deployment.[9]

Lynch demonstrates the lack of stability in Irulan's narration in the opening scene and in the pattern—or lack of pattern—in her subsequent narrative intrusions. The first shot of the film is a close-up of Irulan's eyes. The camera pulls back to a shot of her entire face, and she narrates the background for the film's story. But as Irulan begins to discuss the spice and its central role in the economy of the filmic world, the image of her face disappears from the screen. She subsequently reappears, and then, as she disappears a second time, she quickly reappears again and notes that she forgot to discuss the most important detail—the location of the spice. This omission and correction undercuts Irulan's authority (as films seldom do with their narrators) and subverts the sense of stability that voice-over narration tends to provide for the spectator. The disappearance and reappearance of her image on the screen disconnects voice from image, further destabilizing the spectator in relation to the narrative.[10]

But what is most significant about this opening scene of direct address is the timing of the initial disappearance of Irulan's image. Irulan's face disappears when she talks about the spice and its power. By linking the disappearance of the film's narrator to her discussion of the spice, Lynch implies the incompatibility of subjective mastery and enjoyment. The spice, a substance of pure enjoyment, derails the mastering power of Irulan's narration and even causes her to forget momentarily a crucial part of her presentation. In the fantasy world of *Dune*, enjoyment, not the mastering power of voice-over narration, holds sway. This is also why Irulan's narration during the rest of the film is so inconsistent. After her initial descriptions of the narrative situation, her narration disappears for long periods of time and reappears at random. This is one of the ways in which Lynch departs from his source text, Frank Herbert's novel *Dune*. Whereas Lynch establishes Irulan's narrative voice as unreliable and inconsistent, Herbert uses it as a constant and reassuring presence. This departure from the novel suggests the fantasmatic nature of the world Lynch sets up in the film. Here, the mastering voice no longer holds sway: the fantasmatic world of the film severs the voice from its role in stabilizing our experience. Mastery fails in the fantasy when it comes up against the proliferation of the impossible object.

The role of Irulan's voice in her narration exemplifies Lynch's treatment of the voice throughout his films. For Lynch, the voice functions as an impossible object embodying the ultimate enjoyment. Rather than quelling our desire by providing a sense of mastery, he depicts the voice as an engine for our desire—one of the object-causes that triggers it. Slavoj Žižek claims that *Dune* isolates "the obscene, cruel, superego-like, incomprehensible, impenetrable, traumatic dimension of the voice which is a kind of foreign body perturbing the balance of our lives."[11] This conception of the voice is apparent not only in Irulan's narration but also in the way the voice figures within the film's narrative. In *Dune*, the voice is a weapon that the women of the Bene Gesserit priesthood—and eventually Paul—use to subvert the authority of the conscious will.

When one employs "the voice," one's own voice alters in pitch and tonality, and this alteration allows the speaker to cause others to act in ways that they do not consciously intend. Lynch's presentation of the voice emphasizes its ability to thwart the mastery we usually associate with speech. The sound of the speaker's voice loses the distinctive character of the speaker, becoming deep and completely hollow. What a character says while using the voice lacks the usual timber that we hear in her voice and resounds in a haunting register. It is as if during the implementation of the voice the character's voice detaches from the character herself and becomes an independently existing object. This accounts for its ability to unsettle both characters within the film and spectators watching, as the use of the voice by Paul's sister Alia (Alicia Roanne Witt) attests most clearly. We see Alia, who is just a young girl, use the voice on Baron Harkonnen. The sound of the voice coming from Alia is especially disturbing because its deep sound contrasts to such an extent with her appearance. Furthermore, the voice enables her to destroy the Baron despite his power and superior strength. Rather than working to reinforce a regime of power, the voice challenges and undermines every such regime. Like the absence of Irulan's narrative voice in the extradiegetic realm, the film's depiction of the voice as a weapon within the diegesis confirms its status as a disruptive object-cause of desire.

The voice doesn't just disturb others; it deprives the subject using it of her/his own sense of symbolic identity. To use the voice is to identify with a detached object. Its power to alter the material world derives from this process of the subject recognizing her/himself in an object that has no substance. Few in the film have the power of the voice not just because it is a secret held by a small group but because few can submit to this identification. The loss of symbolic identity, the recognition that one's subjectivity is reducible to an insignificant object, makes the use of the voice especially difficult for men, whose symbolic identity is tied to having the object rather than being reduced to it. Paul, the only man in the film with this ability, learns the voice from his mother.

The weapon that Paul gives the Fremen to facilitate their revolution involves another form of the voice as an object. It is a material weapon, but one fires it by producing a certain pitch with one's voice and altering this pitch in a specific way. He trains the Fremen to manipulate their voices in order to activate the weapon. As with the voice, this weapon requires the subject to identify with the voice as an object—or at least to experience her/his voice as a detached object. This weapon does not appear in Herbert's novel; Lynch adds it in the film, as he manipulates Irulan's narration, in order to stress the radical power of the voice as an impossible object and the proliferation of this object throughout the fantasy world of *Dune*.

Even the return of Irulan's narrative voice fails to reassert a sense of stability to this world. Instability arises from the use of the audible inner voice—we hear thoughts—of so many other characters in the film. This technique, as Michel Chion notes, is "almost unique" in the history of cinema. But Lynch uses it here for a very precise reason: the audible inner voices indicate the absence of a clearly delineated sense of external reality. Because its world is so completely a world of fantasy, in *Dune* one cannot distinguish between the internal and the external— between psychic reality and social reality. This is one of the results of fantasy. Part of what makes fantasy enjoyable is its ability to erase this barrier and to permit us to imagine acts that would have real effects.

The absence of delineation between the internal and the external voice has ramifications for the spectator as well: it further disturbs our ability to gain a sense of mastery over the filmic reality. As Chion puts it,

> The film's inner voices, often spoken softly, belong to the same space as the externalised voices, thus blurring our relation to reality. The reality on show rests on a discourse proffered as if in a dream. Lynch's intention was indeed to make a dream-film, though this is not to say that he wholly mastered the project. The problem with such a flock of mental voices is that they jam the other voiceover, the traditional narrative voice of Princess Irulan, so that she seems like an intruder, out of place, when she returns an hour after the beginning of the film.[12]

Though Chion adroitly analyzes the effect that the inner voices have on the spectator, his criticism of Lynch for the confusion they generate relative to Irulan's narration misses the role that this confusion plays in the experience of the film. By creating confusion between competing voices and thereby undermining the authority of the primary voiceover narration, Lynch creates a film where symbolic authority is lacking. No symbolic authority exists to stabilize the sense of what is real and what is not or to police the barrier between the internal and the external. In this world, there has been no originary loss of the privileged object: one can still have direct access to enjoyment, and as a result, it proliferates.

A world without an originary loss—a world that enables direct access to enjoyment—is necessarily a fantasmatic world. The privileged object does not exist prior to its loss; the loss of this object is the crucial event, which gives it its privileged status and constitutes it as the object embodying the ultimate enjoyment. A world without the originary loss of this object can only exist retrospectively after one has lost it. Fantasy provides the retrospective look that envisions this impossible world prior to the loss of direct access to enjoyment. By nostalgically imagining a time before loss, fantasy produces a world where barriers and limits do not hold.

Inside Is Outside

Both the proliferation of enjoyment and the breakdown between the internal and external manifest themselves prominently in the character of Baron Vladimir Harkonnen. Baron Harkonnen is a figure of pure enjoyment, as both his body and his behavior evince. His body is not only overweight but ravaged by diseases that distort his appearance. Open and oozing sores cover his face. These visible diseases do not transform the Baron into a figure of pity—that is, they do not indicate his failure or inability to enjoy—but instead serve as an index of the extent to which he does enjoy. The diseases appear to be the result of his profligate life, and this profligacy continues to exist in the very open sores themselves. Baron Harkonnen's relationship to his own diseases makes this clear. Rather than being ashamed of his grotesque complexion, Baron Harkonnen takes pride in it. He employs a doctor to nurse his wounds and profess their beauty. At one point, the doctor says to the Baron, "You are so beautiful, my Baron. Your skin, love to me. Your diseases lovingly cared for, for all eternity." This statement (which censors removed from the television extended-length version of the film) reveals that these diseases function as a source of pride for the Baron insofar as they mark his privileged relationship to enjoyment. They also illustrate the breakdown between the internal and external: the diseased parts of the Baron's skin are points at which his skin no longer covers the inside of his body.[13] Through the diseases, the Baron's insides bubble to the surface, suggesting that his body exists without the limits that define the typical body.

The Baron also openly displays his unrestrained sexual enjoyment in almost every action he performs in the film. Most obviously, he flies around while all the other characters in the film remain confined to the ground. Through the way that the film depicts his flying, its association with enjoyment becomes clear.[14] For instance, after he avoids the assassination attempt by Duke Leto that kills his assistant Piter de Vries (Brad Dourif), the Baron circles the room near the ceiling and shouts repeatedly, "I'm alive." An earlier outbreak of even more excessive enjoyment occurs when the Baron first plans the death of Leto. After describing his plan to eliminate the duke, he flies to the ceiling of his chamber where a liquid oil-like substance spews forth from a pipe. While levitating below the pipe, the Baron bathes in the liquid, allowing it to flow over his head and body. Lynch shoots this scene so as to emphasize the sexual dimension of the experience for the Baron. We see the Baron tilt his head back as the liquid falls on him and a look of great satisfaction comes across his face.

He flies back to the ground where his guards hold a young boy. The Baron caresses the boy, then pulls out the boy's heart plug, which causes all the blood to rush from his body.[15] As the boy is dying and as his blood spurts on the Baron, the Baron hunches over him with another expression of sexual satisfaction. For the Baron, this type of perverse enjoyment occurs publicly and at the expense of others who are not sharing his enjoyment (and who even die as a result of it), and yet he experiences no shame in his acts. As his relationship to his diseases also indicates, the Baron prides himself on his ability to enjoy and display publicly this enjoyment. These displays are only possible because of the absence of any symbolic authority in the fantasmatic world that *Dune* depicts.[16]

Everything about the Harkonnen world suggests an absence of any limitation on enjoyment. In the scene where the Baron plots the death of Leto, we see one of the Baron's nephews, Rabban (Paul Smith), crush an insect in a small container and then drink the liquid that forms from this process. After drinking from the container, Rabban simply tosses it aside into an open pool of water. His concern is his own enjoyment, not doing his part to sustain an orderly world. The activities and the décor of the Baron's palace chamber suggest that bodily enjoyment holds a privileged place here. The Baron and his nephews enjoy excessively and show no compunction about the ramifications of this enjoyment on others or the world. None of the restraints on enjoyment that we would expect to govern social interaction are in effect on the Harkonnen planet of Giedi Prime.

The pervasiveness of sexual or bodily enjoyment in Harkonnen society indicates that the fantasy scenario of *Dune* has successfully bypassed symbolic law and prohibition. The unrestrained enjoyment that we see in Harkonnen society and in the Baron himself is the direct result of the very fantasmatic structure that produces Paul's victory and apotheosis at the end of the film. In the primal fantasy that *Dune* enacts that allows the subject to access successfully total enjoyment (in the form of the spice), there can be no symbolic law barring this access. The symbolic law places an interdiction on the kind of total enjoyment that the spice provides, and thus the scenario that would render this enjoyment accessible must lack this law. The result, as Lynch's film shows, is a figure like Baron Harkonnen. He is the price that one pays for access to the inaccessible.

By depicting the Baron and his society in the way that he does, Lynch shows the necessary underside of the classical Hollywood fantasy that we seldom see in the classical Hollywood film. But we should see it. Hollywood film promises us a fantasmatic escape and then exercises great restraint in its depiction. This restraint creates narrative desire by withholding the full deployment of the fantasy; by not exercising restraint in this regard, Lynch occasions a negative reaction from spectators who want to hold on to some of their desire. An absence of restraint allows Paul to realize directly his dream insofar as it breaks down the barrier between dream and reality: Paul dreams of the vast stores of water on Arrakis, of Chani becoming his lover, and of becoming a savior—all of which he realizes. This same absence of restraint facilitates Baron Harkonnen's public display of his private enjoyment. A complete immersion into the logic of fantasy demands the inclusion of the Baron. Rather than hiding this excess, Lynch's film foregrounds it.

The figure of Harkonnen and the obscenity of Giedi Prime are part of the price we pay as spectators for the fantasy that *Dune* proffers. This is not to say that spectators can't enjoy Harkonnen. They can and do.

But our enjoyment of him renders the obscenity of our own enjoyment visible to ourselves. The depiction of the Harkonnen world forces us to see the aspect of our fantasy that we would like to disavow, and yet it is integral to the way that fantasy delivers on its promises. This is what the proliferation of enjoyment in fantasy looks like.

The Worms and the Spice

The fantasmatic world of *Dune* is a world without an effective prohibition and without the restraint on enjoyment that such a prohibition brings.[17] Here, unlike in our experience of social reality, one can have a direct experience of an impossible enjoyment. This absence of restraint on enjoyment provides the key to understanding the role that the spice plays. In the world of *Dune* the spice functions as what Lacan calls *das Ding*, the maternal Thing, the substance of pure enjoyment.

Ordinarily, the Thing occupies the center of our reality, and yet it cannot appear within our experience of reality. Reality itself is constructed around the exclusion of the Thing. As Lacan notes in *Seminar VII*, "*das Ding* is at the center only in the sense that it is excluded. That is to say, in reality *das Ding* has to be posited as exterior, as the prehistoric Other that it is impossible to forget . . . something strange to me, although it is at the heart of me, something that on the level of the unconscious only a representation can represent."[18] In *Dune*, however, the Thing is not excluded from the filmic world but exists within it. Though access to it is dangerous (involving the risk of a lethal encounter with the worms), one can nonetheless reach it. Only in the world of a fundamental fantasy can the Thing exist on the same plane as other objects.

When Paul first encounters the spice, the film registers its link to the ultimate enjoyment: he smells the spice on his fingers, and the screen becomes completely white, as it does when Henry touches the Radiator Lady in *Eraserhead*. Lynch associates the spice with enjoyment through its qualities, effects, and rarity. Irulan's opening narration tells us that the spice is the most valuable commodity in the universe and that it is located on only one planet, Arrakis. The desolate nature of the surface of Arrakis—its near-total lack of water—and the presence of the worms, which protect the spice from spice miners, both serve to make the spice very difficult to obtain. One must constantly put one's life at risk because one must mine in the open desert and every mining operation brings the worms soon after it begins. These difficulties testify to the spice's precious nature. It has such a great value that it cannot be measured against other commodities. But this value does not derive simply from its preciousness.

The chief property of the spice is its ability to fold space, which is the use the Guild navigators put it toward. This use of the spice allows space travelers to traverse immense distances without actually moving: it causes distance itself to disappear (which makes it an ideal substance for Lynch's cinema of proximity). When we enjoy, we momentarily evade the confines and limitations of our symbolic identity; the spice represents the ultimate enjoyment because it allows one to evade the spatial and temporal limitations of reality itself. It provides an actual experience of what Freud calls the "oceanic feeling"—an experience in which one's distance from the rest of the universe evaporates. For Freud, this feeling is always only imaginary insofar as the Thing remains constitutively out of reach.[19] But in the fantasmatic world of *Dune*, the Thing exists on the same plane as other empirical objects without losing its privileged status. This is the feat that the fantasy in *Dune* accomplishes, and it renders visible an impossible experience—total enjoyment.

Much of the negative reaction to *Dune* stems from Lynch's attempt to show the experience of total enjoyment. Most films promise this experience, but almost none depict it. Why not? The depiction of total enjoyment cannot but strike the spectator as absurd and incommensurate with the expectation that precedes it. We prefer just a hint of this ultimate experience rather than the experience itself so that we can continue to anticipate its (infinite) magnitude. But Lynch's film does not allow this. The figures of total enjoyment in *Dune* are the Guild navigators. They exist in constant contact with the spice and use it to fold space, but this contact with the Thing deforms them. In our first view of a Guild navigator in the Emperor's palace, we see a fishlike creature with an enlarged head and a small body. Through close-ups on the undulating mouth and a bulging eye, the disgusting form of this creature becomes evident. An immersion in complete enjoyment transforms the Guild navigators, according to Lynch's vision, into grotesque beasts. This is the spectator's image of the ultimate enjoyment.

Lynch pushes the depiction even further when he shows the Guild navigators folding space so that House Atreides can travel to Arrakis. We see the entire body of a Guild navigator visible in an extreme long shot, and this shot reveals the absurd form of this creature. The navigator does not appear frightening, powerful, or attractive—just silly. The poor special effects in this scene add to this sense. But the silliness of the image does not mark a point of Lynch's failure in *Dune*; it represents the successful depiction of complete enjoyment. When one immerses oneself in enjoyment, one loses one's symbolic anchoring and becomes absurd. One moves beyond the bounds of sense. The subject doesn't enjoy by possessing the object; the object takes control of and deforms the subject.

The absurdity continues in Lynch's depiction of the folding of space. We see the Guild navigator moving through a giant ship that holds the ships that will travel across the folded space. While moving, the navigator shoots a beam of light out of its midsection. Several other streams of light burst forth from the Guild navigator as we begin to hear a religious chant on the audio track, which adds a sacred quality to the experience. The streams of light are visible against a background of swirling and flickering points of brightness. We see planets encompassed by waves of the different streams of light that then return to the Guild navigator itself. Lynch's use of images of bright light and sacred music here create the sense of a completely fantasmatic experience. When space folds, one experiences a kind of enjoyment that one cannot access without the special quality of the spice, but the film reveals this enjoyment as nonsensical. It is difficult to enjoy the depiction of total enjoyment in *Dune* because the excessive images detach this enjoyment from the realm of signification.

As the Thing, the spice is the site of the ultimate enjoyment, but as the embodiment of the ultimate enjoyment, it represents a horror as well—the complete loss of signification and mastery. According to Lacan, Freud's great insight is his grasp of the identity between the highest good and the greatest horror. He shows, in other words, that the object that would provide the ultimate enjoyment, the Thing, is at the same time a forbidden incestuous object. *Dune* initially depicts these as distinct: one must run the risk of the ultimate horror (the worms) in order to obtain the ultimate enjoyment (the spice). But when Paul undergoes his final transformation into the Kwisatz Haderach after drinking the water of life, the film asserts the identity of the spice and the worms—the identity of the ultimate enjoyment and the ultimate horror. By depicting Paul coming to this realization at the moment he ascends fully to his fantasmatic role of the universe's super-being, Lynch illustrates the trauma involved with the complete realization of one's fantasy.

Clearly, the idea of anyone as the universe's super-being is fantasmatic, and yet, when Paul takes up this position, he is able to make a connection that no subject can actually sustain. Grasping the identity of the worms and the spice means seeing the incestuous object, the object that always threatens to swallow the subject, in the object one fantasizes about. Lynch reveals the trauma of this recognition in his depiction of Paul's transformation. We see a variation on the montage sequence that repeats several times in the film: a shot of a drop of water falling into a pool, followed by a shot of a worm mouth opening, and then another drop falling. Lynch cuts back to Paul's face with a look of agony as his voice-over says, "The worm is the spice. The spice is the worm." After this recognition, he has a look of horror and screams, "No!" In a series of shots we see the Bene Gesserit women all register the trauma of the recognition as well: Lynch shows Reverend Mother Gaius Helen Mohiam, Paul's mother Jessica (Francesca Annis), and his sister Alia all bleeding from their mouths. When one recognizes the identity of the worms and the spice, one loses the distance within oneself that makes one a subject, transcending the primordial repression that inaugurates subjectivity itself. This is possible only in fantasy, and even in fantasy we stop fantasizing before we reach this point.

The enjoyment that Paul finds in his fantasy of saving the world is a feminine enjoyment. He tells the Reverend Mother Gaius Helen Mohiam, "Try looking into that place where you dare not look. You'll find me there staring back at you." This place inside herself where women "dare not look" is the site of feminine enjoyment—an experience that overwhelms the female subject to such an extent that she cannot have any knowledge of it. As the Reverend Mother tells Paul early in the film, no man has ever successfully accessed it, though many have "tried and died."

In order to depict Paul's access to feminine enjoyment, Lynch highlights the feminine nature of the spice and the worms. This informs the most important change that Lynch makes to Herbert's novel. Whereas Herbert emphasizes the immense size and phallic nature of the worms, Lynch's images of them focus almost solely on their huge, teeth-lined mouths, an opening that suggests a vagina dentata. Oftentimes, Lynch shoots the worms as their mouths open, and we see the gaping hole that threatens to swallow everything. By giving the worms this vaginal look and associating them with the spice, Lynch suggests that the enjoyment of the spice is specifically feminine enjoyment.

Masculine enjoyment is tied to the social order because it occurs through an identification with the center of this order—the master or phallic signifier. Enjoying like a man means getting off on the illusion of phallic potency. As phallic enjoyment, it never threatens the phallic social order. But feminine enjoyment or jouissance cannot be reduced to this order because it does not depend on its connection to the master signifier. Lacan has feminine enjoyment in mind in *Seminar XX* when he claims, "There is a jouissance . . . 'beyond the phallus.' "[20] This enjoyment transcends the phallic order insofar as it is always outside of itself, always elsewhere. It is the enjoyment that one feels when one is overcome and experiences an event that goes beyond one's ability to register it.[21] One experiences without knowing precisely what one is experiencing. The difference between masculine and feminine enjoyment is the difference between the finite and the infinite. The finite nature of masculine enjoyment renders it quantifiable and containable; the infinite nature of feminine enjoyment renders it diffuse and ungraspable. Whereas masculine enjoyment can—and most often does—assist in the functioning of power, feminine enjoyment necessarily disrupts it.

Though control of the spice appears to provide power, it remains, as the substance of enjoyment, fundamentally beyond any control. In fact, it controls those who try to wield the power that it promises. This becomes apparent in the case of the Guild navigators. Though the Guild uses the spice to retain a monopoly on space travel, the film illustrates how the Guild is actually enslaved to the spice. Not only is the Guild completely addicted to the spice to the extent that it cannot live without it, but the Guild's excessive exposure to the spice has deformed the Guild navigators into grotesque creatures. They exist in giant tanks of liquid and have large vaginal openings in their midsections. This specifically vaginal opening is what facilitates the folding of space. While using the spice to fold space, one enjoys beyond the phallus.

The appearance of feminine enjoyment in a fantasmatic film like *Dune* is not simply happenstance. The thrill of fantasy—even the mass-produced fantasies of classical Hollywood cinema—lies in fantasy's ability to approach feminine enjoyment. Fantasies promise us an enjoyment that goes beyond the acceptable and transcends the constraints of the social order. However, most depictions of fantasy avoid approaching too close and thus allow our experience to remain safely pleasurable. *Dune* becomes unpleasurable because one loses one's safe distance and enjoys too much. The result is the massive disavowal of the film's achievement—a disavowal that extends even to Lynch himself.

The Perfect Ending

The ending of the film shows Paul's triumph both as the new ruler of Arrakis and in his romantic union with Chani. By bringing the two narrative lines of adventure and romance together in the film's conclusion, Lynch follows the classical Hollywood convention, offering a quintessential fantasmatic resolution for the spectator. After the depiction of the military victory, Lynch even includes a gratuitous knife fight between Paul and the Baron's nephew, Feyd-Rautha, which allows the spectator to enjoy Paul's skill with the knife and the gruesome death of the evil Feyd. The film goes out of its way to resolve all sense of dissatisfaction through the fantasmatic conclusion that it lays out.

In the final scene of the film, Paul accomplishes the impossible: he brings rain to Arrakis through a pure act of will. The camera moves toward a close-up of Paul's blue eye that dissolves into the image of the seas of Caladan, suggesting that Paul creates the rain by bringing the water from Caladan to Arrakis. He completes the realization of his fantasy of saving Arrakis by bringing the external world of social reality into the fantasy. The barrier between these worlds disappears at this point. As the rain becomes visible in an exterior shot of Arrakis, we hear Alia using the voice and proclaiming, "And how can this be? For he is the Kwisatz Haderach!" This is perhaps more enjoyment than the cinema has ever created: Paul saves the oppressed Fremen, kills his rival, overpowers the despotic Emperor, creates rain for a desert planet, has his fantasy object Chani as his lover, and ascends to the throne of the universe's super-being—while Alia's distorted voice, representing the impossible object, provides the commentary. The failure of *Dune*, if that is what we want to call it, is its successful enactment of enjoyment for the spectator. Lynch allows us no distance from the enjoyment that we see, and his departure from his source material further indicates this direction in the film.

Like Lynch, Frank Herbert in the novel *Dune* depicts the victory of Paul and the Fremen over the Baron and the Emperor. But Herbert taints this victory in ways that Lynch does not. Herbert explicitly links Paul's conquest to religious fundamentalism, to a jihad that Paul himself tries to avert. Herbert emphasizes Paul's internal conflict about the struggle he unleashes, and thus we cannot view the conclusion as unambiguously as in Lynch's film. In addition, Herbert informs us that the Fremen legend of a savoir who will lead them is in fact an ideological lie, implanted by the Bene Gesserit in order to render the Fremen more docile. By excluding this material that complicates and even undermines Paul's victory, Lynch allows us to enjoy this victory to the utmost. And in doing so, he shows where our enjoyment lies and the costs of this enjoyment. He includes the element of religious fundamentalism present in Herbert's novel—at the moment of his victory, Paul proclaims, "God created Arrakis to train the faithful. One cannot go against the word of God"—but doesn't allow us to maintain distance from it through Paul's internal struggle in the way that Herbert does. In the film version, we enjoy the fantasmatic resolution and then must confront the ramifications of this enjoyment while the novel's distance spares us from this enjoyment altogether. One finds oneself unambiguously on the side of resolution while watching the film and thereby experiences fully the ramifications of one's fantasizing.

Many science fiction films place us on the side of the working-class revolution—or at least revolution against oppression. Even films as mainstream as *Star Wars* (George Lucas, 1977), *Total Recall* (Paul Verhoeven, 1990), and *The Island* (Michael Bay, 2005) sympathetically portray the prospect of revolutionary change. In each case, liberation occurs through the agency of an enlightened avant-garde. The revolutionary elite acts with certainty even when the majority of the population to be liberated doesn't agree with them. But the films de-emphasize this totalitarian dimension implicit in the revolts: we have revolutionary change without coercion. *Dune* makes the coercive force of Paul conspicuous through the fundamentalist dimension of his revolution. The film suggests that if we are seriously embracing revolutionary change, we must accept the coercive form in which it necessarily comes.

By going too far and offering us too much enjoyment, the fantasmatic resolution in *Dune* eliminates the idea of another place, an alternative possibility, more than any of Lynch's other films. Lynch shows us what an impossible complete enjoyment would look like not so that we might embark on a search for it, but so that we might recognize how it has already been realized. The final act in Paul's fantasy provides the key to the film: in order to complete the fantasy narrative, Paul must return to the social reality represented by Caladan to find the rain. The dissolve to an image of the Caladan sea from Paul's blue eye reveals a turn back to the world of desire at the decisive moment in the fantasy. The fantasy of escape can only complete itself by looping back to what it escapes from.

Through its concluding image, *Dune*, Lynch's most overtly political film, asks us to understand political revolution—and the fantasy that drives political revolution—in a new way. As the film shows, we can transform society in line with our fantasies, but this transformation will, in the last instance, insert us back in the social reality that we have fled. There is a speculative identity between the new society we will create and the old one we will have left behind. This is not to say that political change is not worth the effort. *Dune* clearly takes the side of Paul and revolutionary change as opposed to the conservative forces of the Baron and the Emperor. But we must see the revolutionary alternative not in terms of difference but in terms of identity. By doing so, we effectuate a revolution that embraces the necessity of repetition freely rather than blindly succumbing to it.

FOUR Fantasizing the Father in *Blue Velvet*

A Different Kind of Separation?

Chastened by the failure of *Dune* (1984) and his sense that he had lost control of the film, Lynch returned to a smaller scale for his next project. He vowed never again to give up final cut on a picture, and this necessitated making films for less money. But one could not imagine a more resounding response to critical and popular failure than *Blue Velvet* (1986). It became Lynch's signature film: if someone knows only one Lynch film, chances are that the film is *Blue Velvet*. After it appears, David Lynch became *David Lynch*—a cinematic auteur. He even received another Academy Award nomination for Best Director. No prior or subsequent film generated as much popular and scholarly interest or as much criticism (among feminists for the violence toward women, among conservatives for the perverse image of small-town America, and among Marxists for the seeming nostalgia for the 1950s). The interest almost inevitably focused on the conspicuous division between two opposing worlds that Lynch creates in the film.

Following *Eraserhead* (1977), *The Elephant Man* (1980), and *Dune*, the split between the public social reality and its fantasmatic underside seems even more pronounced in *Blue Velvet*. Almost every viewer of the film notices that it depicts "two separate worlds" that we experience as "the real world, that which we can see and hear and touch; and a subconscious, dream world which must remain hidden, so potentially dark and violent are its wanderings."[1] Lynch foregrounds the opposition between these two distinct worlds to such an extent that detecting it doesn't even require a sophisticated interpretive act. As Laura Mulvey rightly points out, "the binary opposition between the everyday and the netherworlds is there for all to see and to grasp."[2] Despite the obviousness of the opposition between filmic worlds—the public reality and its underside—the most visible opposition in *Blue Velvet* does not revolve around desire and fantasy, but between two different modes of fantasy.

The binary opposition that everyone notices while watching *Blue Velvet* is one between two equally fantasmatic worlds: an excessively ordinary public world of Lumberton that coexists with a similarly exaggerated underworld populated by Frank Booth (Dennis Hopper) and his associates. According to Slavoj Žižek, in "the *Blue Velvet* universe . . . we encounter the fantasy in its two poles, in its pacifying aspect (the idyllic family life) as well as in its destructive/obscene/excessive aspect."[3] Through this opposition, Lynch develops more fully what we saw at work in the structure of *The Elephant Man*. But in *Blue Velvet*, the different aspects of fantasy emerge as fully developed worlds rather than remaining, as in *The Elephant Man*, opposing modes of subjective (John Merrick's) experience. As a result, we are able to see their logic in a way we could not in the earlier film.

The public world that we see when the film opens is not "the real world" but a purely fantasmatic one that corresponds perfectly—even too perfectly—to an American ideal. The opening shots show a bright blue sky, glowing red roses next to a shiny white picket fence, and a waving firefighter riding down the street on a red fire engine with a Dalmatian by his side. These images suggest the kind of perfectly realized fantasy world that one never encounters in reality.[4] On the other hand, the horrific underside of this public fantasy is equally extreme. Frank Booth and his gang revel in their perversity and total disregard for the public law. Mere exposure to them endangers the life of Jeffrey Beaumont (Kyle MacLachlan) and results in a severe beating. If the public world of *Blue Velvet* represents an American ideal, its underside represents an American nightmare. What distinguishes *Blue Velvet* from the typical American fantasy is the extent to which it holds these two worlds apart.

Because *Blue Velvet* depicts two competing fantasy worlds, it constantly violates narrative logic in ways that are possible only within the structure of fantasy and in ways that reflect the struggle between the two fantasy worlds. Or, as C. Kenneth Pellow puts it, "Over and over again, Lynch commits blunders (both in his script and in his direction) in the areas of sequence, causation, and consistency."[5] Pellow's scathing criticisms of the film have the ironic effect of detailing precisely how Lynch's film employs fantasy. For instance, according to Pellow, the setting for the film, Lumberton, "is a small town when that's convenient to his theme, and it is a big city when that serves his need."[6] This ability of Lumberton to be at once a small town and a big city indicates not the failure of Lynch's filmmaking ability but the fact that he has situated us on the terrain of two opposed fantasy structures: in the ideal fantasy, Lumberton is a small town, but in the nightmare fantasy, it's a big city. It has the quaintness of the small town and the problems of a big city (drug dealing, murder, etc.). Each of the "vacillations in narrative logic" that we might detect in the film—and there are many—point us in this direction. By presenting us with these two opposed fantasy worlds, Lynch lays bare how fantasy necessarily works.

Fantasy always functions in these two modes, one comforting and the other disconcerting. As Slavoj Žižek notes,

> the notion of fantasy offers an exemplary case of the dialectical *co-incidentia oppositorum:* on the one hand, fantasy in its beatific side, in its *stabilizing* dimension, the dream of a state without disturbances, out of reach of human depravity; on the other hand, fantasy in its *destabilizing* dimension, whose elementary form is envy—all that "irritates" me about the Other, images that haunt me of what he or she is doing when out of my sight, of how he or she deceives me and plots against me, of how he or she ignores me and indulges in an enjoyment that is intensive beyond my capacity of representation, and so on and so forth.[7]

These two modes of fantasy have an interconnected relationship, as we saw in the case of *The Elephant Man*. But *Blue Velvet* further shows us why we cannot simply content ourselves with the stabilizing fantasy: it fails to provide the stability that it promises, and this failure of stability gives rise to the destabilizing or nightmarish fantasy that provides an *explanation* for this failure. Though the stabilizing fantasy fails inherently, on its own terms, the existence of the nightmare fantasy enables us to rescue the stabilizing fantasy and explain its failure with reference to an external rather than an internal cause. It is in this sense that the fantasy of the ideal depends on its underside.

This interdependence of the two modes of fantasy causes us to experience them at the same time and in an interrelated way. In this sense, the division of the two opposed modes of fantasy in *Blue Velvet* separates what we experience together. Just as we normally experience desire and fantasy in an interrelated way, we also experience the two modes of fantasizing—the fantasy of the ideal and the nightmare—simultaneously. That is to say, when we fantasize about our ideal, we fantasize simultaneously about the threats that imperil that ideal. If, for example, we entertain a nostalgic fantasy about small-town America, we also fantasize the imminent destruction of this ideal due to the rise of the large city. In our typical experience of fantasy, the nightmare exists within the same narrative structure as the ideal.

Even cinematic fantasies tend to affirm this marriage of the two modes. A romantic comedy that strives to show a fantasy of an ideal romantic union always rehearses the threats to that union. And a horror film that delves into a nightmarish fantasy stages this nightmare against the background of the ideal that it threatens. This is what gives *Blue Velvet* its initial distinctiveness as a film. By separating the two modes of fantasy, Lynch allows us to see their similarity. Ironically, when the ideal and the nightmare function together, we cannot see the underlying similarity that binds them together; their very interaction has the effect of making them seem completely different. But in the act of separating and opposing them, *Blue Velvet* renders visible this similarity between the ideal and the nightmare that fantasies usually obscure.[8]

Despite the obviousness of the opposition between the ideal world and the nightmare world, as is also true of *The Elephant Man*, this opposition is not the most important one that Lynch constructs in the film. He also creates an opposition between a world of desire and a world of fantasy. Between the two competing fantasy structures, Lynch inserts a space of desire and locates this space in and surrounding the apartment of Dorothy Vallens (Isabella Rossellini). The fundamental divide in the film is thus not, as is often thought, between the proper public world and its criminal underside: they are two sides of the same coin. What is radically different is the space of desire centered around Dorothy's apartment.

The divide between fantasy and desire in *Blue Velvet* is at once a divide between masculinity and femininity. That is, the film opposes masculine fantasy to feminine desire. In this relationship, feminine desire is a desire that no object can satisfy, a void that threatens to overwhelm both the desiring subject herself and the men who become caught within her desire. Masculine fantasy provides respite insofar as it imagines a scenario in which this desire has an identifiable object. The film depicts the struggle between these two positions, and in the process it reveals the inability of fantasy to tame completely the disruption of desire.

Most feminist criticisms of the film focus on the seemingly complete male dominance that it depicts. For instance, Jane Shattuc claims, "As opposed to Hitchcock's melodramas, which often center on a woman, *Blue Velvet* is a man's world; it trades on women as passive objects of male voyeuristic gazes and sadistic impulses."[9] This interpretation accepts the competing fantasies as the sole filmic reality. Though the ideal and the nightmare fantasy appear to dominate the film (and become the focus of most interpretations), Dorothy in fact occupies the central position. And she is not simply central as the object over which men fight. She desires, and the men are left in the position of reacting to this desire, never acting independently.

Unleashed Desire

The idealized fantasy world that opens the film lasts for less than two minutes. After a series of bright fantasmatic images including roses in front of a white picket fence, a fireman waving from a passing engine, and a crossing guard helping children across the street, Lynch depicts Jeffrey's father Tom Beaumont (Jack Harvey) watering the lawn. The image of the father figure watering the lawn is not simply one in the series of idealized images but the key one. The father holds together and anchors the other idealized images.

The father who collapses in this scene is not a figure of prohibition, a paternal authority barring subjects access to enjoyment. He is a good father who enables rather than restricts the subject's enjoyment; he creates a stable relationship to the impossible, privileged object. What's more, he acts as the support for the entire fantasy structure evinced by the bright and cheery montage that opens the film. Because he plays the crucial role in the ideal fantasy, his collapse necessarily appears as a devastating event. Fredric Jameson claims that the film treats Tom Beaumont's stroke as "an incomprehensible catastrophe—an act of God which is peculiarly an act of scandalous violence within this perfect American small town."[10] The nonsensical, traumatic status of this event stems from the idealized father's role in the fantasy. Without him, the fantasy loses its appearance of seamlessness.

Immediately after Tom Beaumont's collapse, the tone of the film undergoes a dramatic change. As he lies on the ground, his hand continues to hold the garden hose, and we see slow-motion shots of the pet dog repeatedly snapping at the jetting stream of water. The subsequent traveling shot at the level of the grass reveals the violent and active insect life that lies beneath the surface of the lawn, as the audio track turns louder and more voracious. The sequence of shots here—as is almost always the case in *Blue Velvet*—illustrates the relationship between the idealized world of Lumberton and its obscene underside represented by the insects. Tom Beaumont's collapse from a stroke creates an opening between the idealized world and its underside where Frank Booth dominates. Whereas the stable father figure keeps this underside hidden, his frailty renders it accessible. But despite the focus of most spectators and critics, what is most important is not this underside but the opening to it.

The sequence of scenes that follow also indicate the relationship between paternal insufficiency and the emergence of an opening to another world. After this unnerving start, we see Jeffrey walking to the hospital to visit his father. He walks through an abandoned lot and picks up a few rocks to throw. This scene is important only insofar as it sets up the next two. Jeffrey sees his father in the hospital, and we see a look of horror on his face as he observes his father's debilitated condition. After the scene at the hospital, Jeffrey again walks through the same lot and again picks up a few rocks to throw. This time, however, while searching for rocks, he finds a detached human ear.

The fact that the hospital scene intervenes between the two scenes at the abandoned lot suggests a causal relationship between Jeffrey's experience at the hospital and what he finds during the second scene at the lot. The absence of the father within the fantasy structure allows for the introduction of desire.[11] Viewing the incapacity of the father allows Jeffrey to see the ear, which marks an opening within the fantasy world of Lumberton. As Lynch himself points out, the specific body part that Jeffrey finds is not simply a contingent element in the scene. He says, "It had to be an ear because it's an opening. An ear is wide and, as it narrows, you can go down into it. And it goes somewhere vast."[12] The opening that the ear provides in the film is the opening of desire itself. It represents a gap in the fantasy structure that allows the desire of both Jeffrey and the spectator to emerge.

In addition to the opening inherent in the very form of an ear, Lynch associates this particular ear with castration and thus with the emergence of desire. Someone has used scissors to cut the ear off the head of a person, and when the medical examiner pronounces the word "scissors," Lynch cuts back to the abandoned lot where we see a close-up of scissors cutting the police tape. This filmic emphasis on the act of cutting further links the ear to the emergence of desire. The cut of castration—or the castration threat—gives birth to desire by separating the subject from its privileged object. It has nothing to do with anatomy but with the subjection of the subject to the exigencies of the social law. The ear thus acts as a threat to Jeffrey, a warning about the dangers of too much enjoyment (which Detective Williams [George Dickerson] repeats to Jeffrey), but at the same time it incites his desire because of the opening that it creates.

After Jeffrey's discovery of the detached ear, the film's form undergoes transformation. Though the fantasy world of Lumberton remains, it loses its perfect coherence and pockets of desire become evident within this world. The evening of his discovery, we see Jeffrey walking in the dark to visit Detective Williams, and then Lynch cuts to a close-up of the ear in which the camera moves toward and apparently into the ear. The camera movement here indicates that Jeffrey himself is plunging into the openness of desire. When Jeffrey leaves Detective Williams's house, Sandy (Laura Dern) confronts him, and it seems as if she emerges out of a void of complete blackness in the middle of the image. This is another of the openings that begin to populate the fantasy world of Lumberton after the collapse of the father figure at the beginning of the film. As they begin to discuss the mystery of the ear and of Dorothy Vallens, Jeffrey and Sandy walk down a street that has the appearance of a tunnel or an opening to some other place. As Janet

Preston notes, tunnel imagery dominates the film, but it becomes especially prevalent as the film's narrative approaches and enters Dorothy Vallens's apartment. She says, "The interior of the decaying apartment building on Lincoln Street in which the victim protagonist, Dorothy Vallens, lives is the most significant tunnel image. It . . . illuminates the theme of initiation into knowledge which coheres much of the film's imagery."[13] Though Preston correctly sees Dorothy's apartment as the culmination of the film's tunnel imagery, a site where openness and gaps exist throughout the filmic space, it does, in itself, provide no knowledge for Jeffrey. In fact, Dorothy's apartment marks a point of Jeffrey's non-knowledge, and this is what has the effect of stimulating his desire.

The non-knowledge, or impossibility of meaning, is epitomized by the mise-en-scène of Dorothy's apartment and the surrounding area. Whereas Lynch depicts both the Lumberton public world and the underworld as colorful and full, Dorothy's apartment is a world of empty spaces and dark voids, a world bereft of the fullness that fantasy adds. When Jeffrey enters Dorothy's apartment using a stolen key, Lynch shoots the scene with very little light. Initially, the screen goes completely black as Jeffrey enters, and then we see Jeffrey walking around in the apartment in near-total darkness. Even after Dorothy returns home and turns on the apartment lights, the lighting in the scene remains dim, leaving dark spaces within the mise-en-scène. Just before she discovers Jeffrey hiding in her closet, Dorothy moves into one of these dark spaces: we know she is in the apartment, but she appears to be in the middle of a void.[14] This type of lighting suggests a world of desire where nothing can be known. Even the external shots of the apartment highlight our lack of knowledge about it through the use of lighting. We learn that Dorothy lives on the seventh floor, and yet in the first external shot of the apartment, the apartment appears to have only three floors. We see the first three floors and nothing but darkness above them. The lighting produces an apartment that is present as a visible absence.

Lynch constructs a rigid barrier between the world of desire within Dorothy's apartment and the fantasy worlds outside. One cannot easily access this apartment: since the elevator is out of order, it requires traversing seven flights of stairs. Lynch further indicates the different world of the apartment by changing the sound when Jeffrey approaches it—

sometimes even eliminating nondiegetic sound altogether. Within the diegesis, a similar sound barrier exists: Dorothy catches Jeffrey in her closet because a flushing toilet prevents him from hearing Sandy honk the car horn four times to warn him. Though it seems as if a contingent event—the toilet flushing—blocks the passage of the sound, it follows necessarily from the barrier that Lynch establishes in the film. Dorothy's apartment is an isolated space in which fantasy breaks down and ceases to provide the explanations that give the world its coherence.

Blue Velvet reverses the trajectory, moving from a world of desire to a world of fantasy that Lynch employs in his first three films. Here, the film initially immerses the spectator in the fantasy and subsequently depicts a space of desire within the fantasy world. This reversal of trajectory—which Lynch would repeat in *Mulholland Drive* (2001)—illustrates that the relationship between desire and fantasy is dialectical rather than temporal. Even though fantasy attempts to solve the problem of desire, this solution emerges simultaneously with the problem, not afterward. Neither desire's question nor fantasy's answer has a temporal priority, which is why Lynch can begin *Blue Velvet* with a world of fantasy and later thrust the spectator into a world of desire when he introduces Dorothy's apartment.

To say that the one site in *Blue Velvet* where fantasy ceases to operate is Dorothy's apartment seems counterintuitive. If a critical consensus exists about any aspect of the film, it concerns the fantasmatic nature of the scene in which Jeffrey observes Frank's sexual assault on Dorothy. Michel Chion points out that "the kind of fantasy on display" here is one that reenacts "the surrealistic sexual theories of children."[15] Echoing Chion, Betsy Berry is one of many critics who specifies this as "the primal scene," which is "both man's and child's most terrifying scenario: the vision of violent coupling between one's parents."[16] Sam Ishii-Gonzales goes even further, noting,

> This episode not only spectacularly evokes the primal scene, it also conjures up the two other fantasy scenarios identified by Freud as the primal fantasies—namely, the fantasy of seduction and the fantasy of castration. These fantasies are not interchangeable, but they often become interrelated or co-existent for the inquisitive subject. This is something *Blue Velvet* makes dramatically clear. Within the confines of Dorothy's living space, Jeffrey Beaumont is confronted

with each of the primal fantasies in all their enigmatic force; not in strict succession, but in continuous fluctuation.[17]

The problem with this otherwise exemplary analysis of this scene—and the others that see fantasy at work here—is that it wrongly identifies the *attempt* to construct a fantasy scenario with the *successful* elaboration of one.

Within Dorothy's apartment, both Jeffrey and Frank Booth confront her desire, and each fails, despite their efforts, to fantasize a way of making that desire meaningful. The film centers around Dorothy's desire and her status as a desiring subject; the responses to this desire remain secondary and after the fact. Throughout *Blue Velvet*, it is completely unclear what Dorothy desires, or if she desires anything at all. As Jeffrey tells Sandy after his encounter with Dorothy's desire, she seems to desire nothing. He says, "I think she wants to die. I think Frank cut the ear I found off her husband as a warning for her to stay alive." As Lynch depicts it in the film, Dorothy's desire is a pure desire: it desires nothing, and it refuses to satisfy itself with any pathological object. The very purity of Dorothy's desire—her unwillingness to accept any fantasmatic substitutes, her refusal of every satisfaction—may lead us to think that she has no desire at all. But pure desire is in some sense equivalent to the complete absence of desire. In both cases, the subject experiences every possible object as inherently unsatisfying.

As the embodiment of desire, Dorothy draws men to her. They want to discover the secret of her desire, what it is that she wants, and the fact that she wants nothing, that nothing can satisfy her, compels them all the more. At the same time, she threatens the men that pursue her because she reveals the void upon which all subjectivity is based. As Jacques-Alain Miller notes, because of her relationship to nothingness, "A true woman . . . reveals to man the absurdity of having. To a certain extent, she is man's ruination."[18]

This ruination becomes evident in Jeffrey's response to Dorothy. When Dorothy discovers Jeffrey in her closet and confronts him, she finds him in a state of desire. She asks, "What are you doing in my apartment, Jeffrey Beaumont?" and "What do you want?" But Jeffrey is unable to answer, saying only, "I don't know." Later, after Frank's sexual assault on Dorothy, she asks him again, "What do you want?" This time Jeffrey responds, "Nothing." Each of these responses indicates that at this moment—while he is in Dorothy's apartment—Jeffrey's desire lacks a fantasy frame through which it might obtain some direction. To say "I don't know" or "Nothing" in response to the question "What do you want?" is not (necessarily) to lie or to proclaim that one does not desire at all. It is rather the way in which one asserts oneself as a desiring subject in the purest possible form. The desiring subject doesn't know what it wants because it wants nothing—the impossible object that exists only insofar as it remains inaccessible. This is why the anorexic who literally eats the nothing is in some sense the pure subject of desire. The subject who can name what it wants has accepted a fantasmatic substitute for this nothing. At this moment in the film, Jeffrey experiences desire without the surrounding narrative that would domesticate it, and he occupies this position because he encounters Dorothy and her desire. And rather than experience desire in this way without the security of a fantasy frame, he asks Dorothy to allow him to leave.

The absence of any clear direction for Dorothy's desire becomes apparent in her behavior toward Jeffrey. Even Dorothy herself has no idea what she wants, and as a result, she does contradictory things. She holds a knife on Jeffrey and threatens to kill him, and yet she forces him to undress and performs fellatio on him. She says to him, "Don't touch me, or I'll kill you. Do you like it when I talk like that?" Throughout this and a later sexual encounter with Jeffrey, Dorothy seems to be performing—often acting like Frank acts toward her. She performs because she doesn't know what she wants, and the performance leaves open the question of what Dorothy actually desires.

One might say, of course, that Dorothy's performance with Jeffrey occurs in response to Frank's abuse, that she plays the typical role of the victim acting out the violence that has been done to her. But such a reading tells us more about the subject who produces it than about Dorothy. It posits supreme agency in male aggression rather than in female desire, which leaves it unable to explain Frank's behavior toward Dorothy. Something about Dorothy clearly disturbs Frank, which is why he goes to such elaborate lengths to perform in front of her.

From the moment Frank enters Dorothy's apartment, he appears to be staging a fantasmatic scenario, acting out a drama for which the only audience (to his knowledge) is Dorothy herself. Emphasizing the performative aspect of Frank's behavior, Michel Chion contends that

"Frank behaves as if he were the actor in a show designed to move the woman sexually. His way of repeating certain sentences may be the outpourings of a maniac, but might it not also be the mechanical repetition of a particular sentence designed to excite her?"[19] Even if Frank does not aim to excite her in a typical way, he does clearly aim to arouse her and to give a direction to her desire. By doing so, he hopes to avoid what Miller calls the ruination that she portends for him as a male subject. As Chion says, Frank attempts to prevent Dorothy "from becoming depressed and slipping into the void . . . by beating her, kidnapping her child and husband and then cutting off the man's ear."[20] In this light, we can see all of Frank's extreme behavior in the film as an effort to domesticate the desire that Dorothy embodies.

While he remains within Dorothy's apartment, however, Frank's attempt to translate Dorothy's desire into his fantasy structure comes up short. Clearly, Frank dominates Dorothy physically, but he never solves the problem of her desire or succeeds in locating her within his fantasy scenario. From her first telephone conversation with him, Dorothy continually fails to enact the fantasy properly; her desire intervenes and disrupts the narrative that Frank attempts to establish. On the telephone, she calls him "Frank," and Frank corrects her, saying that she must address him as "sir." When Frank arrives at the apartment, Dorothy makes a similar mistake. She says, "Hello, baby." Frank responds, "Shut up. It's daddy, you shithead." These slip-ups reveal Dorothy's difficulty with the fantasy structure that Frank lays out for her. She can't perform her role correctly because Frank's fantasy can't successfully locate her desire. She remains a disruptive force that he strives to domesticate.

The status of Dorothy's desire completely changes when she leaves her apartment and appears in the fantasmatic underworld that Frank dominates. Her desire becomes clear: she wants to care for her son, to be a proper mother. Maternity, as a symbolic role, represents a retreat from desire because it fills in this desire's fundamental absence with a discernible object. As Miller points out, "The truth in a woman, in Lacan's sense, is measured by her subjective distance from the position of motherhood. To be a mother, the mother of one's children, is to choose to exist as Woman."[21] That is to say, taking up the symbolic position of mother represents an abandonment of one's desire. When Dorothy evinces maternal concern for her son, she indicates that she has left the terrain of pure desire and entered the world of fantasy. As a mother, she is on male turf: the image of the maternal plenitude is a male fantasy. By kidnapping her son and prompting Dorothy into the position of the protective mother, Frank creates a fantasy scenario in which Dorothy's desire ceases to be traumatic for him.[22]

Fantasmatic Fathers

What the idealized public world of the film and its nightmarish underside share is a father figure that provides support for the fantasy structure. The coherence of this structure depends on the activity of the father, which is why the collapse of Tom Beaumont at the beginning of the film has such dramatic effects. Within fantasy, the father exists in order to domesticate feminine desire and provide a direction for it. He names this desire and thus works to eliminate its resistance to signification.

In this sense, Frank's violence is an attempt to arouse Dorothy's desire—to motivate her to desire something rather than nothing. Like Jeffrey and like the spectator, Frank experiences the trauma of an encounter with Dorothy's gaze and the horror of her desire, and he uses violence in order to provide a solution to this traumatic desire. This is why the spectator can find some degree of pleasure in the character of Frank, despite his disturbing violence. Frank is a fantasy figure and offers relief from Dorothy's desire through the fantasy scenario that he stages for her. Even his sexual assault on her—the film's most famous scene—works to mitigate the trauma of Dorothy's desire by giving it direction and forcing her to make clear what she wants.

After witnessing Frank's assault on Dorothy, Jeffrey returns to Dorothy's apartment on a later night and has sex with her. Lynch films this sex act in a way that indicates its traumatic status. Before they have sex, he asks her, "What do you want?" She replies, "I want you to hurt me." Though Jeffrey initially refuses, telling Dorothy, "No. I want to help you," he ends up striking her. When he does, the screen turns white. After the white screen, we see a distorted shot of Jeffrey and Dorothy having sex in slow motion. This depiction of their sexual act registers how disturbing Dorothy's desire is for Jeffrey. It not only disturbs Jeffrey and pushes him into uncharacteristic violence, but it also disrupts the filmic representation itself. Lynch cannot film this scene in the typical way because it unhinges the field of representation itself. Dorothy's desire for nothing resists all attempts—both Jeffrey's and the film's—to signify it. It produces the failure implicit in Jeffrey's violence and the failure of representation embodied by the white screen.

Seeing the trauma attached to Jeffrey's encounter with Dorothy's desire in this scene allows us to understand the role that Jeffrey's subsequent joyride with Frank plays in his psychic economy. Jeffrey runs into Frank and his gang as he is leaving Dorothy's apartment, and Frank forces Jeffrey to accompany them on a joyride that almost results in Jeffrey's death. Frank exposes Jeffrey to a violent and sadistic underworld in which Frank is the sole figure of authority. When Jeffrey defies this authority and punches Frank (for hitting Dorothy), Frank threatens to kill him and nearly beats him to death. During this beating, a bond between Frank and Jeffrey emerges. Earlier, Frank tells Jeffrey, "You're like me," and before beating him, Frank smears lipstick all around his lips and kisses Jeffrey. The bond between them is their shared retreat from Dorothy's desire. Even though his night with Frank nearly leads to his death, it actually provides relief for Jeffrey after his encounter with Dorothy's desire. The chronology of the film almost seems to suggest that Jeffrey fantasizes the encounter with Frank and the abuse that results in order to find respite from Dorothy. Far better to be beaten by Frank than to face the trauma of Dorothy's unsignifiable desire. Even if Frank horrifies us as spectators, he nonetheless provides a horror that makes sense.

The bond between Jeffrey and Frank is a homosocial one, and the film suggests that this powerful bond develops in response to the trauma of female desire. The violent nature of homosocial bonding—the fraternity hazing rituals, the humiliation of outsiders, and so on—does not derive simply from an excess of testosterone. This violence has a clear meaning: it assures the subjects participating in it that a power exists with the ability to contain the desire for nothing (the desire that we see in Dorothy). The abyss of this desire threatens to swallow men up, but homosocial violence implicitly promises to control it. Even the victims of homosocial violence gain this assurance, which is why they are often as attached to masculinity as the most aggressive men.

Frank also provides relief for Jeffrey insofar as he occupies the position of paternal authority. Unlike the other fathers in the film, Frank, despite his seeming commitment to unrestrained enjoyment, upholds prohibition and supports the symbolic law. This becomes evident during the joyride sequence when Frank stops at Ben's to discuss his drug dealings and allow Dorothy to see her son. Here, despite loudly proclaiming "I'll fuck anything that moves," Frank also enforces codes of civility. When Frank toasts Ben (Dean Stockwell), Jeffrey doesn't say anything. We then see Frank walk over to Jeffrey, punch him in the midsection, and say, "Be polite!" Though this command appears wildly incongruous in the mouth of Frank given what we have just seen him do, it fits with the idea of him as a figure of paternal authority. And as the sole effective paternal figure in the film, his presence offers assurance to Jeffrey that Dorothy can be contained.

Frank equally reassures the spectator watching the film. Even though he is clearly an evil character (a killer, a drug dealer, a sexual predator, a kidnapper, even a drunk driver), Frank remains a thoroughly pacifying figure on the screen. Dennis Hopper's performance as Frank accentuates his humorous qualities even when perpetuating violence. For instance, when he kidnaps Jeffrey and forces him to go to Ben's, he does so through wordplay reminiscent of Abbott and Costello's "Who's on first?" routine. Lynch also uses music to diffuse rather than enhance the threat that Frank represents. Typically, films associate villains with haunting music. The song we associate with Frank—and that plays as he beats up Jeffrey the night of the joyride—is Roy Orbison's "In Dreams," a song that defies an association with villainy. Frank attempts to distort the meaning of the song: we see him in a close-up telling Jeffrey, "in dreams, you're mine," implying that he will haunt Jeffrey like a nightmare. But the very soft and melodious nature of the Orbison song belies this threat and, along with the lipstick smeared on Frank's face, renders it less intimidating. Lynch's depiction of Frank the night of the joyride and throughout the film emphasizes that he functions as a figure of psychic relief rather than trauma.[23]

Jeffrey's flashbacks the next morning confirm that Dorothy represents the real trauma for him, not Frank. Rather than dreaming about his horrific beating at Frank's hands and his near death, Jeffrey remains fixated on Dorothy, seeing her in a flashback saying "Hit me" and seeing himself hit her in response. Dorothy is a traumatic object-cause of desire precisely because no one can fantasize away her desire and she seems to desire nothing. It is against this background of Dorothy's desire for nothing—or the nothingness of Dorothy's desire—that the desire *for* her emerges. As an impossible object, an *objet petit a*, Dorothy represents a far greater threat to Jeffrey than the father figure. Frank can merely kill him, but Dorothy can force him to confront his desire.

Both the ideal father and the nightmare father are fantasy constructions who work to tame the impossible object-cause of desire. Even though these paternal figures do violence to the subject and represent a barrier to the subject's enjoyment, they nonetheless provide a sense of relief. Without the father, the fantasizing subject experiences the unbearable weight of the impossible object intrude into its fantasy screen, causing the very structure of the fantasy to disintegrate. This is precisely what occurs when Dorothy enters the idealized fantasy world—a world where the father has become incapacitated—near the end of the film.

Fantasy and the Traumatic Encounter

The function of fantasy is to render the impossible object accessible for the subject. In doing so, fantasy provides a way for the subject to enjoy itself that would be unthinkable outside of fantasy. However, the act of making the impossible object accessible for the subject involves a danger. This object remains pleasurable only insofar as it remains absent and impossible. An actual encounter dislocates the entire symbolic structure in which the subject exists. Thus, most fantasies are very careful about the kind of access they offer to the impossible object.

Fantasies distort the object by never allowing it to appear in a pure form. We see an image masking the object, not the object itself. Or we see this object indirectly—as it disappears or moves away. The distortion of the object in the fantasy is the result of a failure to play out fully the logic of fantasy. When fully developed, the logic of fantasy leads to an encounter with the object in its real, traumatic dimension, but most fantasies never go this far. The separation of the worlds of desire and fantasy in *Blue Velvet* allows Lynch to avoid this failure that plagues most films. The film displays the fantasy in its entirety, and thus we experience a direct encounter with the impossible object.[24]

The ideological function of cinema depends on the limited access it provides to this object. Films provide a hint of enjoyment through the fantasy scenarios they deploy, but not too much. They remain pleasurable rather than becoming authentically enjoyable and thus threatening. The pleasure depends on an abbreviated deployment of fantasy, one that ends before it reaches its traumatic point. But the trauma is the key to the enjoyment that fantasy offers: when films avoid trauma, they avoid enjoyment. Lynch gives both by continuing the fantasy where other films stop. If it were the typical film, *Blue Velvet* would end when Jeffrey and Sandy proclaim their love for each other while dancing at a party. But just after this scene, Lynch unleashes a traumatic encounter with the impossible object.

Dorothy, her body naked and beaten, appears in the fantasmatic ideal world of Lumberton. This scene begins with Sandy's former boyfriend Mike chasing Jeffrey and Sandy through the Lumberton streets with his car. Lynch shoots this chase so as to create a sense of danger: we see the pursuing car only in a series of long shots that don't allow us to see who's driving. When Jeffrey assumes that Frank is in the car, the film encourages us to agree with him. After Sandy recognizes Mike driving, we experience the same relief that Jeffrey and Sandy do. Tension persists as they stop in front of Jeffrey's house as Mike prepares to fight Jeffrey for stealing Sandy from him, but Mike does not represent a threat like Frank. We are thus unprepared, like the characters in the film, for what happens next.

While Mike is in the process of confronting Jeffrey, Dorothy gradually enters into the back left side of the image. She seems to appear out of thin air, appearing at first as an indecipherable blot that no one— including the spectator—initially notices. When the other characters do notice, they become completely disoriented. Her intrusion into the fantasmatic realm rips apart the fantasy structure. Mike abandons any notion of fighting with Jeffrey and begins to depart. But to lessen the trauma of Dorothy's appearance, he adds, "Who's that, huh? Is that your mother?" On the one hand, Mike's comment seems to support the reading of the film that identifies Dorothy with maternity, but on the other, it attests to the fantasmatic role that the image of Dorothy as mother plays. That this would be Mike's first assumption when he sees her walking through the yard naked and beaten suggests that he is responding with what immediately comes to mind—i.e., with his unconscious fantasy. Mike's comment says more about him as a character than it does about Dorothy and her actual status in the film.

The threat of the fight suddenly seems absurdly insignificant in comparison with the trauma of Dorothy's body. Her body has no place within the fantasmatic public world, and the fantasy screen breaks down. The form in which Dorothy appears—publicly naked and begging for Jeffrey's help—reveals the spectator's investment in the fantasy and demands that the spectator confront her qua impossible object. She doesn't fit in the picture, which is why we become so uncomfortable watching her naked body in the middle of the suburban neighborhood. When Jeffrey and Sandy take Dorothy into Sandy's house, Dorothy clings to Jeffrey and repeats, "He put his disease in me." Dorothy's presence is unbearable both for characters in the film—Sandy begins to cry, and her mother retrieves a coat to cover Dorothy—and for the spectator.

Here the realm of desire intersects with that of fantasy, forcing an encounter with the real dimension of the impossible object without its imaginary guise. The fantasy structure of Lumberton's idealized world can only maintain its consistency as long as it excludes desire. Hence, when Dorothy's desire intrudes into this structure, she shatters it and at the same time shatters the spectator's distance from what's happening. As a foreign body in this mise-en-scène, Dorothy embodies the gaze, and our anxiety in seeing her indicates our encounter with it, revealing that we are in the picture at its nonspecular point, the point of the gaze. For Lacan, "*The* objet a *in the field of the visible is the gaze*."[25] That is, the gaze is the impossible object—not a subjective look but the point at which the object marks the subject's desire. The gaze includes the subject's desire within the visual field as an impossible point irreducible to that field. As this scene illustrates, in the form of the gaze the object looks back at us. Our desire becomes embodied in the traumatic point of Dorothy's body on the screen. *Blue Velvet* uses a strict separation of desire and fantasy in order to depict the traumatic point of their intersection. The film shows that by immersing ourselves in fantasy without the security of the father, we can encounter the impossible object. And it is through this encounter that we enjoy.

A Utopia Without Disavowal

The film concludes with what seems like the restoration of the idealized fantasy, now cleansed of both its nightmare underside and of Dorothy's desire. At Jeffrey's house, we see Jeffrey's and Sandy's family interacting with each other on a sunny summer afternoon. Jeffrey's father stands with Detective Williams in the backyard, his health now restored. Jeffrey and Sandy are together, with her boyfriend Mike no longer a barrier to their romance. What's more, a robin appears on the window ledge, seeming to confirm Sandy's fantasmatic prediction that there will be trouble only until the robins come. There are, however, noticeable stains within this idealized image.

The robin itself, the representative of the ideal, also hints at the continued existence of the underside as we see it eating a bug. This bug serves to remind us of the opening sequence, where Tom Beaumont's collapse opened up the underworld of bug life beneath the surface of the grass. The idealized fantasy thus reveals its failure again, even at the point of its apparent success. The limitation of this fantasy becomes even more evident as the film ends.

The film ends with a final image of Dorothy that suggests that the restoration of the father has secured her desire. She now exists as a mother, with only maternal desires, in the idealized fantasy world of Lumberton. The last image of the film depicts Donnie, freed from Frank's threat, playing with his smiling mother on a bright sunny day. The idyllic scene offers visual confirmation of the clarity of Dorothy's desire, but, as so often happens in a Lynch film, the audio track belies the visual image. The last words of the film are Dorothy singing the song she has sung throughout the film. We hear, "And I still can see blue velvet through my tears." This line suggests that despite the image of Dorothy playing peacefully with her son, her desire cannot fit completely into the maternal role. Here the visual and the audio tracks are completely at odds with each other, as the audio track recalls Dorothy's involvement with Frank. This continued division within Dorothy's desire indicates that neither alternative is entirely satisfying to her. She remains a subject desiring nothing and thereby staining the denouement of the film.

In this way, the film shows us the limit that fantasy cannot eclipse. As *Blue Velvet* makes clear, fantasy works in two different ways to narrate the disturbance that desire brings to the symbolic order, but neither of these ways is fully successful. The ultimate contention of the film is not that we should abandon our fantasies—if this were even possible—because they always fail. What we must do, instead, is pay attention to those moments at which fantasy fails, not to guard against these moments, in order to see that the enjoyment we derive from fantasy depends directly on the moments of failure. It is only at the point at which they fail that fantasies allow us access to an otherwise inaccessible object.

We most often think of the turn to fantasy as a betrayal of desire, as a way of compromising on the purity of desire. On one level, *Blue Velvet* confirms this idea through its depiction of fantasy as a retreat from Dorothy's implacable desire. But on another level, the conclusion of the film indicates how a certain mode of fantasizing can take desire into account and remain true to it. By taking fantasy to its limit, by fantasizing absolutely, one sees desire reemerge in the fantasy. The bug that the robin eats and the sound of "Blue Velvet" on the film's audio track in the final scene bear witness to desire's reemergence. Fantasy allows us to rediscover the desire that it leaves behind so long as we persist in it seriously enough. It is only the halfhearted fantasy that forsakes desire. The absolute commitment to fantasy produces the impossible moment at which betrayed desire returns.

FIVE   The Absence of Desire in *Wild at Heart*

Lost in Fantasy

When *Wild at Heart* (1990) was released on August 17, 1990, Lynch was at a high point of popularity and critical esteem. The television series *Twin Peaks*, created by Lynch with Mark Frost, had just finished its successful first-season run (the pilot episode having aired as a mid-season replacement on April 8), and critics and audiences still recalled favorably the impression of *Blue Velvet* (1986), his previous film. According to most critics and viewers, *Wild at Heart* did not reach the perceived heights of *Blue Velvet*, but neither did it fall to the depths of *Dune* (1984). It won the Palme d'Or, the top prize at the Cannes Film Festival, but those who didn't like the film tended to feel that it went too far in the direction of excess: where *Blue Velvet* had an ideal world that counterbalanced the violent underworld it depicts, *Wild at Heart* had only the underworld.

The typical Lynch film, as we have seen, takes *The Wizard of Oz* (Victor Fleming, 1939) as its model for enacting a strict separation between the world of desire and the world of fantasy. Though *Wild at Heart* contains more overt allusions to *The Wizard of Oz* than any of Lynch's other films, its structure, ironically, has less in common with it than does the rest of Lynch's work. *Wild at Heart* shows Sailor (Nicolas

Cage) and Lula (Laura Dern) talking about the Yellow Brick Road and going over the rainbow, Lula imagining her mother Marietta (Diane Ladd) as the Wicked Witch of the West, Lula wearing a version of Dorothy's ruby slippers, and the good witch Glinda (Sheryl Lee) appearing to Sailor in a vision at the end of the film.[1] Despite these and other allusions, *Wild at Heart* does not depict clashing worlds of desire and fantasy that would correspond to the division between the black-and-white Kansas and the colorful Oz, but immerses us completely in a world of fantasy.

Wild at Heart is *The Wizard of Oz* without Kansas. For this reason, it should not be surprising that all the film's allusions to *The Wizard of Oz* refer to Dorothy's fantasy world and not to the mundane reality of Kansas. *Wild at Heart* presents a world suffocating under the heightened presence of the object and bombarding the subject with excess. Only in a single shot toward the end of the film does Lynch suggest the alternative—the world of desire—that this world of excess obscures. Just after the film's most memorable scene (when Bobby Peru [Willem Dafoe] sexually assaults Lula), we see a close-up of Lula's feet in red slippers. In a direct allusion to *The Wizard of Oz*, Lula clicks the heels of her red shoes in an effort to remove herself from the world of excess and go "back to Kansas"—to a world of desire that bars and provides protection from enjoyment. Yet no such respite exists: unlike Dorothy in *The Wizard of Oz*, Lula clicks her heels to no avail.

The close-up of Lula clicking the heels of her red shoes signifies the absence of the world of absence and desire in the film. In this sense, *Wild at Heart* does continue the division that marks Lynch's other films, but here the world of fantasy has completely subsumed the world of desire. The world of desire is present only through the allusion to its absence.[2] This allows Lynch to explore the ramifications of living entirely in a world of fantasy—a world committed at all times to maximizing enjoyment. Characters do not succumb to a symbolic law demanding the sacrifice of enjoyment for the sake of the social order. The result is not what we might expect: rather than allowing Sailor and Lula to enjoy themselves fully, the fantasy world constantly threatens their enjoyment.

Because the external world has the character of a private fantasy rather than a public realm, Sailor and Lula's private fantasy ceases to be a distinct place apart from the external world. The more the world itself becomes fantasmatic and overwhelms us with images of excessive enjoyment, the more difficult it becomes for us to fantasize. Fantasy depends on a public world of desire that bars enjoyment. We create fantasies—even filmic fantasies—in response to absence of the object that constitutes this public world. In the completely fantasmatic world that *Wild at Heart* depicts, the impossibility that plagues our desire does not exist; the film presents the ultimate enjoyment as directly accessible rather than impossible. Sailor and Lula's fantasy has no problem of desire that it must solve, and thus their relationship ends up simply replicating the external world rather than providing an alternative.

The critique that *Wild at Heart* levels at contemporary society centers on its proclivity for closing off the space for fantasy. We live in a society that bombards us with nonstop excess; the public realm today provides no relief from images of enjoyment and incentives to enjoy. Images that once were confined to private fantasies now proliferate publicly. But the point is not that this societal turn to public displays of private fantasies has gone too far; it doesn't yet go far enough. It seems as if we're suffering from too many people publicly living out their fantasies, but they're living them out in an abbreviated form. Obsessed with the image of enjoyment, we miss the real or traumatic dimension of fantasy. What *Wild at Heart* shows is that the fantasmatic contemporary world requires a more profound commitment to fantasy on the part of the subject if this subject is to experience fantasy in its real dimension, to experience fantasy beyond its visual dimension. The subject constructs fantasy out of images, but these images frame a nonspecular point—the impossible object—that is the source of the enjoyment that fantasy provides.

The Excesses of Wild at Heart

Wild at Heart is Lynch's most excessive film. The film includes more graphic violence, more open displays of sexuality, and more acts of extreme criminality than any other Lynch film. Its excesses cause *Blue Velvet* to seem subdued in retrospect. We see, among many other things, brain matter spill from the head of Bobby Ray Lemon (Gregg Dandridge); Bobby Peru's intense sexual assault on Lula; Bobby Peru inadvertently blowing off his own head with a shotgun; and the sadistic torture and murder of Johnnie Farragut (Harry Dean Stanton). What makes these and other excessive events so disturbing is that Lynch does not provide any alternative space wherein we might establish our bearings as spectators, a space that we could contrast with the excessive events. Instead, the excess pervades each and every scene. Lynch critic Jeff Johnson claims, with some justice, that in this film "Lynch took literally Blake's metaphysical musings about the road of excess leading to the palace of wisdom."[3] Only one character advocates any degree of restraint—Johnnie Farragut—and he dies a horrible death precisely because his restrained pursuit of Sailor and Lula displeases Marietta and leads her subsequently to acquiesce to his murder.

The form of the film evinces a similar lack of restraint.[4] Not only does Lynch include graphic imagery within the frame, but he also constructs the narrative in a way that emphasizes excess. The movement of the narrative suffers continual interruptions due to the film's excessive events. This occurs, for instance, when Sailor and Lula are driving at night through Texas and encounter a car crash. As they stop to investigate, a woman involved in the crash dies before their eyes. The entire scene has an excessive status relative to the filmic narrative because it serves only to interrupt rather than advance the narrative. Instead of moving forward in a linear fashion, the narrative seems to exist in order to bring us to the next extreme image. This dynamic becomes apparent during Sailor and Bobby Peru's attempted robbery. As he shoots this climactic scene in the film, Lynch emphasizes not its role in the narrative but the extreme images that it produces—the aforementioned decapitation of Bobby Peru, and a dog seen walking away with the detached hand of one of the robbery victims in his mouth. Lynch creates a form that highlights the extreme image at the expense of narrative movement, I would argue, in order to illustrate the effect of unrestrained enjoyment. In the filmic world of *Wild at Heart*, there is no normal experience free of the stain of excess.[5]

One of the chief ways that Lynch portrays visually the unrestrained enjoyment that characterizes the filmic world is through the use of fire. Beginning with the film's opening titles, which Lynch displays in white against a black background with flames rising up on it, fire or flames appear throughout the film. Each time that we see fire, characters are enjoying themselves, even—or especially—when another character burns to death. When we see Sailor and Lula have sex for the first time in the film, Lynch includes a close-up of a flame lighting a cigarette.

This image, repeated later in the film, points toward the extreme enjoyment that they seem to experience. At other times, fire illustrates the enjoyment that characters experience during acts of violence. Marietta organizes the fiery deaths of both Uncle Pooch (Marvin Kaplan) and her husband Clyde, and their burning bodies demonstrate the enjoyment that she receives from their violent deaths.

Lynch explicitly links Marietta's excessive enjoyment to the excesses that are ravaging the planet. Early in the film, Lula tells Sailor, "That ozone layer is disappearing. One of these mornings the sun is going to come up and burn a hole clear through the planet like an electrical x-ray." After Lula says this, we hear a woman's laugh in the background and see a close-up of a pained look on Lula's face. The film dissolves to a shot of a house in flames—an image of the death of Lula's father—as the woman's disturbing laugh continues. This image dissolves back to Lula's pained face. She proclaims, "That woman's laugh creeps me out. It sounds like something I heard before. It sounds like the wicked witch." The laugh "creeps her out" because it reminds Lula of her mother's laugh, her mother's obscene display of enjoyment. We know that Marietta is responsible for the fire that kills her husband, and the image of the burning thus also marks her enjoyment. If the planet, as Lula claims, suffers from too much heat and fire, Marietta's excessive enjoyment plays a part in raising its temperature.

Marietta's excessive enjoyment also manifests itself in the spectacle she creates out of herself. We see her drunk, out of control emotionally, and obsessed with destroying anyone who stands in the way of her desire. She demonstrates no respect for the typical barriers that mark relationships, as she follows Sailor, the boyfriend of her daughter, into a men's room and asks him, "How would you like to fuck Lula's momma?" This type of uncontrolled will to enjoy even violates her self-interest, causing Marietta to act in ways that victimize herself. Frustrated with Johnnie Farragut's inability to apprehend Sailor and Lula, she allows Marcello Santos (J. E. Freeman) to have Johnnie murdered even though she's in love with him. After consenting to the murder of her lover, we see Marietta lose all restraint and smear bright red lipstick all over her face. The image of Marietta's face completely covered with red lipstick is so disturbing because it indicates her utter lack of self-control. Even in her feeling of remorse, she does not stop at the point most people do but continues to extremes. Discussing this scene,

Jana Evans Braziel notes, "*Wild at Heart* presents Marietta as a woman who is rapidly spilling over towards boundlessness."[6] The result of this boundlessness—and that of the other characters in the film—is a world in which enjoyment appears as an unavoidable public spectacle.

The intrusion of private enjoyment into the public world becomes most evident in the character of Bobby Peru. Bobby is in Big Tuna making a porn film, and we learn from another character that he was involved in a massacre of civilians in Vietnam. But Bobby's excessive enjoyment is not limited to what he does; his appearance registers his obscene enjoyment directly on the surface of his body. His deformed mouth and teeth resemble a vagina dentata, and Lynch films them in a way that emphasizes their role in Bobby's enjoyment. During his sexual assault on Lula, Bobby repeats "Say 'fuck me.' " As he does this, we see repeated close-ups of his mouth, which looks more like the open mouth of the worms in *Dune* than an actual human mouth. The close-ups suggest an enjoyment that derives not from the sex act itself but from speaking about it. This suggestion soon receives confirmation when Bobby refuses to have sex with Lula after he finally coerces her into saying "Fuck me." His private enjoyment manifests itself in the most public act of all—that of speaking.[7] Whenever he speaks in the film, his coarse language and overly familiar manner renders obvious his intense enjoyment.

Even before his assault on Lula, Bobby displays the public nature of his enjoyment in his dialogue with her. He enters Lula and Sailor's cabin and asks if he can "take a piss in your head." This statement makes public activities that are usually kept private. And his subsequent explanation further displays his obscenity, as he tells Lula that he means her toilet rather than her actual head. He flaunts the extremes of his ability to imagine perversions, even while denying that he will realize them. This publicizing of private enjoyment helps to create a world without a public realm constituted around absence and lack.

Marietta and Bobby serve as the primary figures of authority in *Wild at Heart*, and each pushes Sailor and Lula toward enjoyment rather than away from it. In this sense, they represent the contemporary world's perversion of authority—the maternal superego and the anal father of enjoyment. Whereas traditional authority functions through absence and at a distance from the subject, contemporary authority remains close at hand and exhibits its own suffocating enjoyment as it commands the subject to enjoy as well.[8] Marietta demands that Lula remain within their perverse bond and eschew any other love object, and Bobby drives Sailor to commit a robbery that Sailor doesn't want to commit. The proximity of these two authority figures threatens to suffocate both Sailor and Lula. The excessive enjoyment that characterizes the filmic world of *Wild at Heart* leaves no room for Sailor and Lula to constitute their relationship. To experience too much enjoyment is always to feel as if one is not experiencing enough.

Publicized Privacy

It is tempting to focus on the appealing romance between Sailor and Lula—Michel Chion calls it "the most beautiful love ballad which the cinema has ever whispered into the night"[9]—and contrast this relationship with the threatening external world in which it exists in the film. The relationship, according to this interpretation, provides respite from the unpleasant life existing outside of it. It is harmonious, pure, and innocent, while the surrounding world is degraded, violent, and perverse. Though not as celebratory in his praise of the relationship as Chion, Kenneth Kaleta emphasizes this dynamic: "Mutual security in their union, romantic innocence, underlies the . . . relationship, distinguishing them from the squalor and frenzy of their world."[10] Even critics who see a connection between the relationship and the world surrounding it tend to see this connection resulting from the influence of an impure world on Sailor and Lula. The fault does not lie with their relationship itself. For Martha Nochimson, the distinction between the romantic relationship and the external world in the film breaks down, but it breaks down when the "dissonant" nature of the external world intrudes on them. She claims, "Tensions in Sailor and Lula's relationship are never resolved because, despite their moments of sexual grace, they too are part of the dissonant world as it actually exists."[11] If Sailor and Lula's relationship falls short of an ideal at some point, this is the product not of its own internal failing but that of the society in which it exists.

The problem with this apotheosis of the film's romance and corresponding denigration of the rest of the society that the film depicts lies in its failure to see the fundamental link between the two that the film itself makes. *Wild at Heart* does not oppose Sailor and Lula's romance to the violent world that surrounds it but shows the intimate link between the two. Throughout the film, Lynch works on the level of form to demonstrate the links between the romance and the surrounding world. The film even goes so far as to suggest that the society depicted in *Wild at Heart* lies in such disarray *because of* the approach that Sailor and Lula take to their romance. That is to say, they experience the world as violent and threatening because of the position they occupy, not necessarily because the world is violent and threatening. *Wild at Heart* breaks down the distinction between the merely private fantasy and the external world, allowing us to see how private fantasies work to shape the external world.

Even a film as devoted to the exploration of private fantasy as *Wild at Heart* becomes a film about society at large. Though the political dimension of *Eraserhead* (1977) and *Dune* (1984) is perhaps more evident, *Wild at Heart* shows how the private becomes public and takes on a social import. In this sense, it defies Sharon Willis's complaint that "while Lynch's films are all about struggles with 'the parents inside one's head,' they are about protecting and preserving those internal imagoes, internal censorships. Consequently, they offer the lure of protection from history and politics by imagining that everything comes down to a private psychosexual adventure, or drama. It is all in our heads."[12] In *Wild at Heart* (the film that earns the majority of Willis's criticism), the drama may in fact be in our heads, but our heads are leaking into the outside world.

This becomes most apparent through Lynch's use of music in the film, especially the speed-metal song "Slaughterhouse" by the band Powermad. On the one hand, the song serves as something like an anthem for Sailor and Lula's relationship. It plays when we first see them having sex, when Sailor and Lula dance to the band playing it live, and when they dance to it on their car radio on a deserted Texas highway. According to Annette Davison, "Slaughterhouse" expresses "the strength and passion of Sailor and Lula's love."[13] But the song is not associated only with images of their romance. We first hear this song in the opening scene of the film as Sailor beats Bobby Ray Lemon to death. After a shot of Lemon threatening to kill Sailor and a close-up on Lemon opening his switchblade, the two begin to fight, and just as the fight commences, the violent sound of "Slaughterhouse" commences as well. Davison describes this song as "a loud and grandiose piece of rock music that builds in strength through a combination of the emphatic repetition and variation of thematic figures with percussive interruption."[14] The loudness and building strength of the song creates a sense of breaking free from restraint—and this out-of-control quality characterizes both the romance and Sailor's violence. If "Slaughterhouse" expresses the passion in Sailor and Lula's relationship, it also expresses the way in which this passion exceeds the relationship itself and manifests itself in Sailor's rage toward the external world. Lynch uses the same music for their relationship and for Sailor's lethal violence in order to indicate the absence of a barrier between the relationship and the external world.

Before it establishes the romance between Sailor and Lula, *Wild at Heart* depicts a threat to this romance in the form of Bobby Ray Lemon (and Marietta, who hired him to kill Sailor). This would seem to suggest, following Nochimson's thesis above, that the film highlights the external forces that threaten the purity of the romance. However, though the opening scene shows Lemon and Marietta as threatening figures, it places more emphasis on Sailor's excessive reaction to Lemon's threat. As we hear the pounding music from Powermad, we watch Sailor beating Lemon's head repeatedly against the railing of the stairs. A close-up of blood splattering across the floor follows. Sailor throws Lemon down the stairs and smashes his head against the ground until a pool of blood amasses. After we see Sailor standing victorious over the body, Lynch cuts to a closer shot of the body that makes visible brain matter oozing out of the back of Lemon's head. Rather than displaying remorse, Sailor poses over the dead body and lights a cigarette. The fact that this scene opens the film and thus provides our first insight into Sailor's character suggests its importance for understanding him. Though Sailor is defending himself, the level of violence he employs far exceeds what is necessary. This depiction of excessive violence emanating from Sailor reveals the link between Sailor and Lula's relationship and the violent world that surrounds them. Instead of marking a retreat, their relationship helps to constitute the violent external world.[15]

Lynch himself says that he included the character of O.O. Spool (Jack Nance) making reference to *The Wizard of Oz* in order to indicate the link between Sailor and Lula's relationship and the world surrounding it. *The Wizard of Oz* provides the schema for the fantasy that Sailor and Lula try to realize: they picture themselves on the Yellow

Brick Road heading for somewhere over the rainbow, menaced on their voyage by the Wicked Witch. They transform *The Wizard of Oz* into their own private language, but Spool's presence in the narrative suggests that others have access to this same private language. Spool appears in the film after Sailor and Lula arrive in Big Tuna, Texas, and this appearance seems entirely tangential to the filmic narrative, as does the belabored story he tells about his dog. But when he mentions the dog, he says, "And you may even picture Toto from *The Wizard of Oz*." This statement from a complete stranger discomfits Lula—as it should the viewer—because it indicates that Sailor and Lula's private fantasy life has seeped into the public world. Discussing this moment, Lynch says, "The idea that someone else was speaking about something that Sailor and Lula shared secretly was a double whammy. It fits in with the theme, but it's scary at the same time."[16] Hearing an outsider's reference to Toto, we recognize Sailor and Lula's inability to construct a distinctive fantasy life in a wholly fantasmatic world.

At one point in the film, the distinction between the lovers and the world surrounding them seems most emphatic: as Lula drives the car after they leave New Orleans, she searches for something to listen to on the radio and finds only disturbing news being discussed on every station. Disgusted, she pulls the car over to the side of the road, gets out, and demands that Sailor "find some music" on the radio. After tuning through more talk radio, Sailor discovers a song—"Slaughterhouse" by Powermad, the speed-metal song that played when Sailor killed Bobby Ray Lemon and when Sailor and Lula had sex for the first time in the film. Here, the song appears diegetically (as it did once earlier in the film when Sailor and Lula listened to the band perform it live) and occasions a dramatic change in Lula's attitude. She and Sailor begin to dance wildly at the side of the road as the song blares from the car's stereo.

The music seems to offer some private respite for Sailor and Lula from the violence and tragedy of the external world. But the song itself is just as violent as the discussions on the radio, and, for us as spectators of the film, we associate it with the extreme violence that Sailor displayed as he beat Bobby Ray Lemon to death. This connotation indicates that despite Lula's belief that this music offers an alternative to the "sick" world, Sailor and Lula remain firmly within this sickness while dancing on the side of the road to "Slaughterhouse." Until the end of the film, Sailor and Lula's relationship continues to mirror the external world rather than pose a genuine alternative.

Not Enough Fantasy

Sailor and Lula encounter so much trouble in their attempt to realize their fantasy because they fail to commit themselves fully to it. They want the fantasy to be pleasurable, and thus they cannot sustain it when it isn't. It is this deviation, not the fantasy itself, that produces each of the difficulties they encounter. Rather than warning us about the dangers of fantasmatic enjoyment, the film reveals what results from our inability to follow the logic of fantasy. This failure occurs when we turn our attention toward the Other and concentrate on how the Other sees us. When one fully commits to one's fantasy, one ignores the Other's look altogether, but this doesn't happen in the film, nor does it happen in our seemingly fantasmatic contemporary society.

Wild at Heart belies Lynch's own conservative comments about its serving as a cautionary tale. Commenting on contemporary society, he claims, "Each year we give permission for people to get away with more. We do it by being disorganized, being without leadership, not making decisions fast enough, and not holding true to things that were in place to begin with. Then it gets easier to give more away."[17] From these comments, it sounds as if the excess that *Wild at Heart* depicts is the result of an absence of authority—an absence that has allowed individual subjects too much leeway in realizing their private fantasies at the public's expense. And this is certainly how the film initially appears. But such a view misses the degree of obedience that Sailor and Lula exhibit toward figures of authority.

Sailor and Lula each fail to fully embrace their fantasy for different reasons, and through the depiction of their failure, Lynch reveals the common male and female ways of avoiding the real that fantasy actualizes. Sailor avoids fully committing himself to their fantasy because of his investment in phallic authority. From the very first scene of the film, Sailor sets out to prove his non-castration, to prove that he is potent rather than lacking. He beats Bobby Ray Lemon to death and lights a cigarette over the body in order to underline his triumph. Later, he engages in a similar—though less violent—outburst when another man approaches Lula at a concert. This scene is especially revelatory insofar as it depicts Sailor defending Lula's "honor." Sailor forces the man to apologize to Lula for the offense he has given her. Far from indicating Sailor's devotion to Lula and their fantasy, these actions show Sailor's investment in phallic authority. He acts as he does not for Lula but for the anonymous societal Other—in order to demonstrate his status as non-lacking.

Sailor believes himself free of all the symbolic constraints that bind other subjects. His mantra concerning his snakeskin jacket makes this idea of himself clear: "My snakeskin jacket... represents my individuality and my belief in personal freedom." The problem with this insistence on his individuality is precisely the *insistence* itself. That is, the very fact that Sailor must profess his freedom to the Other testifies to his lack of freedom and to his dependence on that Other to recognize him as a "free" subject. Sailor claims that he suffers from an absence of symbolic authority, noting that he "didn't have much parental guidance." But the film reveals the opposite. Sailor suffers from too much "parental guidance"— the suffocating presence of parental or social authority.[18]

Sailor's investment in symbolic authority and its ideal of non-castration leads him ultimately to go along with Bobby Peru's heist. Bobby dangles the idea of providing for Lula in front of Sailor, and this is enough to win Sailor's acquiescence. He seduces Sailor with the image of a "real man" who could support his woman. At the end of the film, this is also what prevents Sailor from initially going with Lula and his son Pace when they pick him up from prison. Feeling that he can't be the perfect father for Pace, Sailor rejects fatherhood altogether. The very identification with symbolic authority prevents him from fully embracing fantasy.

And where Sailor invests himself in symbolic authority at the expense of fantasy, Lula invests herself in an imaginary authority—her mother Marietta. She recognizes the role that her mother plays in keeping her apart from Sailor, and yet never stands up to her mother or breaks off communication. Her commitment to her imaginary bond with her mother remains stronger throughout the film than her commitment to the fantasy of romantic union with Sailor. She confesses to Sailor, "Maybe my momma cares for me just a little too much," which shows that Lula grasps to some extent Marietta's improper bond with her. But the very way that she puts it—that Marietta cares "too much"— demonstrates her refusal to acknowledge what's at stake for her.

In order to sustain her feelings for her mother, Lula lies to herself and to Sailor about her own knowledge concerning Marietta's activities. In narrating her childhood to Sailor, she recounts Uncle Pooch's rape of her when she was thirteen and the death of her father. Both of these cases reveal that Lula knows about her mother's knowledge of the rape (and her involvement in Pooch's murder afterward) and that she seems to know about her mother's role in her father's death. As Lula discusses Uncle Pooch's rape, we see a flashback of the event, and when she describes how angry Marietta would have been had she known, we see Marietta walking in on the aftermath of the rape and accosting Uncle Pooch. Since this flashback occurs while Lula is speaking, the film suggests that she knows what we see—and has either repressed it or intentionally ignored it. From this, we can suppose that Lula at least suspects her mother's role in the death of her father. This avoidance of the truth about her mother allows Lula to continue to enjoy the security of her bond with Marietta.

To succumb to the logic of fantasy is to encounter a materialization of the gap within the symbolic order. Fantasy, the narrative appearing in this gap, primarily functions to assure us that the gap doesn't exist, that there is an Other outside the system of signification who authorizes it. But because of its location in the gap of the symbolic order, fantasy also has the potential to destroy the assurances of symbolic identity and the comforts of imaginary bonds, forcing us to experience an enjoyment that leaves us exposed and vulnerable. This is an enjoyment that we don't see throughout the film. We see images of Sailor and Lula enjoying themselves, but even when these moments occur privately, the rehearsals of enjoyment are performances for the Other. Joan Copjec suggests that "jouissance flourishes only there where it is *not* validated by the Other."[19] One cannot perform one's enjoyment; one suffers it.

Refusing Any Absence

The problem with the enjoyment that the characters in *Wild at Heart* pursue is that it demands an impossible total presence. The attempt to secure complete enjoyment without loss inevitably produces precisely the experience of loss that one tries to avoid. Complete enjoyment has an imaginary status: we see it—or imagine it—in the Other, but every attempt to realize it brings disappointment. This disappointment is the genesis of psychoanalysis, which comes into being in response to it and reveals that all satisfaction depends on an initial renunciation of the privileged object. As Lacan puts it in *Seminar V*, "it is insofar as the child . . . does not renounce its object that its desire does not find itself satisfied."[20] The initial renunciation provides the avenue through which desire travels. The attempt to sustain a relationship with the privileged object inevitably fails because the object only becomes the privileged object—the object embodying the subject's enjoyment— through its loss. Clinging to the presence of the object thus devalues the object and foregrounds the subject's failure to enjoy.

But the drive to enjoy is not so easily sidetracked. Though consciously the subject may remain fixated on the ideal of complete enjoyment, the unconscious drives the subject toward another form of enjoyment. Since enjoyment can only be partial and depends on the experience of absence, the subject disappointed with the attempt to achieve complete enjoyment soon works unconsciously to create the loss of the object whereby enjoyment will become possible. That is to say, the frustrated subject bent on complete enjoyment engages in a form of self-sabotage that actually deprives this subject of the privileged object that it desires. The subject's proclivity for self-sabotage—dreams that return to trauma rather than imagining its disappearance, the negative therapeutic reaction, and so on—impels Freud to write *Beyond the Pleasure Principle* (1920), in which he discovers the death drive and asserts its primacy. As Freud sees, unconscious self-sabotage is the path that desire takes when it initially chokes on the stifling presence of the privileged object.

Perhaps the fundamental counterintuitive claim of psychoanalysis is that subjects do not act in their own self-interest. Instead, they sacrifice their self-interest in order to create or sustain themselves as desiring. Self-interest has value for the subject because it provides something to sacrifice. By sacrificing one's own interest in an act of self-sabotage, one inaugurates the relationship of desire relative to the lost object. But few consciously engage in the project of self-sabotage: the conscious pursuit of self-interest allows the subject to remain blind to the unconscious sacrifice of it.

This is the dynamic that becomes rampant in a world where everyone is bent on obtaining complete enjoyment. This pervasive will to enjoy infects almost every character in *Wild at Heart*, and Lynch includes the otherwise tangential story of Jingle Dell (Crispin Glover) in order to exemplify the link between the search for complete enjoyment and the violence that characterizes the world of the film.[21] While Lula and Sailor are talking in bed one night, Lula tells Sailor the story of her cousin nicknamed "Jingle Dell," as we see the story unfold in flashback. Jingle Dell earned his name because he wanted Christmas to last all year long, and when it didn't, he concocted a paranoid theory about aliens controlling the earth and stealing the spirit of Christmas. In response to the absence of the spirit of Christmas, he began placing cockroaches on his anus. As Lula recounts this detail, we see an image of Dell's mother finding his underwear covered with cockroaches. Even though this seems like a bizarre and extreme perversion, it follows logically from Jingle Dell's starting point. Lynch has Lula tell this story because it demonstrates in precise terms the trajectory that results from the privileging of complete enjoyment.

Jingle Dell's desire for Christmas to last all year long is a desire for enjoyment without absence. But enjoyment depends on absence, and Christmas allows us to understand this in the simplest way. One's enjoyment is the result of the absence of the privileged day throughout the rest of the year: one enjoys Christmas only as an exceptional day, which means that one obtains from it a partial enjoyment. In order to explain the failure of complete enjoyment, Jingle Dell turns to a paranoid explanation: the Other has stolen this enjoyment—the spirit of Christmas—and thus represents an external barrier to complete enjoyment. This type of explanation allows the subject to preserve the ideal of complete enjoyment as a possibility in the face of its failure. Jingle Dell can tell himself that even though we don't enjoy the spirit of Christmas all year long, this failure is not necessary but the contingent result of an alien agency. In conjunction with this explanation, Jingle Dell begins placing cockroaches on his anus in order to experience enjoyment in some way after missing the complete enjoyment of a permanent Christmas. The masochistic turn to the cockroach appeals to Dell because the cockroach allows him to suffer and, while suffering, he feels the absence of the privileged object, which is the mode in which one can enjoy it. In this way, Dell's turn to perversion provides exactly what his investment in the spirit of Christmas could not—actual enjoyment.[22]

The case of Jingle Dell lays out the pattern that the other characters in *Wild at Heart* follow, albeit less explicitly. Sailor's self-destructive acts—the killing of Bobby Ray Lemon, the robbery committed with Bobby Peru—result from the logic of Jingle Dell. Unable to experience the complete enjoyment he desires despite the presence of Lula, Sailor finds a way to introduce absence into their relationship and thus to make it enjoyable. Lula, for her part, finally submits to Bobby Peru and says, "Fuck me," for the same reason. This scene occurs in the midst of troubles in her relationship with Sailor, and it works to emphasize the experience of absence for Lula. Though they don't go so far as to put cockroaches on their anuses, both Sailor and Lula's behavior mirrors that of Jingle Dell.

The Price of the Happy Ending

Though other scenes (the shooting of Johnnie Farragut, Bobby Peru's assault on Lula) are more memorable than the ending, the film's final scene may be the most disturbing simply because it seems to violate the overall tone of the film and represent a clear instance of Lynch's caving in to popular expectations. Lynch himself expressed awareness that people might say he "was trying to be commercial" by producing a happy ending where Barry Gifford's source novel did not.[23] Lynch's rewriting of the conclusion of Gifford's novel marks a dramatic change. As David Hughes points out, though he made other significant changes in writing the screenplay, "No single aspect of Lynch's adaptation represented a more radical departure from the source material than the ending."[24] Though this type of departure is typical in Hollywood adaptations, we cannot simply chalk it up to Lynch's desire to create a popular film, especially in light of his other films and the other ways in which this film eschews a popular appeal. Why, then, does the film end happily?

Lynch includes the happy ending in order to show just what it would take for us to experience enjoyment amid the contemporary landscape. In order to secure the film's happy ending, Sailor and Lula must fully commit themselves to the real kernel of their fantasy and give up their investment in their symbolic and imaginary relationships. After Sailor walks away from Lula and his son Pace toward the end of the film, a gang of men approach him from all sides and surround him as he walks down the middle of the road. Sailor stops, lights a cigarette, and asks, "What do you faggots want?" This question prompts the gang to attack Sailor, and as he lies on the ground after the beating, he has a vision of the good witch Glinda (Sheryl Lee) from *The Wizard of Oz*. Glinda tells Sailor that Lula loves him and that he shouldn't turn away from love. Sailor protests, "I'm wild at heart," and Glinda responds, "If you're truly wild at heart, you'll fight for your dreams." Though it seems like a maudlin cliché, the corrective that Glinda offers to Sailor here shows how Sailor has misunderstood what constitutes "wild at heart" throughout the film. For Sailor, being wild at heart means embodying an ideal of non-castration, being a real man in the eyes of the Other; but Glinda points out that being "truly wild at heart" involves fully committing oneself to the logic of one's fantasy—"fighting for one's dreams," as she puts it. To do so one must adopt an attitude of indifference concerning the Other's recognition. Glinda's redefinition of the film's titular concept spurs a revolution in Sailor.

In response to his vision of Glinda, Sailor apologizes to the gang and runs to Lula and Pace. The key gesture here is the apology, which suggests that Sailor has given up the ideal of non-castration. Rather than seeking complete enjoyment through refusing any experience of lack, Sailor now recognizes that one can discover enjoyment through lack. One can become wild at heart only through embracing the fantasmatic response to lack. When Sailor psychically turns from his commitment to full enjoyment to a full commitment to fantasy, he is able to return to Lula and accomplish the film's happy ending.

The status of the gang that beats up Sailor in this scene demonstrates the effect of Sailor's own disposition on the world around him. The gang's members first approach Sailor in a way that seems threatening, but the film suggests that they threaten Sailor not because they are threatening in themselves but because he is out to prove his non-castration. The gang, in other words, stands as a blank slate that takes a definite (aggressive) form as a result of Sailor's attitude toward them. Sailor articulates the first actual hostile remark between them with his homophobic slur, and this slur triggers the beating. After Sailor apologizes, the gang evinces no more hostility. Their aggressive demeanor occurs in response to the demeanor and expectations of Sailor himself. When these change, the external world changes too. By giving up his investment in the ideal of complete enjoyment and committing himself instead to his fantasy, Sailor in effect transforms the external world. The perverse and threatening world in which we live is the product of our failure to sustain investment in the logic of fantasy when it touches the traumatic real.[25]

We see a related dynamic in the case of Lula. When she goes to pick up Sailor after his release from prison, Lula receives a call from her mother, who asks her not to go. Lula rejects this idea, and Marietta asks, "Girl, what if I *told* you not to go?" Marietta raises her voice as she says this, and we see a close-up of her face as she screams into the phone. The film cuts to Lula, who says, "Mamma, if you get in the way of me and Sailor's happiness, I'll fucking pull your arms out by the roots!" and slams down the phone. This exchange marks Lula's first open rejection of her mother, and Lula's words themselves indicate her willingness to break the bond that exists between them. Even though Lula isn't literally threatening to pull Marietta's arms "out by the roots," this way of putting her rejection alludes to breaking the hold that her mother has over her.

When Sailor returns to Lula at the end of the film after his own revelation, Lynch cuts back to a picture of Marietta. We see her image disappear as smoke rises from the empty frame. Marietta's photograph disappears in this way because Lula has defied her and broken the bond that exists between them. The bond continued to exist only insofar as Lula sustained it. When she gives this up and commits herself fully to her fantasy, Marietta and her influence dissolve. The fundamental step toward creating the possibility of enjoyment is breaking the bond with the maternal figure. As Lacan puts it in *Seminar XVII*, "The means of jouissance are open on the principle that one has abandoned the enclosed and foreign jouissance of the mother."[26]

The sacrifice of the privileged object is an experience that contemporary subjects are increasingly unwilling to submit to. The insistence on complete enjoyment and on the absolute presence of the privileged object creates an aggressive and violent world in which the subject finds itself increasingly unable to enjoy. Without an acceptance of the initial loss, one loses the space for fantasy.

The disappearance of Marietta's image in the picture frame and the dramatic transformation of the gang surrounding Sailor are moments when the impossible occurs in *Wild at Heart*. A change in Lula and Sailor's relationship to their private fantasy occasions a change in how others treat them. In the act of fully embracing their fantasies, even in their traumatic, real dimension—being "truly wild at heart," as Glinda puts it—they abandon their own isolation from the world. In doing so, they change their world and demand a similar transformation in the spectator as well. Ironically, Lynch suggests that we can come to see the connection between our private fantasy and the external world—their speculative identity—through a deeper immersion in the fantasy itself. To put it another way, we can see the link between our experience in the cinema and our experience outside it only when we immerse ourselves wholly in the former.

According to this way of understanding the film, *Wild at Heart* remains a scathing piece of social commentary, but it loses the conservative inflection that Lynch's own interpretation would give it. The film depicts a degraded society where verbal assaults and extreme violence confront the subject at every turn. But it allows us to locate the origin of this degradation in the prevalence of too much respect for the law rather than not enough. The filmic structure of *Wild at Heart* thereby undermines the typical conservative jeremiads aimed at the licentiousness of contemporary culture and appropriates their appeals. Conservatism (as adherence to the law) becomes itself the source of the problem. The only freedom from the threats that populate contemporary society lies in the full embrace of fantasmatic enjoyment rather than the attempt to curb it.

The Contradictory Status of Laura Palmer

With *Twin Peaks: Fire Walk with Me* (1992), Lynch returned to the television series that ABC cancelled after its second season. This seemed like a safe choice for Lynch: as with *Dune* (1984), the film had a built-in audience among those who watched the television series. Unfortunately, the film had a fate similar to that of *Dune*, and it avoided being a bomb the magnitude of *Dune* only because of the relatively meager size of the budget ($10 million in 1992 for *Fire Walk with Me* versus $42 million in 1984 for *Dune*). Even audiences at Cannes who had embraced the excesses of *Wild at Heart* (1990) booed and hissed at the premiere of *Fire Walk with Me*. Lynch's decision to create a prequel rather than a sequel and his insistence on shooting the film from the perspective of the murder victim in the series, Laura Palmer (Sheryl Lee), had the effect, in the mind of many fans and critics, of retroactively ruining the television show they enjoyed.

Fire Walk with Me begins with a traumatic event that marks its break with the television series that shares its name. The credits appear on a snowy television screen, and as the camera pulls back to reveal that we've been seeing a television screen without any picture, a woman screams, and an axe plunges into the television. Here, not only does the film reduce the television to a snowy screen transmitting nothing, but it also destroys it. The violent death of Teresa Banks (Pamela Gidley) in this scene is simultaneously the violent death of the *Twin Peaks* television series. The opening of *Fire Walk with Me* thus announces that the prequel to the series will be fundamentally different in structure and theme. The difference manifests itself most directly in the perspective from which we experience the town of Twin Peaks.

In the television series, Laura Palmer serves as a structuring absence that organizes the desire of the other characters and the spectator (who wants both to understand Laura and to find the solution to her murder).[1] Her desire is the impossible object, the *objet petit a*: the series follows the investigation of FBI Special Agent Dale Cooper (Kyle MacLachlan) into Laura's murder, but the actual focus for Cooper and viewers is Laura herself, specifically what she desired. The investigation leads Cooper to all of Laura's friends, acquaintances, and lovers, yet leaves viewers in the dark about the location of her desire. Each character thinks that she or he has a privileged insight into Laura's desire, but no one offers an adequate answer. She remains, even after the solution of her murder, a mystery to be solved. Insofar as she exists just outside our grasp, she embodies the impossible object.

The series focuses on Laura because she seems to represent perfectly the predominant fantasy of femininity. She is popular, smart, generous, attractive, and sexy, yet she retains a sense of innocence. She occupies a central place in the fantasies of the men (and women) of Twin Peaks, which has the appearance of being a mythically perfect American small town. Lynch places Laura and her desire at the center of the series and the film to explore the fantasy structure that continues to shape American society.

In *Fire Walk with Me*, Laura continues to embody the impossible object, but the difference between the series and film resides in the location of this object. Where the series leaves it perpetually out of reach, the film allows this absent object to become present. Rather than remaining a mystery that we can desire and fantasize about, Laura Palmer becomes a fully realized character. According to Michel Chion, her character, in contrast with the other characters in the film, seems real. He says, "In this world of character types, the one figure which ordinarily would be treated like an image-object is Laura Palmer, and yet it is her character which Lynch wished to present in three dimensions."[2]

This three-dimensional portrait stands out all the more when we contrast it with the way that the television series treats Laura.

Through the depiction of Laura Palmer in the film, Lynch subjectivizes the impossible object-cause of desire, and he allows us to experience from the perspective of the object itself. Put another way, the object-cause of desire in this film cannot be regarded merely as an object as it can in most other films. This reversal marks the radical innovation of *Fire Walk with Me* and makes it Lynch's most important and original film. Where Lynch's other films permit a momentary encounter with the impossible object, this film constructs our experience through it. The impossible act occurs throughout the experience of watching the film. Through its deployment of the fantasy surrounding Laura Palmer, the film places us in the impossible perspective of the object within this fantasy. From this perspective, we grasp the speculative identity between subject and object. Whatever difference we want to attribute to the impossible object disappears in the closed circuit of this type of identity. In the act of experiencing from the perspective of the impossible object, we do not simply come to recognize the objectified woman as "a coherent person."[3] Michel Chion's claim that Lynch portrays Laura as a three-dimensional character does not go far enough. I would argue instead that Laura is a fully realized subject in the film insofar as we see the hole inside her. At the core of her subjectivity exists a fundamental emptiness, and no one in the film is able to relate to her or connect with her because of this emptiness.

Even though Laura occupies the position of the fantasy object, she doesn't find any fulfillment or sense of identity from the role. She embodies the ideal of contemporary American female beauty, yet she derives no enjoyment from the position that her attractiveness allows her. What stands out about her is precisely her inability to find any of the roles available to her satisfying. She moves through a variety of roles—homecoming queen, girlfriend of a football star, whore, drug user, meals-on-wheels volunteer, and so on—but cannot fully invest herself in any of them. She inhabits each briefly and easily shifts to another, even when this other role contradicts the earlier one. She can, for instance, mock her secret lover James (James Marshall) derisively one instant, and an instant later genuinely express love for him. The film does not present this type of activity as an indication of Laura's hypocrisy: she doesn't inhabit one identity and then hypocritically feign that she inhabits another. Her subjectivity is an emptiness that remains irreducible to any identity.[4]

Lynch conveys the emptiness of Laura's subjectivity through the performance of Sheryl Lee, whom critics have rightly applauded for her portrayal of Laura. Not only does Lee move almost instantaneously from the attitude of the spiteful vamp to the loving girlfriend, but she does so in a way that makes clear that beneath the different identities is a void rather than a coherent personality. She destroys the fantasy image that fans of the television series bring to the film, revealing that Laura does not really have the hidden allure that others imagine her to have.[5] This becomes visible only because Lynch immerses us fully in the fantasy from her perspective.

Lee's performance illustrates that the inadequacy of the identities available to her is not the result of Laura's fullness of character that cannot be so narrowly confined but instead results from a fundamental absence. The object at the center of our most profound cultural fantasy has an emptiness where the fantasy posits a fullness. When Laura adopts an identity, the absence transforms into an illusory presence that can deceive other characters but not the spectator. Lynch shoots these transformations specifically to make us aware of them. This becomes most striking in two scenes, one involving her boyfriend Bobby (Dana Ashbrook) near the beginning of the film and the other involving James near the end.

On the first day we see Laura, she has sex clandestinely with James at school while Bobby searches for her. When he finally sees her walking home, Bobby accosts Laura for disappearing and demands to know where she was. A look of contempt comes over Laura's face, and she says, "I was standing right behind you, but you're too dumb to turn around," and then says to her friend Donna (Moira Kelly), "If he turned around, he might get dizzy." As she speaks, Laura begins to chuckle, and Bobby resumes his questioning: "Where were you? I'm not kidding around. Who were you with?" Rather than appease him, Laura simply tells Bobby to "Get lost." But when he threatens to break off their relationship, she undergoes a complete transformation. Her mocking look disappears, and she stares at him with a half-smile and glazed look. She says, "Come on, Bobby. Come on. Come on." This change of heart alleviates Bobby's worry, allowing him to walk away, hopping around with excitement and professing his great love for her.

What stands out about this scene is the posture that Laura adopts after her change of heart. The look that she gives Bobby is not what we would expect: rather than looking directly into his eyes to console him, she stares straight ahead at his chest, never once making eye contact with him. Lynch shoots the conversation in a standard shot/reverse-shot manner that makes clear the seeming misalignment of her look. This look testifies to Laura's absence of personality. It is almost as if she cannot look into Bobby's eyes because she has no coherent position within herself from which she could make normal intersubjective contact with another person. This absence of personality colors the content of her consolation. She doesn't tell Bobby where she has been or even that she loves him. She simply repeats the meaningless phrase "come on." At the moment Laura appears to be ready to reveal herself to someone, she reveals instead that she has nothing to reveal.

The later scene with James follows a remarkably similar trajectory. After James expresses his desire to save Laura, she slaps him and proclaims her contempt for his sentimentality. But again she undergoes an instantaneous transformation and takes James into her confidence: "You don't even know me. There are things about me . . . Even Donna doesn't know me." While saying this, she looks over James's head, not into his eyes. When she finally looks down and makes eye contact, it is only to inform him that she isn't there. She says, "Your Laura has disappeared." James tries to comfort her, but she again changes her attitude, giving him the gesture of the middle finger and saying with disdain, "I think you want to take me home now." Each time that Bobby or James tries to connect with her as a coherent person, she responds by showing them—and us as spectators—that she has no such identity with which to connect. As a pure void, she lacks the symbolic anchoring that other characters in the film believe they have.

The cultural fantasy surrounding someone like Laura Palmer depends on a belief in her plenitude. She inspires male (and female) dreams because she seems to be the perfect woman and to embody a mysterious knowledge of the ultimate enjoyment. But beneath this image of perfection *Fire Walk with Me* reveals not just a flawed reality, but an emptiness. A flawed Laura would nourish the myth by humanizing the object, and it would allow us as spectators to feel compassion for her. But an empty Laura leaves the spectator no such outlet. And yet, Laura is the central figure through which we engage the film. In doing so, we identify not with her as a substantial character but with her as an emptiness, experiencing the impossible perspective of the absent object. Lynch is not shattering the central American cultural fantasy but demanding that we endure the objective position within it.

A conversation between Laura and Donna early in the film reveals Laura's lack of anchoring and her awareness of it. Donna asks Laura, "Do you think if you were falling in space you would slow down after a while or keep going faster and faster?" Laura responds, "Faster and faster. For a long time you wouldn't feel anything. Then you would burst into fire—forever. And the angels wouldn't help you, 'cause they've all gone away." The mise-en-scène here adds to the idea that Laura is falling through space: during the entire conversation, she lies drooping over the arms of a chair in her parents' living room, which gives her the appearance of floating in air. Just after Donna asks her question, Lynch includes a close-up of Laura as she gulps, registering her awareness of her status as a subject. The image of the gulp registers emptiness in a way that no signifier can, suggesting it rather than trying to name it. This exchange anticipates remarkably the path that Laura follows in the film. Unlike Donna, Laura has nothing to slow her down or stop her from falling; she exists without any external authority that might stabilize her.

The emptiness of Laura's subjectivity stems from the contradictions that her position as the impossible object-cause of desire forces her to live out. She grasps the illusory nature of each identity because she simultaneously experiences its opposite. In a sense, having too much identity permits her to exist without identity. She embodies in one person all the contradictory male fantasies about women: she is innocent, and she is a whore; she is the homecoming queen, and she is addicted to cocaine; she is a loving maternal figure, and she is a cold-blooded manipulator. The foundational opposition here is that of the virgin and whore, and male fantasy works by identifying different women in each of these positions. By collapsing the two, by depicting the identity of the virgin and the whore, Lynch brings the two separate fantasy worlds of *Blue Velvet*—the stabilizing fantasy and the threatening fantasy—into one. The result is a fantasy object that becomes destabilizing for everyone who encounters it insofar as it cannot be reduced to either of the oppositions.

Laura's first appearance in the film plays with these oppositions. The film's first shots of her present her in a completely idealized way. In a tracking shot, we see her walking to school down the sidewalk of an idyllic neighborhood with leafy trees hanging over the sidewalk and perfect green lawns. She holds her books cradled against her chest, a posture suggestive of schoolgirl innocence. She goes by the house of her best friend Donna to pick her up on the way to school. In addition to the visuals of this scene, the sound track plays the sentimental "Twin Peaks Theme," which contributes to the idealization of Laura. Lynch uses the conjunction between the visual and audio tracks to build up the ideal that will quickly turn into its opposite. Very soon after arriving at the high school, Laura betrays this idealization: she leaves Donna and snorts cocaine in a bathroom stall. The trajectory of this sequence aims very explicitly to establish Laura in the role of the idealized high school girl and subsequently undermine this image. What the sequence shows is not that Laura is really a drug user and not an innocent schoolgirl; she is both at the same time.

In the figure of Laura, the fantasy of the pure virginal woman coincides with the fantasy of the licentious and sexually available woman in order to reveal how both fantasy figures are ultimately the same. *Fire Walk with Me* takes us so far into the predominant fantasy that we see the dual nature of its object. This is precisely the recognition that patriarchal ideology will not allow and that the patriarchal subject cannot tolerate: to see the speculative identity of these two figures is to see impurity even in the ultimate purity, and vice versa. Structurally, both the virgin and the whore occupy the same position, and fantasies involving the one always have the other existing in the background. The point is not that one recognizes a virgin only through the contrast with a whore (though this is certainly the case) but that one only enjoys the fantasy of the virgin when the idea that she is actually a whore silently accompanies this fantasy—and the reverse is true for enjoying the fantasy of the whore. Even within the realm of fantasy, enjoyment depends on the idea of something more beneath the object—the hidden secret of the object. In this sense, fantasy as we typically experience it doesn't reveal secrets but perpetuates them by doubling itself into the ideal and the nightmare, each containing the other hidden within it.

This doubled aspect of fantasy informs the structure of *Blue Velvet*. However, in that film, we see how the two fantasy worlds—the ideal and the nightmare—parallel each other and how each works to domesticate desire. *Fire Walk with Me* effects a leap forward in understanding the relationship between these two types of fantasy. It reveals their interdependence and ultimate identity.[6] The latter film eviscerates all the distinctions that our fantasies typically enact and thrive on. The fantasy of the ideal and the fantasy of the nightmare remain pleasurable for the subject only insofar as they remain distinct. This is why *Fire Walk with Me*—and its depiction of Laura Palmer in particular—is so disturbing. By filming *Fire Walk with Me* from the perspective of the subjectivized impossible object, Lynch offers us the opportunity to identify with it. In the act of doing so, we would recognize the identity of the ideal and the nightmare. This is a recognition that Laura herself must make along with us as spectators, and it marks the possibility of an ethical subjectivity.

The Hostility of Deer Meadow

Once Laura Palmer appears thirty minutes into *Fire Walk with Me*, the form of the film undergoes a dramatic change. After the murder of Teresa Banks that opens the film, *Fire Walk with Me* opens into a world of surfaces in which we never unravel the mysteries that these surfaces seem to hide. Even for those who have seen the television series, the first part of the film retains a sense of impenetrability. From the opening scene depicting Agent Chester "Chet" Desmond (Chris Isaak) arresting sexily attired women outside a school bus of screaming children to Dale Cooper's discovery of "Let's Rock" written across the windshield of Chet's abandoned car, the events that occur here defy explanation within the terms that this part of the film itself offers. It is only when we view it through the lens of the second part—the world of fantasy—that it begins to make more sense.

After the familiar opening shot of the "Welcome to Twin Peaks" sign, the second part of the film begins with the image of Laura Palmer. Subsequently, Laura dominates this part of the film, appearing in almost every scene. The impossible object appears as a presence. In contrast, the first part of the film begins with the murder of Teresa Banks and a shot of her body wrapped in plastic and floating on a river—the sacrifice of the privileged object constituting it as an absence. Lynch emphasizes the constitutive role of Teresa Banks in this section through the unusual use of a caption. When we see the floating body, a caption stating "Teresa Banks" appears in the bottom part of the screen. This is unusual on two counts: first, the caption is superfluous because FBI Regional Bureau Chief Gordon Cole (David Lynch) almost immediately identifies the murder victim in his conversation with Chet Desmond, and, second, cinematic convention dictates that a caption would be used in this instance to identify the place where the body is floating, not the name of the victim herself.[7] This minor toying with convention on Lynch's part—and the use of an identifying caption itself, which suggests documentary authenticity—serves to emphasize the status of Teresa Banks here. Teresa Banks becomes the absent object-cause of desire, and the entirety of the first part of the film focuses on investigating her. Her absence opens up other mysteries, but she remains at the center of the film.

Whereas the second part of the film subjectivizes the impossible object, the first part leaves this object completely absent. Here, Lynch constructs a world of desire in which every image and situation seems threatening because the characters (and we as spectators) see it without any fantasmatic depth. What we see in the first part of the film, the dilapidated and hostile town of Deer Meadow, contrasts negatively with the pristine and hospitable town of Twin Peaks. As David Hughes puts it, "Lynch gave the town a shadow self in Deer Meadow, with its corrupt and belligerent police force (contrasting with the Twin Peaks sheriff and his deputies), a diner with an unpleasant hostess and no special (a far cry from the 'Double R' diner), and a sleazy and unkempt trailer park (about as far from the luxurious Great Northern as you could get)."[8] The malevolence of Deer Meadow emerges in response to the experience of lack that predominates there. All of the characters experience the absence of the privileged object and suspect others of either trying to steal or having stolen what little enjoyment they do have.

In the scenes in the trailer park where Teresa Banks lived, we see the rampant dissatisfaction and hostility that runs throughout the world of desire. Here, the trailers are in a dilapidated condition, and the tenants lack even the most basic necessities. While Chet Desmond and Sam Stanley (Keifer Sutherland) are talking with Carl Rodd (Harry Dean Stanton), the manager, a woman living there approaches Carl and complains about her persistent lack of hot water. The writing on the door of Carl's trailer indicates his lack of receptivity to such complaints and to all interaction with the Other. It reads, "DO NOT EVER DISTURB BEFORE 9 *AM* . . . *EVER*." When Agents Desmond and Stanley knock on Carl's trailer before 9 A.M., they draw their badges in response to the threat implied by the sign and by Carl's loud and angry grumbling inside. Carl initially perceives and is perceived by the Other as a threat, an attitude that characterizes a world of desire.

The absence of a fantasmatic dimension to this world creates a sense of distance between the spectator and all the characters, even the hero of the first part of the film, Agent Chester Desmond. Though the film aligns us as spectators with Chet because he heads the investigation, it also alienates us from him when we see his behavior. He mirrors the threatening posture that others demonstrate to him, going so far as to twist the nose of a hostile deputy in the Deer Meadow sheriff's office. What's more, he amuses himself at the expense of his naïve coworker, Agent Sam Stanley, who evinces no hostility toward him. At Hap's Diner, we see a shot of Chet looking at Sam's arm holding a cup of coffee. He then asks Sam for the time, knowing that Sam will turn his wrist instinctively in order to check his watch, which would cause him to spill his coffee (and this is what occurs). Through the depiction of this otherwise insignificant action, the film shows us that even the hero partakes of the generalized hostility in this world. Distance separates us from every character, just as it separates the characters from each other.

The world of desire that Lynch constructs is a world in which subjects experience their alienation in the signifier without the respite of fantasy. Subjects exist on the level of the signifier alone. As a result, an idea is encoded for no reason other than for the simple act of encoding itself. This is because the act of encoding—the act of producing a signifier—is the only type of enjoyment that one can experience in this world. Gordon Cole uses a dancing woman, Lil (Kimberly Ann Cole), as a code to explain the Teresa Banks case to Agents Chet Desmond and Sam Stanley. As they drive to Deer Meadow after seeing Lil's performance, Chet deciphers the code with Sam. Among other things, he tells Sam that Gordon Cole has indicated the local authorities won't be cooperative, that the sheriff's uncle is in a federal prison, that the case will involve a great deal of legwork. The problem with this coding and decoding is that none of this information requires a code in the first place. If, as some viewers of the film postulate, Cole was worried about someone overhearing him due to his habit of speaking loudly, he could have simply written this information straightforwardly in a report or note to Chet and Sam. Nothing necessitates a code because Cole isn't trying to deceive anyone; he simply creates—and undoubtedly enjoys—the code for its own sake. There is, strictly speaking, no reason for it except enjoyment.

Cole's near-total deafness further accentuates the enjoyment that occurs in the act of signification during this part of the film. Because Cole cannot hear well, he screams when engaging in conversation, never once talking in a normal tone. Cole's screams draw our attention—and the attention of the other characters in the film—not toward what he says but toward the exaggerated act of speaking itself. Cole fits perfectly within the world of desire because he exists for us as spectators on the level of the signifier rather than on the level of the signified. In this sense, his deafness corresponds directly to his proclivity for using obscure and unnecessary codes.

The senseless enjoyment of signification itself extends beyond Gordon Cole to other characters in the first part of the film. At Hap's Diner where Teresa Banks worked, Chester Desmond and Sam Stanley question Irene (Sandra Kinder), the hostess. During their conversation, Irene builds up the desire of the investigators (and the spectator) by creating the idea that there is something to be known when there is actually nothing. She tempts Chet and Sam by hinting that she has a theory about the killing of Teresa Banks, but her theory is simply that "her death was what you'd call a freak accident." Irene even adopts this same tack when taking the agents' food order. She asks them, "You want to hear about our specials?" When they nod, she continues, "We don't have any." In both of these cases, Irene deliberately creates a desire that she knows will not be satisfied; she creates a desire knowing that there is nothing—no-thing, the *objet petit a*—that could satisfy it.

One of the patrons at Hap's interrupts the agents' interview of Irene with a statement that functions in the way that Irene's statements do. From a table across the diner, the man says in a raised voice, "Are you talking about that little girl that got murdered?" Like Irene's comment that she has a theory about the killing, this question contains within it the promise of some revelation. But when Chet asks him if he knows anything about the murder, the man responds, "I know shit from shinola," a response that clearly tells nothing and reveals that the man knows nothing (even as it seems to promise that he does know something). The man subsequently repeats his original question, but Chet ignores him the second time because he knows that the question is creating a fiction to conceal that the man is hiding nothing. As Cate Racek points out, "in Deer

Meadow, the secret is on the surface. There is no depth here, just the desire that will not fit into their lacking dialogue."[9] Both this old man at Hap's and Irene resemble Gordon Cole insofar as all three use the signifier to create a sense of mystery where none exists.

The world of desire that Lynch creates in *Fire Walk with Me* is not a world where enjoyment seems completely absent. This distinguishes *Fire Walk with Me* from his three subsequent films, all of which focus entirely on the extreme dissatisfaction that predominates in this realm, in the experience of the social reality without recourse to fantasy. In this film, Lynch reveals that a certain kind of enjoyment is possible without fantasy. Though, as Lacan puts it, "the signifier is what brings jouissance to a halt," there is also a certain jouissance that corresponds to the act of signification itself.[10] The characters in the first part of the film access this type of enjoyment, even though their world lacks the enjoyment that derives from fantasy. The presence of this enjoyment of the signifier itself gives the first part of the film a sense of mystery. This senseless enjoyment of sense-making creates the impression of hidden depths and a secret knowledge, but as long as we remain within the world of desire, the secret is ineffable. One could watch the first thirty minutes of *Fire Walk with Me* on its own multiple times and never solve its mysteries because it creates mysteries that exist for their own sake. It is only when the film moves to Twin Peaks and the world of fantasy that we can fill in the gaps of the world of desire.

Incest as the Fantasmatic Solution

One of the chief complaints about *Fire Walk with Me* is its lack of coherence, the disconnection between the first and second parts of the film. Jeff Johnson notes that "the aesthetic integrity of the narrative in *Fire Walk with Me* is seriously flawed,"[11] and even a proponent of the film like Michel Chion admits that "formally, the film does not succeed in joining together all its disparate elements."[12] But when we understand the two parts of the film as contrasting worlds of desire and fantasy, this incoherence disappears, and we can see how the second part of the film provides a fantasmatic solution to the question that the first part poses. The story of Laura Palmer's last days allows us to make sense of the murder of Teresa Banks and the disappearance of Chester Desmond. Lynch uses the turn to the fantasy world of Twin Peaks to expose the structural conditions underlying the oppressive and violent social reality represented by Deer Meadow.

Where the deployment of fantasy in *Eraserhead* (1977) reveals the sacrifice at the origin of capitalist reproduction, in *Fire Walk with Me* it illustrates the invisible forces that create a hostile social reality. Because fantasy narrates the dissatisfaction of the social reality to render it satisfying, it has the ability to expose what our ordinary experience of this reality obscures. The second part of *Fire Walk with Me*, the elaboration of the fantasy world, explains why places like Deer Meadow are so threatening and why women like Teresa Banks are murdered. But the fantasy has this explanatory power only insofar as Lynch follows it to its end point.

Just on the level of the film's narrative alone, the fantasy world of Twin Peaks solves the mystery of Teresa Banks' murder in a very straightforward way. Through Leland Palmer's flashback, we learn that Leland (Ray Wise), inhabited by BOB (Frank Silva), killed Teresa Banks after she set up a sexual rendezvous with herself, Leland, and two girls, one of whom turns out to be Laura. Lynch shows Leland walking to the motel room, and as he turns a corner he sees Laura and Ronette Pulaski (Phoebe Augustine) sitting on the bed talking. Before we see him retreat, Lynch intersperses a brief close-up of Laura laughing. Leland paces away from the room, and then Lynch juxtaposes a close-up of Leland's panicked face followed by another close-up of Laura laughing. When Teresa taps him on the shoulder, we see Leland betray his panic to her by telling her that he can't participate, that he "chickened out." Seeing Leland's abrupt reaction, Teresa suspects that Leland knows one of the girls, and, after learning about his relation to Laura, begins to blackmail him. It is at this point that he kills her.

This information—that Teresa Banks found out that Leland was the father of Laura and threatened to expose his illicit activity to her and to the public—actually tells us all that we need to know to make sense of most of the narrative complexities of the film. Like the death of Laura Palmer later in the film, the death of Teresa Banks results directly from BOB's absolute aversion to publicity. BOB kills only when the woman he is enjoying threatens to expose his activity. But this is not an act of self-protection on BOB's part; as the embodiment of a psychic force, he need not worry about being arrested or going to jail. Publicity does endanger not BOB's liberty so much as his mode of procuring enjoyment.

The film presents BOB as a transcendent force that operates through subjects without regard for the restraints that limit human behavior. His appearance suggests his status in the film: he has long stringy gray hair, a straggly beard, and wide malevolent-looking eyes. The film's form registers his disturbing and unreal presence. When Laura sees him looking for her diary behind her bed, he appears in a series of quick jump cuts. Later, when he is raping her, the film cuts back and forth between the image of BOB and Leland. His appearances disrupt the form of the film itself and the spectator's pleasure in viewing.

BOB's enjoyment stems from illicit sexual and violent encounters. But he enjoys himself only as long as his identity remains secret, which is why Lynch only allows the spectator to see him for an extended period of time in the otherworldly Red Room. He kills Teresa Banks when she discovers who Leland is and kills Laura when she recognizes the connection between BOB and her father. In both cases, he resorts to killing in order to remain unexposed. Both BOB's resistance to publicity and his ability to transgress prohibitions suggests, I would argue, that he occupies a position outside the system of signification and its rules. This is the position of the exceptional signifier, the signifier of exception, what psychoanalysis calls the phallus. The phallus, according to Lacan, "can play its role only when veiled."[13] Any publicity threatens the potency of the phallus because its power is illusory. Its posture of autonomy masks its dependence on the societal Other.

The position of phallic authority carries with it an illusion of independence. We believe that this authority rules through its greater strength and superior force of will. But it remains fundamentally dependent on the support that the social order as a whole provides for it. Collective obedience instills an air of invincibility in the figure of phallic authority. If it ever loses this support, it loses the entirety of its power and disintegrates. But public support depends on no one's recognizing the illusory nature of the phallic authority's power. Such a recognition would render collective obedience impossible, which is why the phallus requires the veil.

The association of BOB with the phallus suggests why Mrs. Tremond's grandson appears wearing a phallic mask (a mask with an elongated nose). He appears at the moments in the film when BOB is on the verge of being exposed—for instance, when Leland sees Laura in the motel room when he shows up for an orgy—and he thus reveals to us the precarious status of the phallus. Beneath the mask there exists not the powerful figure of BOB but just a little powerless boy. The image of Mrs. Tremond's grandson wearing the phallic mask illustrates that phallic power is nothing but the mask.[14]

Throughout the first part of the film, BOB remains a hidden force, functioning undetected through Leland. But the turn to fantasy in the second part of the film exposes the phallus and undermines its power. In fantasy, the phallus becomes visible as the figure that enjoys without restriction, the figure able to access the unapproachable object. This occurs through BOB's repeated sexual encounters with Laura. In order to access Laura, BOB takes the form of her father Leland. Of course, he could have easily inhabited some other male figure such as Bobby or James, but he chooses Leland. By inhabiting Leland, he transgresses the ultimate law, the founding law of society as such—the prohibition of incest.

By depicting the relationship between Leland and Laura as the fantasmatic answer to the questions posed by the world of desire, Lynch identifies fantasy as such with incest. Every fantasy is, in a sense, an incestuous fantasy: in order to provide enjoyment, fantasy must enact a scenario for accessing the privileged—that is, the prohibited—object. The subject fantasizes about obtaining something off-limits, and the model for this object is the familial object that the symbolic law bars. But fantasy remains bearable for the subject only insofar as the subject fails to recognize its incestuous dimension. The subject must deceive itself concerning the object's proximity and see an object that is too close as existing at a safe distance. Through fantasy, the subject accomplishes the impossible, enjoying an object that must be simultaneously close and distant.

One of the primary criticisms of both the television series and the film centers on the depiction of incest and specifically BOB's role in it. In short, the depiction of BOB as the perpetuator of the incestuous rape of Laura lets her actual father, Leland Palmer, off the hook. He becomes nothing but the staging ground for the activity of a supernatural force, not a rapist and killer himself. It is Diane Hume George who gives this critique its most detailed elaboration. She says,

> *Peaks* participates in excusing male violence toward women, mythologizing their behavior as possession by evil forces that originate outside of the self. Safely relegated to supernatural and irresistible

status—even Coop cannot, in the end, resist the cosmic force represented and embodied by BOB—the "evil" does not reside in normal, troubled, tragic human lives, but in helplessly possessed male victims who do not know what they are doing and cannot be held responsible.[15]

According to this account, Lynch depicts natural beings as nothing but the victims of the "supernatural." But this critique depends on a naïve interpretation of figures like BOB and the Man From Another Place (Michael J. Anderson). If we are attentive, *Fire Walk with Me* actually demonstrates that BOB and the Man From Another Place function as structural rather than supernatural forces. Yes, BOB certainly acts through Leland, the ordinary man, but this in no way exculpates Leland. He and other ordinary men are guilty for their role in perpetuating the functioning of the structure.[16]

The turn from the world of desire to the world of fantasy clarifies the structural role that the Red Room plays. In both worlds of the film, it occupies a transcendent place where the constraints of time and space don't apply (which is why Annie [Heather Graham] can appear to Laura and tell her about Dale Cooper before Annie has even met Dale). This transcendent place exists because the system of signifiers always contains a gap that doesn't exist within that system. The system produces its own beyond in the form of the absence that it cannot signify as a result of language's inability to say everything. The role that this absence plays becomes clear through the film's depiction of the Man From Another Place.

The fantasy fills in the gaps in our knowledge about the Man From Another Place and offers an explanation of the role that he plays (both in the film and in the television series). He appears first when Agent Phillip Jeffries (David Bowie) briefly shows up in the Philadelphia FBI office after having disappeared for three years. Phillip tells the agents there about his experience in the room over the convenience store, and as he recounts the experience, we see a series of images of this room, which contains the Man From Another Place. The first word that we hear from him appears at the time to be a signifier without a signified: "garmonbozia." Outside of the *Twin Peaks* universe, "garmonbozia" is a nonsensical word, a word without meaning in any known language, though it has spawned many outrageous theories among *Twin Peaks* fans as to its linguistic derivation. But even within the terms of the film itself, the word has no clear connection to what's going on. At this point in the film, the word is a pure surface for us as spectators and has the effect of producing the desire for the absent sense, which the turn to the fantasy world provides.

At the end of the film after Leland has killed Laura, the Man From Another Place and MIKE confront BOB and Leland. Together, the Man From Another Place and MIKE repeat the word "garmonbozia," but this time it appears within a sentence, which provides a context for determining its meaning. What's more, the subtitles include a translation of the word. The Man From Another Place and MIKE say together to BOB and Leland, "I want all my garmonbozia," and the subtitle reads, "I want all my garmonbozia (pain and suffering)." When he hears this demand, BOB touches Leland and then makes a throwing gesture with his hand, after which a splattering of blood appears on the floor. Now "garmonbozia" has a meaning and plays a clear role in the action of the film. Here the function of fantasy becomes visible in a precise way: fantasy fills in the absence that exists on the level of the signified and gives the signifier a sense of depth. This scene within the fantasy not only defines what was for us a nonsensical term, but it also explains the relationship between the Man From Another Place and BOB that the first part of the film left completely ambiguous.[17]

The Struggle Between Life and Death

The Man From Another Place defies explanation more than any other of the many strange characters in *Fire Walk with Me*. He does not reside in the ordinary human world nor does he even make appearances there like BOB. We see him only in the otherwordly Red Room. His diminutive size and seemingly inexplicable behavior—his unusual eating habits, his dancing, his strange statements—appear to be nonsensical features of the film, features Lynch includes for their own sake. But he only seems nonsensical because we as spectators aren't used to watching a film that attempts to explore fantasmatically the structures of the unconscious. Thus, the Man From Another Place and the film in general make sense only if we turn to the insights of psychoanalysis.

Within the fantasy world of *Fire Walk with Me*, we learn much more about the Man From Another Place than we do in the first part of the film. Assisted by the picture that Mrs. Tremond gives to her, Laura enters the Red Room and sees the Man From Another Place and Dale Cooper. The Man From Another Place asks, "Do you know who I am? I am the arm and I sound like this." He then makes a whooping sound by moving his hand back and forth over his mouth. With this statement, he identifies himself as a body part that exists disconnected from a body. The nonsensical whooping sound suggests his disconnection from the system of signification. When we later see MIKE without an arm and the Man From Another Place standing where the missing arm should be, this idea of the Man From Another Place as the detached body part becomes even more evident.

According to Lacan's understanding of subjectivization, part of the body detaches itself as a result of the body's submission to the signifier, which renders the body incomplete. The signifier imposes itself on the subject as a cut on the body, and this detached body part becomes the libido, the source of the drive in the subject. Under the sway of the drive, the subject seeks this detached part of the body—"the part of himself, lost forever, that is constituted by the fact that he is only a sexed living being, and that he is no longer immortal."[18] In this light, we can understand The Man From Another Place occupying the position of the libido, the lost body part that institutes the drive in the other characters. The drive that the Man From Another Place institutes is the death drive, a drive that continually returns to and repeats the experience of loss. Because the experience of loss originates and continues to inform the drive, every drive, according to Lacan, is a death drive. He says, "the drive, the partial drive, is profoundly a death drive and represents in itself the portion of death in the sexed living being."[19] *Fire Walk with Me* shows the power of this death drive over the characters in the film; it is the ultimate source of all the activity that we see, though a competing force emerges through the figure of BOB.

As a figure of phallic authority, BOB appears to be an irresistible force. He inhabits Leland Palmer and engages in illicit sexual and violent activities without repercussions. But the end of the film shows us that even BOB, the figure of phallic authority, acts in response to the Man From Another Place and follows the dictates of the death drive. BOB inhabits Leland not in order to dominate but in order to access the lost object through the incestuous relation with Laura. In this way, the phallus serves the drive, even as it proclaims its potency and independence. Lynch represents the counterintuitive nature of the primacy of the drive over the phallus through the actors he has playing the Man From Another Place and BOB. Michael J. Anderson is a dwarf and appears as a friendly, nonthreatening figure. Frank Silva, who plays BOB, towers over Anderson and is the most terrifying character in the film. But after Leland kills Laura, the dependence of the latter on the former becomes absolutely clear.

In the Red Room, MIKE and the Man From Another Place face BOB and Leland (who hangs suspended in midair). When MIKE and the Man From Another Place demand their garmonbozia from BOB, BOB seems to reach into Leland, extract blood from him (which is perhaps Laura's blood), and splatter this blood on the floor. All along BOB has seemed like a figure of authority and power, but when he does the bidding of the Man From Another Place, he betrays that his activities merely feed the drive, allowing it to continue to enjoy. This act of feeding becomes literal in the next shot. We see an extreme close-up of the Man From Another Place's mouth as he eats creamed corn (which the film associates with enjoyment) off a spoon. Earlier, at the moment of Laura's murder, we see a brief shot of the Man From Another Place laughing wildly. BOB's activity doesn't bring enjoyment for BOB himself, but it does allow the Man From Another Place to enjoy.

If the Man From Another Place enjoys BOB's violence, he is not the cause of it. The phallus represents an attempt to short-circuit the drive, to obtain enjoyment without suffering from the absence that characterizes the drive. In *The Indivisible Remainder*, Slavoj Žižek sees the phallus as a response to this absence. He says, "the Phi, the signifier of phallic power, phallus in its fascinating *presence*, merely 'gives body' to the impotence/inconsistency of the big Other."[20] As the detached body part, the Man From Another Place represents the gap within the Other, and BOB, as the phallus, tries to fill in this gap. Žižek explains further the movement from the gap in the Other to the phallus, which is the movement from the Man From Another Place to BOB:

The passage from S($\mathbb{A}$) to the big Phi is the passage from impossibility to prohibition: S($\mathbb{A}$) stands for the impossibility of the signifier of the big Other, for the fact that there is no "Other of Other," that the field of the Other is inherently inconsistent; and the big Phi "reifies" this impossibility into the Exception, into a "sacred," prohibited/unattainable agent who avoids castration and is thus able "really to enjoy" (the primordial Father, the Lady in courtly love).[21]

The Man From Another Place and BOB are locked in a struggle between absence and presence, between an enjoyment based on circulating around the lost object and an enjoyment based on actually having this object.

Trying to have the object in the way that phallic power does is an attempt to enjoy without lack. When MIKE pulls his truck next to Leland and Laura in their car and begins yelling at them, he accuses Leland/BOB of trying to enjoy illicitly. Though barely audible above Leland's revving engine, MIKE says, "You stole the corn! I had it canned above the store. Miss, the look on her face when it was opened. There was a closeness. Like the Formica table top. The thread will be torn, Mr. Palmer. The thread will be torn." The bizarre nature of MIKE's rant suggests that Lynch obscures what he's saying with engine noise in order to hide the fact that he isn't saying anything—that MIKE speaks nonsense. But psychoanalysis renders this seemingly incoherent statement sensible. MIKE indicates that Leland's incestuous activity is a theft of enjoyment—a stealing of the corn—and that it cannot continue because "the thread will be torn." Phallic authority's effort to enjoy without the tearing of the thread, without loss, inevitably fails. The phallus never successfully possesses the privileged object, but merely engages in an endless pursuit of this object, a pursuit that results in the satisfaction of the drive.

The struggle between the Man From Another Place and BOB is the struggle between the death drive and life. *Fire Walk with Me* shows, following Freud, the priority of death over life. It is the life force that perpetuates violence in the film, not the death drive. The phallus attempts to preserve its connection to the object and to guard against loss, but the impossibility of possessing the object leads phallic authority to acts of destructiveness, acts that end up serving the death drive.

The insight of the film into the relationship between the death drive and phallic authority stems from how it depicts the structure of fantasy. In our ordinary experience of social reality, phallic power has the illusion of autonomy; we see its displays of potency rather than its secret dependence, which becomes apparent only in fantasy. Lynch organizes the film around the fantasy object, Laura Palmer, and fully immerses us in the fantasy that centers around her. This has the effect of making visible the underlying structure of the social order because she—or her desire qua object—is the absent center of that order.

The Master Exposed

Shooting *Fire Walk with Me* from the perspective of the impossible object has the effect of exposing the dependence of paternal authority on this object that it despises and abuses. Lynch displays this dependence by placing Laura at the center of the film and showing figures of paternal authority constantly reacting to her. Occupying the position of phallic authority provides a certain kind of enjoyment for the man, but at the same time it structurally deprives the man of access to feminine enjoyment. Thus, no matter how much power a phallic authority has, it always experiences its lack of this other type of enjoyment. This is what we see in the case of BOB. BOB rapes Laura Palmer—and has done so since she was twelve years old—because he wants to experience the feminine enjoyment that he imputes to her. He wants to experience from her perspective. As Laura tells Harold Smith (Lenny von Dohlen) after she discovers that BOB has taken pages from her secret diary, "He wants to be me, or he'll kill me." Just after Laura leaves Harold, we hear BOB say to Laura, "I want to taste through your mouth," as the visual track dissolves from a shot of the ceiling fan to a shot of Laura to a shot of a red curtain. Laura experiences BOB's desire to embody her and partake of the enjoyment he attributes to her.

The problem is that BOB—and phallic authority as such—cannot ever capture this elusive enjoyment. As Serge André puts it, "Even if he has had sexual pleasure and given it to his partner, he can never be sure of having possessed her, that is to say, of having participated in the *jouissance* that is *hers*."[22] In fact, the more that BOB has Laura, the more he feels that something escapes. This is why he must keep coming back. Though he has had Laura since she was twelve, he still longs to taste through her mouth, not having yet successfully done so. Her enjoyment remains elusive for BOB because she herself doesn't possess it; it is an enjoyment of the Other. According to André, "That the specifically feminine part of *jouissance* is articulated at S($\cancel{A}$), beyond the phallic contribution made by her partner, means that a woman takes pleasure in herself as Other to herself."[23] But BOB fails to grasp this and thus continues to believe that he can pin down Laura's enjoyment and possess it. Lynch's elaboration of the ultimate male fantasy thus has the effect of exposing the failure of phallic power.

BOB's misunderstanding about Laura's enjoyment manifests itself in the demand he addresses to her: "Fire walk with me." In *Blue Velvet* (1986), *Wild at Heart* (1990), and *Lost Highway* (1997), fire provides an image of the ultimate enjoyment. The films depict subjects burning with enjoyment or encountering fire as they approach enjoyment. But in each case fire represents enjoyment from a male perspective, from the perspective of male fantasy. Feminine enjoyment cannot be reduced to an image—even one of fire. In *Fire Walk with Me*, we don't see any instances of fire, despite the film's title, because the film locates us within Laura's perspective, not that of the male who is fantasizing. This is another way in which the film thwarts the expectations of spectators. As Michel Chion notes, "The film does not totally fulfil the contract with the public which is suggested by its title" because "the role of fire in the film is minimal."[24] The absence of fire in the film is not simply an error on Lynch's part or an insignificant omission; it reveals that Laura doesn't enjoy in the way that the male fantasy expects of her. Her enjoyment remains enigmatically presented within the film's mise-en-scène, leaving us completely unsure whether she enjoys herself or whether she merely feigns enjoyment on occasion.

The uncertainty of Laura's enjoyment introduces uncertainty into the lives of the men who encounter it. This occurs most conspicuously with BOB, who returns to Laura due to his inability to possess her with any certainty. We see this happen on a lesser scale with Bobby, just after Bobby shoots and kills Deputy Cliff Howard (Rick Aiello) during a drug deal. Bobby panics after killing the deputy (who was delivering the drugs), but Laura, high on cocaine, laughs uncontrollably at Bobby's panic and at the deputy's death. While laughing, she claims, "Bobby killed Mike." Laura's statement is manifestly untrue; both she and Bobby see plainly that the dead man is not Bobby's friend Mike but a stranger. Nonetheless, Bobby becomes confused. He responds, "This isn't fucking Mike. Is this Mike?" The doubt that enters into Bobby's mind here is the result of the uncertainty that Laura's enjoyment introduces into the male psyche. Laura places doubt in Bobby's mind where there was absolute certainty, and she does this in the midst of a display of enjoyment.

The uncertain status of Laura's enjoyment leaves BOB in the position of seeking something that he can never know if he has or not. As a result, BOB, the figure of phallic authority in the film, ends up being completely dependent on Laura. His nightly assaults do not represent his agency but rather his lack of it. BOB spends the entire film *reacting* to Laura, attempting to inhabit her and experience what she experiences. He ends up killing her because she defies his authority and insists on a mode of enjoyment that one cannot possess.

Accepting the Ring

The ethical challenge for Laura Palmer in *Fire Walk with Me*—and the fundamental problem for the spectator—is not accepting her own symbolic death. Throughout the film, she quickly and courageously embraces her own emptiness as a subject, and the spectator must adopt this position from the moment of her entrance into the film. But what Laura resists acknowledging is the emptiness of the Other. Laura's reluctance to see the nonexistence of the Other explains both her attitude toward Donna and, more importantly, her inability to recognize her father as BOB.

Throughout the film, she takes solace in the idea that Donna is unlike her, that Donna actually has a substantive identity. When she sees Donna adopting her lifestyle and falling into the void that she occupies, this completely traumatizes Laura. After Donna accompanies her on a night of drinking, drug use, prostitution, and an orgy, Laura becomes irate with Donna for imitating her. She says, "I don't want you to be like me." Insofar as Donna remains a normal small-town high school girl, she provides a sense of security for Laura and allows Laura to continue to believe that Donna is anchored in a way that she isn't. Donna sustains for Laura the ideal of the non-lacking Other.[25]

To recognize the identity of BOB and Leland would be to acknowledge her father's lack, and this is what Laura cannot do until the end of the film. It takes so long and so much evidence to convince Laura because of the trauma inherent in this acknowledgment. Her suspicions start early in the film when she sees BOB in her room and runs outside the house. A moment later, her father comes out, thereby indicating that he was the person she saw. Later, while riding in the car with her father, MIKE screams to her, "It's him! It's your father!" But Leland revs the car engine so that Laura can barely hear what MIKE is saying. She only becomes convinced when BOB becomes Leland during the sex act itself.

Lynch shoots this scene in a way that conveys the trauma that the revelation has for Laura. We see BOB sneak into Laura's bedroom through an open window and begin to have sex with her. She repeats four times, "Who are you?" during the sex act. After the fourth time, we see a shot of Laura's face as a look of horror comes over it and she screams, followed by a reverse shot showing her father's face where BOB's was. At this point, the screen goes completely black until it shows a shot looking down directly into a bowl of cereal (which has the appearance of vomit). The entire consistency of Laura's world seems to break down: the images lose their coherence and become blurry, the clock on the wall in Laura's classroom begins to spin out of control, and so on. In her room, the angel disappears from the picture hanging on the wall. All this chaos results from Laura's encounter with the lack in the Other. Seeing her father as BOB, she can no longer believe in the pristine Other that has a substantive identity. Now she looks out into the Other and sees the same emptiness that exists within herself.

But the film does not end with the trauma of Laura's encounter with the lack in the Other. Instead, the trauma actually becomes the basis for Laura's emergence as an ethical subject and her defiance of BOB. In this sense, the complaint that Laura is simply a victim of male fantasies misses the mark. According to Laura Plummer, Laura Palmer is nothing but this: "Laura's transgressions of social law—snorting cocaine and being a sexually active teenager—originate in the abuse of her father. That is, Laura Palmer is merely reactive; she has no agency. She is only punished."[26] What Plummer fails to see is the radicality of Laura's gesture at the end of the film. Laura defies the phallic power of BOB in a way that no other character in the film does. When Leland takes Ronette Pulaski and her to the railroad car, MIKE rolls the ring from the Man From Another Place into the car with Laura at the moment Ronette escapes. Laura puts the ring on her finger, a gesture that defies BOB's authority. Just after she puts the ring on, Leland screams, "No! Don't make me do this," before he kills her. The act of putting on the ring seems to force Leland/BOB to kill Laura rather than just sexually assaulting her as he usually does.

By taking the ring, she accomplishes the impossible. She aligns herself with the Man From Another Place against BOB, with death against life. She marries herself to the death drive. The ring has a structure almost exactly like that of the drive: a closed loop organized around a central absence. In the act of taking the ring, the subject affirms and embraces absence, which undermines BOB's authority. But we immediately see the cost of the impossible act: the embrace of the death drive costs Laura her life. When BOB kills Laura, he removes the ring and places a letter under the nail of the finger that formerly held the ring. This gesture reveals in another way the difference between the Man From Another Place and BOB—or the difference between the drive and the phallus. Whereas the drive circulates around an absence, the phallus attempts to fill in this absence—the hole left by castration—with the materiality of the letter.

Laura can accept the ring in the railroad car because she has reached the point where she no longer hopes. It is to this point that the fantasy depicted in *Fire Walk with Me* leads us. It allows us to experience the emptiness of both the object and the Other. In doing so, we escape the idea of an escape. When Laura puts on the ring, she no longer has any investment in life, and BOB's hold over subjects depends entirely on their investment in life. As she had told James earlier that night, "There's no place left to go." The embrace of the death drive is what BOB cannot tolerate: it separates Laura from him and places her beyond his control, guaranteeing that he will not possess her. Laura finds a solution here through the embrace of the death drive. Through this act, she breaks the hold that phallic authority has over her and frees herself as a subject. BOB kills her almost as soon as she slips the ring on. But in the instant of her impossible identification with the death drive, she achieves the ethical position that the film itself privileges.

In this way, the fantasmatic dimension of *Fire Walk with Me* places an onerous demand on the spectator. One must first see oneself in Laura, the impossible object, and then one must follow her down the path of ethical subjectivity. Ethics here means embracing the absence of an outside, the recognition that "There's no place left to go," no elsewhere where we could imagine things are better. Adopting this position, one finds the outside within the inside, the infinite within the finite. Or, as Hegel suggests in his analysis of Christianity, one recognizes that the kingdom of heaven is Main Street.

SEVEN Finding Ourselves on a *Lost Highway*

The Fantasy of Sense

After the critical and popular failure of *Twin Peaks: Fire Walk with Me* (1992), Lynch took a long period of time off from feature filmmaking. His follow-up film, *Lost Highway*, did not appear until 1997. He spent much of this time thinking through and exploring possible ideas for a new project—throwing ideas at the wall, as he would put it. When the right idea came, it came from the random phrase "lost highway," which appeared in the novel *Night Moves* by Barry Gifford (who also wrote the novel *Wild at Heart* on which Lynch based his film). Struck by this phrase, Lynch proposed cowriting a screenplay with Gifford unrelated to the novel. The film was their first collaboration as cowriters, and, despite Gifford's influence, it did not return to the relative clarity of *Wild at Heart* (1990) but continued down the path laid down by *Fire Walk with Me*.

Lost Highway is as difficult to experience as *Fire Walk with Me*, though for different reasons. On the level of our immediate cinematic interaction with the film, it presents us with images so bright that we close our eyes or look away, and voices so distorted that we wish we could close our ears. These difficulties, temporarily unpleasant though they may be, become but minor bumps in the road when we contrast them with the interpretive difficulties that the film's narrative incoherence—or seeming incoherence—presents. As Anne Jerslev rightly points out, "More than *Twin Peaks: Fire Walk with Me*, *Lost Highway* takes the form of a radical departure from classical principles of coherence, unity and closure."[1] It is tempting, on a first viewing, to chalk these difficulties up to Lynch's obscurantist proclivities and to conclude that the narrative is unconventional just for the sake of being unconventional, or that the point is simply that there is no point.[2] But if this is the case, then *Lost Highway* hardly seems worth the 135 minutes that a viewing requires, let alone any efforts spent in making sense of it. This conclusion seems to have been that of audiences and critics alike, most of whom rejected *Lost Highway*, just as they did *Fire Walk with Me*.[3] Even if the difficulties of the film serve to conceal something profound in the film's narrative, they are not necessarily worth the trouble. The film's obscurity, in that case, would still not clearly be necessary. The only serious justification for the difficulties of the film's narrative lies in their structural necessity. Its difficulties derive from making evident an underlying logic of fantasy that is operative, though certainly not apparent, in the filmic experience itself. Because the narrative of *Lost Highway* brings the logic of fantasy out into the open, it necessarily strikes us as incongruous, as a film without a narrative altogether.

More than in Lynch's other films, the division of *Lost Highway* into opposing worlds of desire and fantasy dramatically affects the sense of the film. The chief effect of this separation is that the film doesn't seem to make sense at all. Fantasy, though it is opposed to "reality," nonetheless provides an underlying support for our sense of reality. Without this support, we can no longer be sure of our bearing within the social reality—our sense of the meaningfulness of that reality. The separation of desire and fantasy also makes clear the way in which fantasy acts as a compensation for what the social reality doesn't provide. Fantasy provides the illusion of delivering the goods, but *Lost Highway* ultimately makes clear that it fails to do so. In this sense, fantasy is not an escape from an unsatisfying social reality but a way of repeating it. The subject turns to fantasy to escape the deadlock of desire but inevitably encounters the deadlock in a new form. One fantasizes oneself a different person, but the traumatic disruption of the impossible object-cause of desire remains. Even in the act of accomplishing the impossible, one always returns back to one's starting point.

The separation between fantasy and social reality in *Lost Highway* manifests itself most apparently in the transformations that its protagonist undergoes. He first appears as Fred Madison (Bill Pullman), later becomes (while in prison awaiting execution for the murder of his wife) someone entirely different, Peter Dayton (Balthazar Getty), and then becomes Fred Madison again. In opting to have different actors play the characters of Fred Madison and Peter Dayton, Lynch establishes a readily visible distinction between the experience of desire within the film and the experience of fantasy.[4] The transformation between the two, which occurs without explanation, baffles characters within the film as well as audiences without. We can grasp what's happening in *Lost Highway* only if we see the sudden transformation of Fred Madison into Peter Dayton as fantasmatic: Peter Dayton *is* Fred Madison within Fred's fantasy. The entire scenario surrounding Peter Dayton that follows in the film thus becomes the elaborated structure of this fantasy.[5]

Through the wide visual divergence between the world of Fred and the world of Peter, Lynch establishes them cinematically as worlds of desire and of fantasy, respectively. From the first shot of the film, Lynch gives Fred's world a sense of the unknown. Rather than beginning with an establishing shot, the film opens with a close-up of Fred, which inaugurates the mystery. None of the subsequent shots help to clarify things, and the entire depiction of Fred's world leaves the spectator without any sense of time or place. Fred's world lacks the visual fullness, the depth, of Peter's; there is a sense of emptiness here, which Lynch establishes through the use of a minimalist décor and subdued lighting in Fred's house. This emptiness provides the space for desire—something seems lacking, thus impelling the movements of desire. The desiring subject and the desiring spectator emerge through the confrontation with an absence of meaning, and this absence is ubiquitous in the first part of *Lost Highway*.

By minimizing the depth of field in the shots of Fred's world, Lynch creates a sense of flatness in that world. Everything seems to be taking place on the surface, without any depth. The use of color and sound also add to the feeling of depthlessness: the colors are drab (black, gray, taupe, dark orange), and there are long periods of silence without any background sound. This world is mysterious precisely because it is a world of surfaces, and where we would expect to find depth, we find only a void (silence or darkness). While he lights all the main rooms of the house with low, though adequate lighting, Lynch leaves the hallways completely dark, indicating this void beneath the surface, the void from which desire emerges. Such darkness is absent in Peter's world. From the moment Peter appears, the mise-en-scène is wholly different: bright lighting, more colorful furniture and décor, and no empty spaces. The depth of field underlines the fuller look. Lynch shoots Peter's world much more traditionally than Fred's, so that it is not pervaded by mystery in the way of the latter. This absence of mystery—this sense of a turn toward realistic cinema—lets us know that Peter's world is wholly fantasmatic. A world of pure desire would be completely mysterious in this way because it would offer us no possibilities for making sense of the desire of the Other (which is the function of fantasy).

Enduring the Desire of the Other

Rather than turning to fantasy, as one might assume, to avoid contemplating his impending execution, Fred does so in order to gain respite from the desire of his wife Renee (Patricia Arquette), which continues to haunt him despite the fact that she seems to have died. From the beginning of the film, Renee's desire works to generate Fred's desire—precisely because he has no idea what she wants, let alone how to give it to her. She seems to have, somewhere within her, some hidden kernel of excessive enjoyment that Fred can't access. Bill Pullman's performance and Lynch's placement of Fred within the frame help to make clear that Fred posits a secret, mysterious enjoyment in Renee. On two separate occasions when Fred approaches Renee, the shots depict him emerging from a completely darkened corridor in the house (echoing similar shots in *Blue Velvet* [1986], such as when Sandy [Laura Dern] first appears). Desiring is, in a sense, being in the dark about the desire of the Other—or feeling oneself in the dark. Bill Pullman's delivery of Fred's lines also makes clear that Renee's desire mystifies Fred. When responding to Renee's questions or conversing with her, Pullman uses unusually long pauses and a puzzled expression in order to demonstrate Fred's sense of bewilderment. The sum of these effects helps to illustrate that Fred feels himself confronted with a mystery that he cannot fathom—the mystery of what Renee wants.

At the beginning of *Lost Highway*, Renee is a mystery to Fred, and he interprets this sense of mystery that pervades her as a veil, beneath which lies her hidden treasure, her secret enjoyment. On the first evening depicted in *Lost Highway*, Fred asks Renee if she's going to the club that night (where he plays the saxophone in a jazz band), but she decides not to go. This decision, ostensibly innocent, is for Fred filled with meaning (because he sees it as a veil hiding something), but he doesn't know what kind of meaning (because he can't see beneath the veil). He then proceeds to interrogate her:

> FRED: What are you going to do?
> RENEE: Read.
> FRED: . . . Read? . . . Read what?
> (RENEE *laughs*)

As Fred, Bill Pullman delivers this final line with two belabored pauses, suggesting that he is uncertain whether or not Renee is telling the truth.

Renee's cryptic response and subsequent laughter when asked to specify do not help Fred to solve the mystery of her desire. The laughter seems to indicate that Renee has something up her sleeve, but whatever this might be, Fred feels himself completely barred from it. We can sense this feeling in Fred's voice when he tells Renee, after she laughs, "It's nice to know I can still make you laugh." He takes some degree of solace in the fact that he seems still to have some part of what she wants, but his overall feeling here is one of being alienated from her desire, an alienation that quickly turns into suspicion. From the club that night, he calls home, checking up on Renee, but she doesn't seem to be there to answer. Lynch cuts between a shot of Fred calling from the club and a shot of the phone ringing at Fred and Renee's home with no one answering. The editing of this shot sequence extends the sense of mystery pervading Renee. By including the shot of the phone ringing in the seemingly vacant home, Lynch attempts to involve the spectator in Fred's suspicions about Renee. It is not clear that Renee isn't there, but nonetheless this is Fred's belief—and ours, if we follow the proddings of Lynch's camera—a belief premised upon seeing Renee as veiled. But when he gets home, he finds Renee sleeping peacefully in their bed by herself. This episode leaves Fred and the audience with a hint that Renee is desiring, but with no idea about *what*. But in coming up against the mystery of Renee's desire, Fred reveals something further.

Through Fred's relationship with Renee, *Lost Highway* illustrates how we come into existence as desiring subjects. Fred's sense of bewilderment about Renee's desire, his constant efforts at interpreting what it is she really wants, is actually the mark of his own emergence as a desiring subject. His constant efforts to interpret Renee's words (and even her silences and laughs) indicate that Fred himself desires. In attempting to interpret Renee's desire, Fred constitutes himself as desiring. Desire is an effort to figure out what the Other wants from me. As such, it is a perpetual question that can never be answered because it would have to be answered with words, i.e., with another veil or screen that necessarily gives the illusion of hiding desire. Even asking the Other to demonstrate her/his desire physically in an effort to elude language would come up against the same stumbling block: as beings of language, even our gestures function as signifiers, which means that they are opaque and appear to hide desire.

If Fred came right out and asked Renee what she wanted, whatever answer she gave would seem to Fred as if she were hiding something further, the something that she really wanted. This is why Lacan claims that desire "cannot be indicated anywhere in a signifier of any demand whatsoever, for it cannot be articulated in the signifier even though it is articulated there."[6] Desire is the result of our insertion into language, but nonetheless it can't be named by that language. Thus, insofar as he holds fast to his desire (i.e., insofar as he continues to try to interpret Renee's desire), Fred is doomed to be stuck with a question that doesn't have an answer, no matter how far he pursues that question. The endlessness of desire and its perpetual question make it unbearable and nearly impossible to sustain.

This unbearable quality is why we don't experience desire without a correlative fantasy. On its own, desire requires that we persist in a radical uncertainty relative to the Other. As a result, most narratives dilute desire with a dose of fantasy, providing characters and situations that readily make sense. But even narratives replete with uncertainty necessarily betray some investment in fantasy, or else they would cease to be narratives altogether. Narratives allow us the respite of knowledge, thereby delivering us from desire's complete uncertainty, even as they receive their energy from desire. We can see the unbearable quality of desire in Fred's response to Renee's desire and, by extension, to his own. It doesn't take long for Fred to begin to view desire itself with suspicion. We should resist the temptation of blaming this response on the ambiguity with which Renee presents Fred. As Martha Nochimson rightly points out, "Fred is doomed by his relationship to Renee not because of *her* inconsistencies but because of *his* obsessions."[7] Fred retreats from desire itself—not particularly Renee's desire.

The Entrance of the Superego

One way to retreat from desire is to turn to the law, to identify with the law as a bulwark against desire. Whereas fantasy offers an imaginary answer to desire's question, the law attempts to arrest the very process of questioning itself, along with the disturbance it provokes. In its effort to keep desire in check, the law takes up a position of an observer vis-à-vis desire. It observes desire in an effort to keep it to a minimum, to eliminate its disruptive effects on the functioning of the social order. In order to better observe desire, the law has a representative within the psyche, the superego, that watches over the subject from the inside. The superego is the psychical agency of self-observation, and though it is a part of the psyche, its attachment to the law makes it seem as if the superego comes from the outside. In *Lost Highway*, the videotape that appears on Fred and Renee's front porch on the film's second morning indicates the presence of some observing agency. Like the superego, whoever is observing their house with a video camera seems to be an intruder, an alien figure.

The superego is, in one sense, at the source of the feeling of being watched, though its ultimate source lies in our sacrifice of desire to the law. The manifestation of the superego appears in the film, not coincidentally, just as Fred has begun to become more suspicious about Renee's desire. Feelings of suspicion and jealousy are a response to desire, a suspicion of desire itself—indicative of an investment in the law. Fred's suspicion indicates a failure on his part to sustain desire's question, and it is this failure that provides a burst of energy to the superego, resulting in the videotape at the door. In giving up his desire, Fred opens the door to the superego, "inviting" it into his psyche. The superego develops insofar as we give up desire: the more we give up desire, the stronger the superego's command that we give up more desire becomes.[8] In *The Metas-*

tases of Enjoyment, Slavoj Žižek offers an explanation of this relationship: "[The] superego draws the energy of the pressure it exerts upon the subject from the fact that the subject was not faithful to his desire, that he gave it up. Our sacrificing to the superego, our paying tribute to it, only corroborates our guilt."[9] The tape's presence tells us that Fred's abandonment of his desire has energized his superego, but its presence also spurs Fred's suspicions, which means it doesn't provide him any relief. The turn away from desire to the law is not, properly speaking, a turn away from desire at all. The more the subject seeks refuge in the law, the more heavily it experiences its own lack.

Law and desire work hand-in-hand to keep the subject's attention focused on the Other and the question of the Other's desire.[10] As long as the subject takes its bearings from the Other's desire, it remains on a thoroughly ideological terrain in which the Other completely determines the subject. In this position, the subject sees only symbolically circumscribed avenues for action rather than a real opening to act. Such openings appear as impossibilities for the subject tied, through the dialectic of law and desire, to the question of what the Other wants. But *Lost Highway* doesn't end with this stale alternative.

The evening after Fred and Renee receive the first tape, Fred posits an increasingly greater desire to Renee, "seeing" her present at the club that night with another guy (Andy, as we learn later). Later that night, Fred tries to have sex with Renee, but is unable to—and unable to give her what he thinks she wants. And from Renee's response, we can see that this isn't the first time. Fred's impotence—or simply his inability to satisfy Renee sexually—further empowers his superego because it makes him feel even more estranged from her desire and even guiltier. We get confirmation of this when Fred, just after their failed sexual experience, recounts a dream to Renee. He tells her, "There you were lying in bed. It wasn't you but it looked like you." Instead of her face, in the dream-image we see the face of the Mystery Man (Robert Blake), who turns out to be—we don't know this yet at this point in the film—the one responsible for the videotape.[11]

The Mystery Man's face appears suddenly in Fred's dream sequence in the place of Renee's face, an effect that adds to the horror it provokes, illustrating the way in which the superego represents the Father in his most ferocious form. Fred sees the face that has been observing him (i.e., the superegoic face) in the place of his wife's. The superego lodges itself between Fred and Renee, further cutting off Fred from Renee's desire and his own. It blocks the path of Fred's desire, keeping watch over any desire to transgress its prohibitions. Furthermore, the superego continues to make itself felt with greater and greater strength, as the next morning's videotape shows. Unlike the tape of the previous morning, on this tape the observing camera enters Fred and Renee's house and travels down the hall toward their bedroom, finally dissolving into static as the image of them sleeping in bed appears.

That evening at a party, the film reveals the significance of this increasing intrusion. Fred runs into the Mystery Man, who approaches Fred and tells him that he is at Fred's house *now*. Fred, of course, finds this "crazy," but the Mystery Man is able to prove his claim by offering his cellular phone to Fred so that he can call home. And sure enough, the Mystery Man answers the phone in Fred's house, even though he is also standing in front of Fred at the party. When Fred asks him why he's there, the Mystery Man replies, "You invited me. It is not my custom to go where I am not wanted." In this response, the Mystery Man provides another piece of evidence that he occupies the position of the superego.[12] Just like the Mystery Man, the superego is an intruder from an external place into an internal one. As Freud points out, "the part which is later taken on by the super-ego is played to begin with by an external power, by parental authority."[13] The superego is the result of any internalization of the father (or, more specifically, of the Name of the Father) as an agency of prohibition. In the formation of the superego, "external restraint is internalized."[14] The superego is, like the Mystery Man in the film, in two places at once—inside and outside.

The film makes even more evident this extimate quality of the Mystery Man through a manipulation of sound. Lynch's work with sound is often the most inventive aspect of his filmmaking, as we can see in this instance. He uses sound (or the lack of it) to make clear the bond between Fred and the Mystery Man. When the Mystery Man approaches Fred in order to speak with him, the background noise of the party dims to become almost inaudible, as if, in the midst of this crowded party, the Mystery Man and Fred are having a private—intrapsychic—conversation. When the Mystery Man walks away after their conversation, the background noise returns again to normal, suggesting that we have moved back from the internal to the external. The internalization of the law through the agency of the superego reveals something important about the subject's relation to desire. This internalization is not so much an imposition of authority as the result of a sacrifice made by the subject. The superego follows from the sacrifice of desire, which is why, in a sense, Fred did invite the Mystery Man into his home, as the latter claims. In giving up his desire, Fred offered an open invitation to the superego.[15]

On the drive home from the party, Fred gets, as it were, a last chance. He asks Renee about Andy (the host of the party and the guy with whom Renee had been flirting), and she tells about a job that Andy once told her about. Beyond that she can't remember. Once again, she presents him with an enigma: the "job" remains a complete mystery, which sends Fred's desire racing. But under the increasing pressure of the superego he cannot continue in the uncertainty of this open question (i.e., what does Renee want?). The next morning's videotape—the first one Fred watches without Renee—depicts the results: Fred hacking away at Renee's body in their bedroom. Compelled by the pressure of the superego, Fred attempts to eradicate desire's incessant and unbearable question.

Even though the superego is, for psychoanalysis, the advocate for morality within the psyche, it nonetheless demands Renee's murder. How does this square with the idea of the superego as a "moral" agency? Morality always comes down to—and this is why Lacan contrasts it with an ethics of desire—the command to sacrifice the object because the object's ambiguity is what keeps pushing desire forward. Morality aims, in short, at arresting the disturbance that desire causes. This is why, at the close of *Seminar XI*, Lacan says of the moral law that it "culminates in the sacrifice, strictly speaking, of everything that is the object of love in one's human tenderness—I would say, not only in the rejection of the pathological object, but also in its sacrifice and murder."[16]

Just murdering Renee is not enough to sate the appetite of this morality because she isn't identical with the object-cause of desire. That object is a part object—part of her, not the whole of her. Thus, we see Fred, after having killed her, dismembering Renee's body in an effort to find this object somewhere in her body. The object, however, is not simply in Renee (as Fred believes when he is mutilating her); it is, as Lacan would put it, "in her more than her." Consequently, the mutilation is doomed to fail, and despite his destruction of Renee, the object remains just as ineffable as ever. He doesn't discover her "secret." Killing Renee in no way makes things easier precisely because he can't really kill her—or at least that part of her which is the object-cause of desire. As the film subsequently shows, the death sentence he receives is the least of his worries.[17]

Fantasizing Reality

Despite her "death," the problem of Renee's desire continues to haunt Fred with increasing vehemence while he's in prison. One doesn't just get rid of the trouble that desire stirs up, and the fact that we later see her alive again merely confirms this. The more one tries to destroy this object, the more it continues to haunt. This is why killing Renee only makes things worse for Fred. In his prison cell Fred falls apart, buckled by the desire that he could not destroy by murdering Renee. It is at this point that Fred attempts to quell desire in another way—giving up desire for fantasy, which results in his transformation into Peter Dayton. While most films, at some point in the narrative, depict a similar turn from desire to fantasy (when they enact some sort of resolution), *Lost Highway* actually enacts this turn within the formal structure of the film itself—replacing one character (Fred Madison) with another (Peter Dayton). At this point, the film itself fully immerses itself in fantasy, which has a paradoxical effect: because the film becomes immersed in Fred's fantasy—taking it so seriously as to effect a transformation in his character—it jolts the spectator out of viewing comfortably through the lens of fantasy.

By highlighting the radicality of the transformation that fantasy occasions, Lynch returns us, as spectators, to the unbearableness of desire. Through the transformation into Peter, it is this unbearableness of Renee's/his desire that Fred is trying to escape. In the fantasy that follows, Fred conceives an answer to the question of what Renee wants, and though it is not always pleasant for him (or for Peter Dayton), it does allow him to get a handle on the enigmatic object. Fantasy provides an explicit staging of the Other's "secret." If desire is a perpetual question, fantasy is an answer, a solution to the problem that desire presents, which is why fantasy, even if it is masochistic, provides a sense of relief.

The commonsensical definition of fantasy—escape from reality—can't explain fantasy's unpleasant dimension. In his explanation of

Fred's transformation into Peter, Tim Lucas invokes this definition, claiming that "after realizing what he's done, Fred cannot face the overwhelming realities of the murder and his conviction, and his denial extends to the obliteration of his own identity."[18] This description of the turn to fantasy posits a preexisting reality which fantasy seeks to deny. But Fred, as far as we can see in the film, doesn't seem all that troubled by reality. Rather, it is desire that troubles him. This is why there is a clear continuity between his state before the murder and after; it is difficult to see how the murder has changed much, other than making Renee's desire even more impenetrable.

Furthermore, if fantasy is supposed to offer respite from the unpleasantness of reality, it seems that Fred should demand at least a partial refund. Renee's enigmatic desire may be disconcerting, but in his fantasmatic alternative, he *knows* that Alice (Patricia Arquette again, here a platinum blonde) is the mistress of Mr. Eddy (Robert Loggia)—not exactly a pleasant alternative. But we don't turn to fantasy for happiness or for respite from reality; we turn to it for respite from the torments of our desire.

Fantasy fills in the gap that haunts the social reality, but in doing so reveals that there is something not encompassed by this reality—a traumatic real. The very fact that we must have recourse to fantasy—that the social reality doesn't satisfy us—testifies to the existence of a real that haunts our reality. If the social reality were without fissure, if it could account for everything, it would not have a fantastmatic underside. And the turn to fantasy, the transition, makes the real evident because it reveals, however briefly, the point of fissure within the social reality. The real is the transitional point at which fantasy emerges. Again, because *Lost Highway* holds social reality and fantasy apart, the transition between them—contact with the real—becomes apparent where our everyday life obscures it.

The moment of transition to fantasy in *Lost Highway* is a traumatic moment: the camera (from Fred's point of view) is moving down the middle of a highway and then swerves, heading straight for Peter, who stands by the side of the road. In the background, Peter's parents and girlfriend Sheila come running and screaming in terror. Following this encounter between social reality and fantasy, we see Fred writhing in pain on his cell floor—evidence of him enduring an experience of the void that haunts reality. The void then appears momentarily on the screen as a mysterious (vaginal) opening that expands and threatens to envelop the spectator—only to disappear almost instantaneously. Just as it seems to envelop us, the fantasy takes hold, and we find ourselves on seemingly solid ground. And this traumatic real does leave its mark: the oozing wound on Peter's head serves as a reminder. Just as Fred's splitting headaches indicate the presence of the traumatic real in the world of desire, Peter's head wound indicates its presence in the world of fantasy. In the former case, trauma is always in the future, about to happen; in the latter, it has always already occurred. In other words, trauma haunts the world of desire as the possibility that is right around the corner while it haunts the world of fantasy as a past event that that world can never escape. We can also see the sign of the trauma's presence in the refusal of Peter's parents to speak about "that night," revealing that the fantasy necessitates that certain things remain unspoken. Keeping the traumatic real unspoken allows fantasy to create a world seemingly without fissure.

In fantasy, we produce an image of ourselves as we want to be—an ideal ego or imaginary identification. Peter Dayton fulfills this function for Fred Madison first of all in his ability to enjoy women in a way that Fred cannot. As the police tell us, Peter "gets more pussy than a toilet seat." What's more, in the figure of Peter, Fred can see himself as innocent, a victim of dark and sinister forces and of a corrupted woman. And yet, Peter is not an innocent naif: he has a criminal record, a large group of cool friends, and an active sexual relationship with his girlfriend Sheila. In other words, Peter represents both innocence and sophistication—an idealized, though contradictory, image. Through the turn to Peter, Fred realizes an impossible identity.

Like Peter, his parents have a double quality to them. They both wear leather jackets and dark sunglasses—which suggest that they are "hip"—while they drive a wood-paneled station wagon and watch with fascination documentaries about strawberries—characteristics that suggest the seeming innocence of *Leave It to Beaver*. These oxymoronic characteristics in both Peter and his parents indicate emphatically that they are part of a fantasy construction. This fantasy cannot allow Fred to see himself as so innocent as to be a dupe, but neither can it allow him to see himself as in any way culpable. Only by walking this fine line can fantasy assist Fred in escaping from his desire.

Fantasy not only offers us the image of ourselves as we want to be, it is also the basis for our sense of being situated in a "real world" rather than a mysterious one plagued by uncertainty. This is clear in the contrast between Fred and Peter. Whereas Fred seems to exist completely outside of any personal history or social relations, Peter has what seems to be a "full" life: parents, friends, job, (criminal) history, etc. Mystery pervades Fred's world. As Reni Celeste points out, "The first world encountered in this film is enveloped in the mood of suspicion, silence, clues that have no meaning and acts that have no agent."[19] In contrast to Fred, Peter doesn't live in a vacuum, but within a rather clearly defined social setting.

If it is the case that Fred's world is one of desire and Peter's world is one of fantasy, then this suggests that all the background elements that give our existence its sense of completeness are fantasmatic. The ability to grasp oneself in a specific sociohistorical setting is fantasmatic because it makes us feel secure—rooted, connected to people, place, and time. Fred's existence has no such stability; it is the free-floating existence indicative of a world of desire without fantasy. In Fred's world, we have no way of getting our bearings, no clear markers to latch onto, so that we should even hesitate to call it a "world" at all. Peter's, on the other hand, offers us clear points of reference. In depicting this contrast, Lynch shows the extent to which a "sense of reality" actually has little to do with reality itself. It depends fundamentally upon a well-developed "sense of fantasy."[20]

This contrast is perhaps most apparent in the stylistic differences between the two worlds. Whereas Lynch shoots Fred's world with minimal depth of field, with monochromatic tones, with low, yellow lighting, and with long periods of silence, he shoots Peter's world using the traditional conventions of Hollywood realism. The moment after the transformation from Fred to Peter, the style of the film undergoes a wholesale change. The prison, flat and drab when Fred occupied it, acquires depth and color. Peter's cell has a light shining through the window that wasn't shining into Fred's cell, and the first shot of the prison corridor has a depth of field that contrasts with the flatness of Fred's world. When Peter arrives at his parent's home, the lighting, depth of field, and colors seem much more like what we are used to seeing than in the shots of Fred and Renee's home. The first shot of Peter at his home depicts him wearing bright colors (red and white) and sitting on a lawn chair in the brightly lit backyard. This mise-en-scène marks a complete departure from that of the first part of the film, a departure that indicates the evanescence of mystery.

In Peter's world, spectators have something to hold onto, a sense of depth beneath the surface rather than just emptiness. The constant background music also helps to provide this sense of depth, but it is the dialogue that makes it especially apparent. Here, unlike in Fred's world, actors speak their lines without lengthy and awkward pauses, in a manner that suggests "real" conversation. This realism in the dialogue helps to produce a world in which everything makes sense and in which we are not bombarded by a constant aura of mystery. In this way, the turn to Peter's world provides the same kind of respite for spectators that the turn to Peter provides for Fred. By shooting Peter's world—the world of fantasy—in a realistic style, Lynch makes evident the fantasmatic underpinnings of our sense of reality. He shows, in other words, that it is precisely the fullness and depth—the feeling of "life"—of the filmic experience that are fantasmatic. The sense of depth we associate with reality is wholly a product of fantasy, an indication of a retreat from desire.

The escape from desire becomes most apparent in the transformation of Patricia Arquette's Renee into Alice Wakefield. We know that a link exists between Fred Madison and Peter Dayton because after both transformations—Fred into Peter and Peter into Fred—the one occupies the same physical space that the other had occupied. In the case of Renee and Alice, no such clues exist. However, because Patricia Arquette plays both roles, there is at least an indication—which will get substantiated—that Alice is a fantasized version of Renee. The transformation of Renee into Alice allows Fred (as Peter Dayton) to solve the deadlock of Renee's desire and conceive, on the level of fantasy, of a way of enjoying her. Whereas Renee's past and her desire remained a mystery to Fred, Peter is able to enjoy Alice because he knows what she wants. In Alice, desire finds its satisfaction, albeit only an imaginary satisfaction. Unlike Renee, Alice, as a fantasy object, is knowable. In other words, in the fantasy one finds a solution to the desire of the Other. This difference is most apparent in Alice's association with Andy. Though Renee seemed—at least to Fred's mind—to have some illicit involvement with Andy, she provided Fred no details, other than proclaiming that they were "friends" and that Andy once told her about a "job," the specifics of which slipped her mind. With Alice, all of the questions find answers.

After Peter becomes aware of Alice's involvement with organized crime and pornography, he wants to know the reason for this involvement. While they are together at the Starlight Motel, he asks, "How did you get involved with these fucking people, Alice?" In response, Alice repeats, word for word, Renee's description about meeting Andy and him telling her about a job, except that Alice remembers the job and describes it to Peter. Whereas Renee's account is wholly ambiguous—and thus elicits Fred's desire—Alice provides the intimate details of the job, allowing Peter a share of her enjoyment. The job consisted simply of one of Mr. Eddy's gangsters putting a gun to her head while she took her clothes off in front of Mr. Eddy. Alice's description horrifies—arouses—Peter, who now has confirmation about what it is that Alice wants. He asks her, "Why didn't you just leave? . . . You liked it, huh?" Though Alice's story upsets Peter, it also offers him a fantasized answer to the question, "what does the Other want?"; it allows him to conceive of the Other enjoying. The answer, not surprisingly, is the phallus, represented by Mr. Eddy, the site of power within this fantasy construction. The phallus functions to signify the Other's desire.

We Can Only Go So Far

The phallus gets in the way of Peter's enjoyment of Alice. Whereas Fred could not enjoy Renee because he had no idea what she wanted, Peter cannot enjoy Alice because Mr. Eddy stands in the way and has expressly prohibited Peter from enjoying her. When he becomes suspicious of Peter and Alice's relationship, Mr. Eddy pays Peter a visit at Arnie's Garage, where he implicitly warns him about "making out" with Alice, telling him,

> I'm sure you noticed that girl who was with me the other day—good-looking blonde, she stayed in the car? Her name is Alice. I swear I love that girl to death. If I ever found out somebody was making out with her, I'd take this [his gun], and I'd shove it so far up his ass it would come out his mouth. And then you know what I'd do? . . . I'd blow his fucking brains out.

Mr. Eddy's warning suggests that he, as the father, will jealously guard his privilege of enjoying the woman.[21] He defends this privilege by brandishing his heavily phallicized gun and threatening castration for the wayward son.

Though the father does prohibit Peter from enjoying Alice, his fantasized existence does at least allow for the possibility of Alice's enjoyment, the satisfaction of her desire, and in this way, the presence of the father (and the phallus) provides respite from the desire of the Other. No matter how threatening the father may be, he is always a relief, but only a fantasized relief, as the film makes clear. By having this father figure emerge only through the fantasy, *Lost Highway* shows that his status is necessarily fantasmatic, an indication that the subject has abandoned its desire. As Lacan notes in *Seminar XXIII*, "the father is a symptom."[22] Fred Madison fantasizes the father's existence because he offers a way of structuring his enjoyment via the fantasy and thus also offers a respite from desire. When Mr. Eddy appears in the fantasy structure as the agent of prohibition, he signals—as the father always does—that Fred has retreated from his desire.

Within the structure of fantasy, the father provides the anchor upon which we can ground meaning and get our bearings. This is the function of the father: he is the point from which everything else can be made sensible. With the assistance of this paternal function, fantasy transforms what doesn't make sense into what does—questions into answers. But the answers it provides—the way it structures our enjoyment—are never pleasant, because it always structures enjoyment as something prohibited. It is not just that Fred has a self-destructive fantasy and should try to come up with a more positive one. The destructiveness lies in the nature of fantasy itself.

As Peter tries to enjoy Alice for himself, to violate Mr. Eddy's prohibition, the limits of the kind of enjoyment possible through fantasy come clearly into view. Alice talks Peter into a plan that would allow him to enjoy her, that involves robbing and killing Andy (Mr. Eddy's hireling). When Peter enters Andy's house to carry out the plan, he encounters enjoyment everywhere: there is a pornographic film with Alice in it playing on the far wall and a loud voice is chanting nonsensically.[23] Getting so close to this enjoyment horrifies Peter, and, after Andy—a barrier to it—dies, Peter sees a picture of Mr. Eddy, Andy, Renee, and Alice, a picture that indicates the breakdown of the barrier between fantasy and social reality. He wonders if both Renee and Alice are the same person, and though Alice tells him that they're not, Peter begins to get a splitting headache, suggesting that he's not so sure.[24] As he gets too close to the possibility of enjoying his object through the fantasy, the real object (Renee) begins to intrude into the fantasy, thereby making the horror of enjoyment more and more evident.

After seeing the picture of both Alice and Renee together, the fantasy starts to unravel with the intrusion of the social reality. Peter, with his head aching, goes upstairs looking for a bathroom but finds instead a hotel room. When Peter opens the door, he sees a wildly distorted image of Renee having sex. (Watching the film, it is difficult to determine whether it is Renee or Alice, though the screenplay indicates that it is Renee. The ambiguity suggests the further breakdown of the fantasy.) Renee calls out to him, in a distorted voice, "Did you want to talk to me? Did you want to ask me why?" As she says the word "why," Renee's voice becomes completely garbled, indicating that the sense of what Renee is saying here becomes overwhelmed by the enjoyment of the voice itself—an enjoyment beyond the meaning of the word. The film indicates the overwhelming presence of enjoyment here not only through the distortion of Renee's voice but also through the distortion of the image and of the narrative itself.

Until this moment, Peter Dayton's fantasmatic narrative has had a certain consistency, the semblance of order. But when Peter walks upstairs in Andy's house looking for a bathroom and finds Renee having sex in a motel room, enjoyment breaks free within the fantasy construction, and the fantasy is starting to teeter. Horrified by this encounter with enjoyment, Peter quickly shuts the door, eager for some sort of respite. With Andy out of the way, nothing stands in the way of Peter's enjoying the fantasy object. But when nothing stands in the way of this enjoyment and the fantasy can no longer keep it at a safe distance, Alice/Renee—the difference is evaporating—becomes unbearable for Peter, just as Renee was unbearable for Fred. Rather than providing respite, the fantasy leads the subject down the path that he tried to escape.

When Alice and Peter drive out to the desert to sell the jewels they've taken from Andy, the fantasy finally dissolves completely. While waiting for their buyer to arrive, Alice and Peter begin to have sex in front of their car's shining headlights. Peter comes as close as he can get to enjoying his fantasy object unencumbered by the threat of the father. Lynch even communicates this proximity to enjoyment through the form of the film: the screen becomes so bright that the audience can barely continue watching.[25] Peter has gotten too close to the fantasy object and destroyed its ontological consistency.

While they are having sex, Peter repeatedly tells Alice, "I want you, I want you." After a few minutes, Alice gets up, says to Peter, "You'll never have me," and walks into the nearby cabin. As she enters the cabin, Peter transforms back into Fred Madison. At the moment when Peter is about to "have" Alice, he loses her: the fantasy dissolves, and he falls back into his identity before the fantasy. This transformation reveals, as Slavoj Žižek notes, "that the fantasmatic way out was a false exit, that in all imaginable/possible universes, failure is what awaits us."[26] Getting too close to "having" the fantasy object triggers the dissolution of the fantasy. Peter can only "have" Alice insofar as he doesn't, insofar as Mr. Eddy's prohibition bars him from completely enjoying her himself. This is a crucial scene in the film because it reveals so clearly the limitations of fantasy. Though it appears to promise us direct access to the object, fantasy always fails to achieve this access. The moment at which we would actually enjoy the object directly in the fantasy, the object gets up and walks away, and the fantasy structure itself dissolves. Fantasy requires some distance if it is to remain pleasurable and stable.

The Compulsion to Repeat

After the dissolution of the fantasy, Fred once again encounters the Mystery Man as he goes in the cabin to look for Alice. Fred inquires about Alice to the Mystery Man, but the Mystery Man refuses to recognize Alice's existence. As a superegoic force, he demands all of Fred's enjoyment for himself, not even allowing him the small ration of enjoyment the fantasy provides him in compensation for his sacrifice of desire. The Mystery Man tells Fred, "There is no Alice. Her name is Renee. If she told you her name was Alice, she was lying." After forcing Fred to acknowledge the nonexistence of the fantasy object (an object of enjoyment), the Mystery Man begins to question Fred and to pursue him with a video camera. He asks, "And your name? What the fuck is your name?" In chasing Fred with a camera and demanding that he pronounce his name, the Mystery Man attempts to compel Fred to fully reject fantasy for the social reality, a reality in which one's name indicates one's place.

Once Fred takes up this place, it signals a successful internalization of the law and installation of the superego as the internal agency of the law. It also signals the disappearance of all enjoyment, even the enjoyment attached to the fantasy. The presence of this enjoyment blocks the identification with the father, which installs the superego within the psyche because it sustains the father as an external barrier to the enjoyment of the fantasy object. Only with the dissolution of the fantasy can the internalization of the father as superego fully take place.[27]

After the fantasy has dissolved and Fred has accepted his symbolic mandate, he is able to kill the father (Mr. Eddy) with the help of the Mystery Man because the father is, at this point, but a remnant of the fantasy. After Fred has internalized the paternal authority, the Mystery Man can shoot Mr. Eddy in the head because external authority is no longer necessary to control Fred's behavior; he has thoroughly introjected this authority now in the form of the superego. When the Mystery Man shoots Mr. Eddy, the bearer of the law, we see an enactment of what Lacan describes in *Seminar I*: "The super-ego is at one and the same time the law and its destruction."[28] The superego is the completion of the father's function and thus renders the father unnecessary. Not only is the father unnecessary, but he also offers a potential for subversion that the superego doesn't. As an external authority, it is far easier to transgress the father's authority than that of the superego. When the authority of the external father becomes unnecessary and the authority of the superego becomes firmly entrenched, we can be sure that the subject (Fred, in this case) has completely given up his desire, sacrificed it to the law. In making this sacrifice, Fred gains access to the father's secret, the secret of the law, and this secret is what the Mystery Man whispers into Fred's ear after he kills Mr. Eddy.

What is the law's secret? That the law is nothing but its secret, that the father never really was alive with enjoyment, except in the fantasy of the son. This becomes evident when the Mystery Man, just prior to shooting him, presents Mr. Eddy with a video screen that displays the latter in his obscene enjoyment. What we see on the screen, however, is not Mr. Eddy enjoying himself, but him watching other people enjoy. The father, the master of enjoyment, turns out to be capable only of watching others enjoy, not enjoying himself. In this sense, the fact that Mr. Eddy is a pornographer makes perfect sense. While we may imagine—i.e., fantasize—that the pornographer is constantly awash in enjoyment, he is actually constantly awash in the enjoyment of others, an enjoyment that he merely observes. The Mystery Man lets Fred know that the Father has never held the secret of enjoying women, as Fred had previously supposed, and that Mr. Eddy is an impotent pretender. As Lacan puts it in *Seminar VII*, "If for us God is dead, it is because he always has been dead, and that's what Freud says. He has never been the father except in the mythology of the son."[29] In other words, Mr. Eddy's enjoyment, his vitality, only existed within Fred's fantasy, insofar as Fred supposed its existence. Fred can now know this secret of the law because he has already sacrificed his object, and, having made this sacrifice, he represents no threat to this law. It is thus only after having sacrificed our enjoyment to the law that we learn this is a sacrifice made in vain.

In practice, of course, such a completely successful interpellation— even if only temporary, as in this case—never actually occurs. That is, we never get to the point where we no longer require the external representative of the law. It occurs in *Lost Highway* because the film holds social reality and fantasy separate. Except for Lynch's excessively normal perspective, the process of accepting one's symbolic mandate never works in a pure form, completely unaccompanied by fantasy. Fantasy doesn't completely dissolve, but continues to function as a supplement to this process. Because wholly accepting one's symbolic mandate requires a forfeiting of one's enjoyment, it tends to arouse discontent, as we see in the case of Fred. At the moment of submission to the law— the moment of the superego's complete introjection—Fred should be a perfectly docile subject. He is bereft of even imaginary, substitute enjoyment. Instead of being docile, however, Fred responds with a renewed effort to subvert the power of the law. Without the supplemental, substitute enjoyment which fantasy provides, part of the control that the law has over Fred evaporates. We thus see the way in which the imaginary enjoyment that fantasy provides assists in the process of creating contented, docile subjects. This becomes apparent in *Lost Highway* as we see what happens when fantasy is absent.

At this point, Fred thinks that if he can communicate the secret of the law to himself prior to the sacrifice of his desire, then he will be able to act upon his recognition. In depicting Fred in an attempt to communicate with himself, Lynch is again separating what we usually experience as something seamless. Fred exists here at two different moments:

one after his successful integration into the social order and one prior to it. The latter moment is, in actuality, inaccessible to us, though we constantly imagine that we are accessing it. This is why the film shows Fred as he drives home and tells himself through the intercom of his house, "Dick Laurent is dead"—thereby repeating the opening scene of the film (but this time from outside the house). In telling himself that "Dick Laurent is dead," Fred is trying to make clear to himself that the father (Dick Laurent/Mr. Eddy) who he supposes to be enjoying women is already dead. If he could communicate this, he would save himself the sacrifice of the object to a dead authority. But the communication misses the mark. Rather than allaying Fred's suspicions that someone else is enjoying Renee, this remark made through the intercom actually serves to multiply them (if not to trigger them itself)—again launching Fred on the path we have just witnessed for the last two hours.

The Fred Madison who knows the truth flees down the lost highway after informing his counterpart about Dick Laurent's death, and as the film ends, he begins to have another breakdown, another flight into a new fantasy. The shot of Fred's breakdown ends the film, and it indicates that the cycle we have seen will play itself out again and again. He can escape into fantasy, but it will never provide the relief it promises.

By bringing the film around again to the place where it begins, Lynch reveals that the relationship between desire and fantasy is underwritten by certain constancy. We alternate between the experience of desire and that of fantasy: fantasy succeeds where desire fails. Desire keeps the object out of reach, and fantasy offers us access to it. But what *Lost Highway* shows is that in the last instance there is no difference between success and failure: even when we construct a scenario that allows us to have the impossible object, we cannot possess the key that renders the object enjoyable. Having the impossible object embodying the ultimate enjoyment shows us the extent to which we really don't have it. The speculative identity of our social reality and our private fantasies becomes apparent through the failure immanent in success. Both social reality and private fantasies circulate around a fundamental impossibility, though they figure this impossibility in opposing modes. As we alternate between them, we continue to endure the impossibility of the object.

Of all Lynch's films, *Lost Highway* seems to have the most critical attitude toward fantasy. The fantasmatic escape becomes an avenue through which the subject returns to the social reality it escaped; fantasmatic success becomes identical with failure. But these qualifications of fantasy's power should not be seen as part of an indictment of fantasy as such. An absolute commitment to fantasy is, even in *Lost Highway*, the controlling force in Lynch's filmmaking. It is only the commitment to fantasy that reveals the absence of an alternative and the failure inherent in every success. Paradoxically, without the turn to fantasy, we would remain duped by the alternative possibility that fantasy promises and appears to provide. The turn to fantasy illustrates for us the identity of where we're escaping from and where we're escaping to, and by seeing their speculative identity, we can transform our relationship to the ruling symbolic structure. We can stop contenting ourselves with fantasizing an alternative world and instead work to reveal this alternative world that is already in our midst.[30]

EIGHT The Ethics of Fantasizing in *The Straight Story*

An Absolute Commitment to Fantasy

In 1999, Lynch, a director known for images of extreme violence and explicit sexuality, and David Mamet, a director known for witty, profanity-laced dialogue, made films that received G ratings from the Motion Picture Association of America. On this level alone, Lynch's *The Straight Story* and Mamet's *The Winslow Boy* represented dramatic departures for each director. It almost seems as if they made these films in order to confound audiences and critics. The irony of the G rating (uncommon for any mainstream adult release) for a Lynch or Mamet film created the kind of shock that both aimed to produce within their films when one simply saw an advertisement for them. Lynch became acquainted with the script for *The Straight Story* through cowriter Mary Sweeney, his longtime romantic partner and editor, and part of its appeal for him was perhaps the incongruity of the story and the expectations surrounding his name.

Most viewers of Lynch's films regard *The Straight Story* as an exceptional film.[1] It seems to stick out among Lynch's films because, as the title suggests, it lacks the weirdness and the formal eccentricities that one expects from these films. Even the narrative, which recounts the trek undertaken by Alvin Straight (Richard Farnsworth) on a lawnmower to reach his estranged brother, is straightforward, in direct contrast to Lynch's previous film *Lost Highway*, which has the most complex narrative structure of any of Lynch's films. The mise-en-scène, the editing, the shot composition, the sound—all these elements lack Lynch's usual excessiveness. *The Straight Story* seems almost entirely free from the fantasmatic distortion that characterizes a Lynch film and provides an arena for the exploration of the hidden underside of contemporary society.[2]

But what appears to be an absence of fantasmatic distortion in *The Straight Story* is misleading. The deception results from the nature of the fantasy it presents—the American heartland as a site of authentic community—and the extent to which we cannot see the film as fantasmatic indicates the extent of our investment in the fantasy that it presents. The exaggerated purity of the American heartland in the film is an index of the film's fantasmatic distortion, indicating that this distortion is fully at work in *The Straight Story*. The film's central character commits himself to the logic of fantasy in a way that no character in another Lynch film does. Alvin Straight constructs a fantasy whereby he can travel by himself hundreds of miles, despite a disability that prevents him from driving, and reunite with his estranged brother Lyle (Harry Dean Stanton). Alvin never deviates from his effort to realize this fantasy despite the trauma attached to it, and his commitment has a direct effect on the structure of the film.

The point is not that we must take the title of *The Straight Story* ironically and view the film through this lens. As Nicholas Rombes points out, the temptation to interpret Lynch's films as ironic reflects our own cultural immersion in irony as spectators rather than anything about the films themselves. He claims, "Lynch's films were among the first to move beyond postmodernism's ironic, parodic appropriation of historical genres and narrative conventions, and . . . to this day readings of Lynch as 'ironic' persist because irony has become the dominant form of reading in a culture that recognises narrative (historical, political or otherwise) as mere performance."[3] The urge to interpret Lynch ironically reaches a peak with *The Straight Story* because the alternative seems to require agreeing with fierce Lynch critic Jeff Johnson's assessment that "Lynch's vision of America in *The Straight Story* [is] even more mythical than the Republican National Committee's."[4] If we interpret the film as ironic, we can at least imagine some distance between the filmmaker of *Blue Velvet* and this vision. The ironic interpretation also inserts distance between the spectator and the screen, protecting us from what we see there. We thus appear to be stuck, as are many critics of Lynch, between an ironic reading and a reading that dismisses Lynch as a thoroughly reactionary filmmaker.

There is a difference, however, between the myths of the Republican National Committee and the filmic fantasy that David Lynch constructs in *The Straight Story*. Though neither the title nor the film is ironic, it is avowedly—and this is what Johnson misses as a viewer of *The Straight Story* and of every Lynch film—fantasmatic. This means that the film encourages us to view the world that it depicts as a world of fantasy. It does this in the way that Lynch's films typically do—by creating a divide between a world of desire and absence and a contrasting world of fantasy. What Johnson calls the "absurd realism" of the fantasy world does not reinforce but reveals the fantasmatic status of the typical myths of the American heartland.[5] Lynch presents his mythical image of the heartland not as reality but as the result of an extreme fantasmatic distortion.

This does not mean that Lynch aims to deconstruct these American myths in order to destroy their ideological effectiveness. *The Straight Story* neither affirms nor undermines the image of America it proffers. Instead, the film illustrates precisely what it would take to construct such a mythical world. One can have the mythical America, but one must create it through adopting the proper attitude toward fantasy.

The appropriateness of the title of *The Straight Story* stems from Lynch's belief that one arrives at the straight through fantasmatic distortion. That is to say, we construct our reality through a fantasy structure that strips away the mystery inhering in our quotidian experience. Fantasy fills in the gaps of our daily lives and thereby secures our feeling that this experience is "real." Without fantasy, our reality would be bizarre, mysterious, and ultimately incoherent—precisely akin to the world of desire in a Lynch film. In this sense, it is entirely appropriate that Lynch's most authentically fantasmatic film bears the title *The Straight Story*.

Material Lack

Unlike Lynch's other films, the distinction between the world of desire and the world of fantasy does not manifest itself as much on the level of film form as through the situation of the main character Alvin Straight. Though the first thirty minutes of the film work to establish an attitude of desire through mise-en-scène and editing, more importantly it focuses on Alvin as a disabled, lacking subject.[6] Lynch establishes a world of desire through his initial depiction of Alvin's infirmity and his inability to care for himself. Each scene in the beginning of the film highlights this inability and reveals it as irremediable. From these scenes, it is clear that the only possible solution for Alvin will be a fantasmatic one.

After establishing shots of a field and a small town main street, the narrative of the film commences with a scene that reveals Alvin as a figure of lack and emphasizes the role of absence in this filmic world. We see a shot of a white house with a woman sunbathing in the yard next to the house. After the woman gets up and walks into the house next door, we hear a thud emanate from the white house. The woman returns to her lawn chair having missed the sound and resumes sunbathing. A friend comes looking for Alvin, and we find out that the sound was Alvin falling—and he is still lying prone on the floor.

Lynch introduces the protagonist only on the film's audio track as a thud, visually present in the scene as an absence. Even the sound of his fall remains unheard within the diegesis because the neighbor goes into her house at the exact time of the fall. In addition, the type of sound— the thud of him falling to the floor—that marks Alvin's debut in the film bespeaks his incapacity. Not only is he unable to walk even with the aid of his cane, but he can't manage to signal for assistance when he does fall. When Alvin's friend Bud (Joseph A. Carpenter) finally enters the house and sees Alvin helpless on the floor, we see Bud, the next-door neighbor Dorothy (Jane Galloway), and Alvin's daughter Rose (Sissy Spacek) having a discussion while Alvin remains on the floor. The extended time that Alvin lies on the floor *after* someone has found him renders this helpless position even more conspicuous than it otherwise would be.

Immediately after this scene, we see Bud driving Alvin to the doctor. The very fact that Alvin requires someone to drive him attests to his lack of independence, but the way that Bud drives him underlines this point. We see Bud, Alvin, and Rose in Bud's old car just as they are about to arrive at the doctor. Bud is driving slower than the average person might walk, and when he finally stops the car, he races the engine in neutral. Not only is Alvin unable to care for himself, he must rely on others who can barely care for themselves.

His pathos lies in the gap between his actual situation as a subject and how he represents himself to others. Outside the doctor's office he stubbornly resists going to see the doctor (Dan Flannery) and once inside categorically rejects tests, X-rays, and a walker. We have already seen Alvin incapacitated, and this defiance seems more comic than heroic: by professing his strength and independence, he highlights his near-total dependence on the Other for both physical aid and symbolic recognition. The doctor says, "If you don't make some changes quickly, there will be some serious consequences," but Alvin reports to Rose, "He said I was going to live to be a hundred." He is all the more the figure of lack insofar as he attempts to avoid facing the incontrovertible facts of his situation and replace those facts with a pose of self-assurance.[7]

The first part of the film emphasizes our lack as spectators as well because it emphasizes what we don't see rather than what we do. We experience the key scenes in this part indirectly: the primary action occurs outside the frame, and we hear it while seeing something else. As he often does, Lynch creates desire through a disjunction between the visual and audio tracks. By leaving the central action outside the frame, Lynch places the spectator in the place of the desiring subject and encourages us to recognize ourselves as lacking. Absence becomes present in our experience of the film. This occurs when Alvin falls at the beginning of the film, and it happens again when we learn about Lyle's stroke, the event that triggers Alvin's journey.

The scene begins with a shot of Alvin and Rose sitting in the house looking out a window at night during a storm. We see the storm here indirectly, through the expressions on the faces of Alvin and Rose, as well as through the flashes of lightning that briefly illuminate the room. As they look out the window, the phone rings in the kitchen, and the film cuts to Rose walking to answer it. During the telephone conversation that she has, however, we return to a visual of Alvin looking out at the storm, as we hear Rose talking in the background. Because we only hear Rose's side of the conversation, the amount of information we receive is limited. She says, "Hello . . . this is . . . Rose . . . yeah . . . yeah . . . Oh no . . . Uncle Lyle . . . When? . . . OK . . . I'll tell him . . . yeah . . . OK . . . bye, bye." Her stutter has the effect of making this cryptic conversation even more so, but it is apparent that something has happened to Uncle Lyle. When she returns to Alvin, Rose tells him, "That was Bobby . . . Uncle Lyle had a . . . a stroke." Just as Rose says this, a flash of lightning brightens the room, and a clap of thunder sounds.

The delay between apprehending that an important event has occurred and learning what this event is characterizes a world of desire. For the desiring subject the object never appears exactly where—or when—the subject anticipates it. This disconnect between the subject and its object has the effect of constituting an object as *the* object. The privileged object is the privileged object insofar as we arrive too soon or too late to apprehend it.

Perhaps the scene that draws the clearest contrast between the opening world of desire and the world of fantasy in *The Straight Story* is one with no relation to Alvin's journey. When we see it initially, it seems to be nothing but a moment of Lynch's typical weirdness, a moment without any narrative importance. After Alvin learns of his brother's condition, we see a shot of Rose talking on the phone at night while looking out the kitchen window. Lynch cuts from a shot of Rose looking to a shot of what she sees out the window: a ball rolls into the frame, and a boy runs to pick it up and stands with it in the middle of the frame. After seeing the boy, we see Rose again looking out the window contemplatively. Viewing the film for the first time, one can have no idea why Rose is looking at the boy in the way that she is or why Lynch includes this scene in the film. In this world, the spectator experiences her/himself in a state of non-knowledge, attempting to decipher the desire of the Other (that is, the film itself) that informs the inclusion of the scene. The world of fantasy, in contrast, fills these gaps and provides the spectator with a sense of knowing the whole story.

Near the beginning of Alvin's fantasmatic journey, we learn the background of this mysterious scene. Alvin tells runaway teen Crystal (Anastasia Webb), whom he befriends, the story of Rose's children. Because of a fire that badly burned one of Rose's four children while Rose had left them with a babysitter and because of her mental disability, the state took custody of all her children. Hearing this account of Rose's history allows us to revisit the seemingly nonsensical scene of the boy picking up his ball and to understand the meaning that this image held for Rose. But as spectators we penetrate the mystery of the scene only after we have entered the world of fantasy. By establishing this contrast between an initial experience of non-knowledge and a later experience of full knowledge, Lynch affirms in a way that he often does the distinction between the world of desire and the world of fantasy. This distinction holds not just for Alvin as a character within the filmic diegesis but also for us as spectators relating to the film as a work of art.

Narrating What Isn't There

What *The Straight Story* makes clear is that fantasy appeals not because it solves our desire but because it explains what desire leaves inexplicable. This becomes apparent when we consider how the world of fantasy allows us to understand the earlier scene where Rose stares out the window at the boy holding a ball. Most fundamentally, fantasy serves as a mode of understanding. The turn from a world of desire to a world of fantasy is not a turn from the lack of the impossible object to the full presence of this object. Fantasy places the lack in a narrative context that renders it sensible. Once we turn to fantasy, we cease to be haunted by a nonsensical lack and begin to confront one that we can understand. Lack loses its ontological character and acquires a meaning.

Alvin's fantasy does not return him to his youth or reunite him with an impossible love, and in this sense perhaps it is a less ambitious fantasy than we usually find in a Lynch film. However, it does allow him to accomplish a task that appears impossible from within his symbolic coordinates. Everyone within the filmic reality dismisses the possibility of Alvin's traveling hundreds of miles on a lawnmower to see his brother. His friends mock him for even considering it, and his daughter Rose lists all the factors (his disability, the distance, and so on) that make the trip impossible.[8] Even Tom (Everett McGill), the salesperson who sells Alvin the mower that will take him on the journey and who expresses warm sympathy toward him, says that he has always thought of Alvin as an intelligent guy until he heard about this scheme. Not one other character in the film believes that Alvin has any chance of accomplishing what he sets out to do.

When the film turns from the world of desire to the world of fantasy, we do not see a radical change in mise-en-scène as we do in *Lost Highway* and Alvin does not appear as a different actor in order to accomplish the impossible. We do, however, see some significant changes on the level of film form as Lynch introduces the fantasy world. The beginning of the fantasy occasions a change in music as Angelo Badala-menti's "Alvin's Theme" begins to play. The camera tracks slowly along the middle of a road looking straight down on the middle line and then pans over to Alvin's mower driving down the side of the road. After a pan to the road stretching out in the distance, the camera tilts to the blue sky and finally back to Alvin's mower. This series of pans leads to a sequence of sweeping helicopter shots of the Iowa fields, including one showing a combine harvesting crops. This introduction to the fantasy world emphasizes its grandeur and beauty. Whereas relatively small sets characterized the world of desire (Alvin's house, the interior of the general store, the main street of the small town), Lynch establishes the setting in the world of fantasy as vast open space replete with possibility. The use of long panning shots, which begin with Alvin's trip, helps to create this sense of openness as well. This shift in the film's form suggests that the turn to fantasy allows Alvin to transcend the limitations that were so conspicuous in the beginning of the film.

The expansive external world might serve to emphasize Alvin's smallness and the hopelessness of his task, but Lynch visualizes no disjunction between Alvin and the environment during his trip. As Joe Kember notes, "Representation in *The Straight Story* persists in this acquiescence and subordination to the environment. Aerial shots travel across harvest scenes, and subjective shots reproduce Straight's progress across the country."9 The landscape during the journey clearly holds a place for Alvin as a presence where the limited world of his hometown of Laurens accommodated him primarily as an absence.

The most important changes occur within Alvin himself. While in the midst of accomplishing the impossible within this fantasy, Alvin undergoes a complete transformation. Though he remains disabled and now requires two canes just to walk, he ceases to be a pathetic figure when he enters the world of fantasy. He becomes a hero struggling to accomplish the impossible and offers wise advice to a young runaway, befriends numerous people during the trip, and is able, for the first time, to confess his guilt about a friendly-fire incident that occurred during World War II to a fellow veteran.

The new image of independence is perpetuated by his systematic refusals of assistance: he won't sleep in the Riordans' house or accept a ride for the rest of the trip, for example. He even leaves money under the phone for a long distance call that he makes at the Riordans' house.

When his mower breaks down, he has Rose send him his social security check in order to pay for the repairs, and when the Olsen twins (Kevin Farley and John Farley) fix it, he bargains with them for a better price. Though he remains old, age no longer incapacitates him but actually ennobles him, providing the wisdom and experience that other characters lack. Though we don't witness any external transformation in Alvin between the beginning of the film and his journey, he nonetheless becomes a totally different kind of subject when he enters the fantasy world of the journey.

But this transformation doesn't occur all at once. Initially, Alvin's fantasy includes a failure, as the first mower that Alvin uses to attempt the journey breaks down after only a few miles. If the beginning of Alvin's trip to see his brother represents the film's turn to fantasy, the inclusion of the initial failure of the trip seems strange. The failure of Alvin's first effort to reach his brother reveals the nature of his attitude toward the impossible task he faces. He is willing to endure whatever humiliation he encounters because his focus is on the impossible task, not on the Other watching him. He embodies the full commitment to one's fantasy.

When the first mower breaks down, Lynch shows Alvin having just left his hometown of Laurens. A large truck passes and creates such an extreme gust of wind that it blows the hat off his head. He stops the mower to retrieve his hat, and when he returns, the mower will not start. This sequence draws attention to Alvin's castration in a way similar to what we saw in the world of desire. The image of the powerful truck contrasts with the weakness of Alvin, who can't even keep his hat on in the face of the truck's might. Unlike in the world of desire, however, the fantasy offers Alvin a way of overcoming this weakness.

After Alvin returns to Laurens, humiliated, with his mower on the back of a truck, he approaches Tom, the John Deere salesperson, about purchasing another mower. This transaction affirms Alvin's position within the fantasy because it affords him a privileged status. Tom treats Alvin differently than his other customers, offering Alvin his own personal mower, which, despite being made in 1966, remains "a good machine." Not only does Alvin receive special treatment, but Tom and Alvin's conversation about the mower also affirms the value of old machines, provided that their owners have maintained them. This claim functions metaphorically as an affirmation of Alvin's potency: in the fantasy world, he resembles the sturdy old mower, not the frail old man from the first part of the film.

The fantasmatic trip does not simply allow Alvin to become independent and to overcome the weakness he displayed in the world of desire. It continues the image of him as a weakened, lacking subject, but within the fantasy he has the capacity to fill this lack. Lynch does not just divide the film between the world of desire and the world of fantasy; he also divides the filmic fantasy itself between Alvin's experiences of lack and his experiences of overcoming it. The former occurs primarily while Alvin travels on the road—as, for instance, when his first mower breaks down—and he finds respite at the various points where he stops his journey. The fantasy thus establishes a narrative movement from traumatic experience on the road to the mitigation of this trauma at the stopping points. The fantasy stages trauma only in order to solve it, whereas the world of desire provides no such solution.

This dynamic occurs when hundreds of cyclists race past Alvin on the road. When the first cyclist passes him, we see a look of shock on Alvin's face, as he jerks the mower to the side in fear, and the many cyclists that follow draw attention to Alvin's slow pace as they speed past. The juxtaposition between the speed of the cyclists and Alvin's lack of speed visibly depresses him, and he once again experiences his castration. But that night Alvin stops at the campsite, where the cyclists engage him in conversation. At the end of the conversation, one of the cyclists asks, "What's the worst part about being old?" Alvin responds, "The worst part about being old is remembering when you were young." This statement has a fantasmatic quality to it because it gives Alvin the last word with the young cyclists, and this last word places the cyclists on the same plane as Alvin. Lynch introduces a cut immediately after Alvin says this, making it literally the last word in the scene. The cyclists are not able to reply, and in fact, no reply seems thinkable. The fantasy structure permits Alvin's revenge on the cyclists for their vitality. We recognize—as the cyclists do themselves—that their youth and agility is fleeting and that they too will soon become old and incapacitated.

A similar act occurs soon after the encounter with the cyclists. A woman speeds past Alvin in her car, but just after she disappears from the frame, we hear a horn honking and tires screeching. A close-up of Alvin's face reveals a horrified look as he sees the woman hit a deer. Before she drives off weeping in her damaged car, the woman tells him, "I have hit thirteen deer in seven weeks driving down this road . . . and I love deer." In the subsequent scene, we see Alvin cooking the deer for dinner, and later he places the antlers on top of his trailer as a kind of trophy.

The narrative trajectory from trauma to triumph reaches its high point when Alvin's mower breaks down toward the end of his journey. Heading down a steep hill, the belt on Alvin's mower breaks, leaving him with no way to slow the mower as it speeds down the incline. Though the mower finally comes to a stop at the bottom of the hill, the incident scares Alvin and displays one more time his powerlessness. Lynch captures Alvin's feeling of terror with close-ups of a panicked look on his face and close-ups of his hands frantically trying to stop the mower.

After this scare, Alvin meets a community of people that welcomes him and embraces him as a hero in a way that we did not see in Laurens. When Alvin loses control of his mower, five residents of the town of Clermont—Danny Riordan (James Cada), Darla Riordan (Sally Wingert), Johnny Johnson (Jim Haun), and Janet Johnson (Barbara Kingsley), and Verlyn Heller (Wiley Harker)—are sitting on lawn chairs watching the local firefighters practice extinguishing a fire on an old abandoned house. This exercise—and the fact that it has the status of a spectator event—reveals the dull nature of life in Clermont. Alvin's arrival injects vitality into this community, and everyone here treats Alvin with a great deal of respect. Whereas the people of Laurens saw the journey as a sign of Alvin's foolishness, the residents of Clermont show reverence for Alvin and the magnitude of his undertaking, despite their misgivings about it. The trauma that occurs when Alvin loses control of his mower leads to the discovery of this community where he can find support and respect. This is how Alvin's turn to fantasy provides a narrative for his experience of trauma. It doesn't remove the trauma of his experience of incapacity—in fact, it augments it—but it does reveal trauma as part of a narrative that has a successful conclusion.

Fantasy and Humiliation

Alvin's fantasy does not simply provide a way for him to narrate and navigate his infirmity; it also demands that he expose himself to the Other and especially to his estranged brother Lyle. This is the ethical dimension of fantasy: when we fantasize, we open ourselves to an experience of humiliation because we value our own private enjoyment over our concern for the Other's recognition. Fantasy has this ethical dimension because of the paradoxical attitude that fantasizing subjects adopt toward the Other. They retreat from the Other into private worlds when they fantasize, but this disregard for the Other also creates an unintended openness. Even as fantasy disguises our subjection to the Other and creates an illusion of independence, it facilitates an encounter with the traumatic real insofar as it manifests the innermost part of our subjectivity externally. In the midst of fantasy, we risk experiencing our subjectivity without its support in the Other, without all the narratives of identity that provide us with a sense of self. We become nothing but our mode of obtaining enjoyment. The real kernel of the fantasy is the moment at which we fully identify with the impossible object and completely externalize our subjectivity.

When one is completely absorbed in fantasy, one experiences one's supreme vulnerability to the look of the Other, and nothing is more humiliating than being seen in the middle of fantasizing.[10] To respond to this look and accommodate the Other, the subject would necessarily have to abandon the private fantasy for the sake of public recognition. The humiliation of the Other's look leaves the subject with a choice: remain within the fantasy and endure the Other's look or retreat from the fantasy and seek the Other's recognition. By traveling hundreds of miles on a lawnmower to see his brother Lyle, Alvin exposes himself to frequent ridicule. His effort seems both impossible and ridiculous, and even those most sympathetic to Alvin find the idea of traveling by lawnmower absurd. But while Alvin is in the midst of this fantasmatic journey, he must simply endure the Other's look and the feelings of shame that it engenders.

When Alvin talks with Crystal, the runaway teen, one night on the side of the road, we see directly the humiliation that he must endure. She looks at his mower and trailer and says, "What a hunk of junk." Instead of answering with an explanation that might validate himself in her eyes or by countering her claim, Alvin simply says, "Eat your dinner, missy." Any other response would be an attempt to preserve or explain his actions in a manner that accommodates him to the Other. Even rejoining with an insult or a self-deprecating statement would be in furtherance of insinuating himself into the Other's expectations. Alvin's response evinces the recognition that an integral part of fantasy is the humiliation that it brings. He must remain committed to the logic of the fantasy and not turn back to the Other in order to avoid this humiliation.

The humiliation in the face of the Other reaches its high point at the end of the fantasy when Alvin arrives at his brother's house. The aim of the fantasy is reconciliation with his brother. As Alvin tells the priest (John Lordan) whom he meets just before arriving at Lyle's, "I want to make peace, look up at the stars like we used to do so long ago." In order to accomplish this, however, Alvin must abandon his pride and approach his brother despite the argument that separated them years earlier. When he arrives at Lyle's house, Alvin places himself in a position of supreme vulnerability. Despite all his effort during the journey, he has no idea whether Lyle will accept or reject his gesture of reconciliation.

The vulnerability that Alvin must endure here explains what occurs when he finally turns down the road where Lyle lives. After turning onto this road, Alvin's mower stalls, and it seems as if he won't be able to complete his journey despite coming within a few hundred yards. A series of dissolves depicting Alvin waiting on his mower give the impression that he waits for several hours until a man driving a large tractor arrives. After speaking with this man, Alvin tries to start his mower again, and it starts, allowing him to drive the rest of the way. Lynch includes this scene not simply to add suspense to a film otherwise bereft of it, but to show Alvin's reluctance to experience the humiliation of meeting his brother. Alvin could have tried to start his mower long before the tractor arrived, but he didn't because he was wary of continuing.

Alvin does continue to Lyle's door, and instead of rejecting him, Lyle weeps at the enormity of Alvin's act. This ending marks the successful conclusion to Alvin's fantasy, and the film's concluding shot—a tilt up to the night sky full of stars—reveals that he has obtained exactly what he claimed to want (looking up at the stars together with his brother one more time). But this conclusion does not represent the real kernel of the fantasmatic experience. That occurs at the moment when Alvin stands outside Lyle's house and yells for his brother, exposing himself completely to possible humiliation. To fantasize is always to expose oneself to the Other through the act of externalizing one's innermost subjectivity. It is Alvin's embrace of this experience that transforms him into an ethical figure, and his ethical act does not remain isolated but changes his world.[11]

What renders the ethical dimension of fantasy visible in Alvin's case is his willingness to immerse himself fully in his fantasy. All subjects fantasize, but most of us use fantasy as a private enclave, a retreat that succors us in light of the disappointments we experience. We make sure that our fantasies don't intrude too far into our public lives. This serves as self-protection, but at the same time, it works to eliminate fantasy's ethical possibilities. But through the character of Alvin, Lynch demonstrates that a different attitude toward fantasy is possible. We might devote ourselves entirely to our fantasmatic project and publicly insist on our private fantasy.[12] In doing so, we simultaneously shatter the limitations that formerly governed us and, at the same time, open ourselves to the Other.

Private Fantasy as Public Ethic

The Straight Story is a film replete with beauty—the physical beauty of Iowa fields and the moral beauty of the American small town. In both cases, we see this beauty not because it actually exists but because, as viewers of the film, we are looking through the lens of Alvin's fantasy. Alvin's total commitment to this fantasy distorts our vision in such a way that we see a beautiful world surrounding him. Lynch demonstrates the way that private fantasy can have an effect on the public world.

Our private fantasies tend to cause us to see an evil or corrupt public world that is the result of someone else—or some force—perverting the public world by realizing there a private fantasy. Hegel calls this attitude the law of the heart. The subject embodying the law of the heart has a private vision about what is best for the public world and sees only a corruption of that vision in what actually exists. As Hegel describes it, such a subject "speaks of the universal order as a perversion of the law of the heart and its happiness, a perversion invented by fanatical priests, gluttonous despots and their minions, who compensate themselves for their own degradation by degrading and oppressing others, a perversion which has led to the nameless misery of deluded humanity."[13] In short, the law of the heart is a paranoid view of the public world, and this paranoia stems from the subject's belief in its own purity. Corruption is rampant, but the subject bears no responsibility.

The Straight Story, in contrast, sees no evidence of corruption in the public world. It is an anti-paranoia film. This is because Alvin is free of worries about the excessive enjoyment of others. Alvin is so committed to his own fantasy, to his own way of organizing enjoyment, that he doesn't envy the enjoyment of others. He sees a nonviolent and welcoming world where most contemporary subjects see threats and menace.

Our view of the other as embodying excessive enjoyment is always *our* view: it tells us much more about our own subjectivity than it does about how much others are really enjoying.[14] The enjoyment of others bothers us—we perceive it as excessive—when we have given up on our own enjoyment. The image of excessively enjoying others is an attempt to kick-start our own enjoyment, to regain the experience that we feel ourselves to have lost. We enjoy through others as we allow the enjoyment of others to bother us. The envy that we experience is itself a mode of enjoying, which we can see in the fascist's exaggerated response to the image of the enjoying minority.

The problem with this mode of enjoying is that it fails to recognize itself as such. The envious subject feels itself deprived of enjoyment rather than ensconced in it—always on the outside of enjoyment rather than within it. To this subject, the enjoyment of others does not appear simply as something that others have and the subject itself does not, but as something others have at the subject's expense. The image of the enjoying other bothers someone precisely because she/he experiences this enjoyment as an indication of her/his own failure to enjoy. If one is enjoying, one passes over the enjoyment of others without finding it disturbing. This is what the envious subject, the subject who obsesses about enjoyment of others, is unable to do.

The Straight Story shows Alvin avoiding any tendency toward envy through his commitment to his own fantasmatic enjoyment. No film in Lynch's career has engaged in social commentary without appearing to as much as this one. He seduces us into viewing *The Straight Story* as the touching narrative of an individual triumphing over adversity (as in thousands of Hollywood films), but what he really authors is a critique of contemporary American paranoia. The target is not the corruption and violence that plagues the society; instead, it is the position that sees and condemns this violence from the perspective of its own insulated superiority.

In order to best understand the relationship between private fantasy and the public world in *The Straight Story*, we must contrast it with Lynch's other road film, *Wild at Heart*. On the one hand, they seem like radically different films, perhaps more different than any two Lynch films. *Wild at Heart* contains more graphic violence, sex, profanity, and criminality than any of his other films, and *The Straight Story* is his only G-rated film. Their only common trait seems to be the genre (the road film) to which they belong. On the other hand, there are fundamental thematic similarities. Both films concern, in a way that no other Lynch films do, the relationship between the subject's commitment to fantasy and the external world that the subject encounters. Like *Lost Highway* and *Mulholland Drive*, these films are companion pieces, each showing subjects taking up an opposite attitude toward fantasy.

Given the excessiveness of *Wild at Heart*, it would seem that this film depicts a fuller investment in fantasy than *The Straight Story*. But as we have seen in our investigation of *Wild at Heart*, this is not the case. The extreme depiction of the external world in *Wild at Heart* is the result of a failure to be fantasmatic enough, a failure to sustain an investment in fantasy. The relatively tame and habitable public world depicted in *The Straight Story* results from Alvin's complete commitment to his fantasy. By committing himself to his fantasy, Alvin alters the way that he perceives and interacts with the external world, and this has the effect of changing it.

Neither film attempts to represent contemporary society as it really is. Both view this society from the perspective of the fantasy structure of the main characters. Sailor and Lula's failure to invest fully in their fantasy produces a threatening external world of chaos and violence. Alvin Straight's complete investment in his fantasy creates a world in which people treat each other with kindness, respect, and fairness. The external public world becomes ideal *because* we see it through the lens of Alvin's fantasy. The strength of his commitment to his fantasy leaves him indifferent to this world and to its perception of him, and this alone transforms its very nature.

At no time during his journey does Alvin experience a threat among those he encounters, nor does he worry about what most of us would think about when making such a journey. When Alvin stops at the Riordans' house, Darla Riordan asks Alvin about the dangers of the road. Alvin tells her that he finds nothing at all frightening about traveling on the open road, especially in light of facing the Germans in World War II. We would expect this type of response from Alvin, given his actions during the journey itself. He never locks his trailer, uses any security devices, or tries to protect himself or his belongings in any manner at all. Because he experiences the Other from the perspective of his fantasy, he simply cannot envision a threat there.[15]

It would be too simple to say that Alvin sees a welcoming world because he expects to see such a world. Expectations alone would not be enough. Alvin experiences the world as fundamentally nonthreatening—he escapes the paranoia that is rampant in contemporary American society—because he finds enjoyment within his fantasy and insists on following this fantasy despite the difficulties it brings. Through the figure of Alvin, Lynch suggests that our paranoia about violent others out to steal our enjoyment is the result of a collective failure to commit ourselves fully to our own fantasmatic enjoyment. If we did so, we would no longer feel the need to protect ourselves from the dangerous other.

In *The Straight Story*, Lynch depicts an America that is indeed, to return to Jeff Johnson's attack, more mythical than the Republican National Committee's version. But Lynch also reveals this mythical America as mythical—as the product of a turn to fantasy. In addition, he shows the price that one must pay for an America where others cease to be threatening. One must, like Alvin Straight, fully invest oneself in the logic of fantasy and follow this logic to the encounter with the traumatic real. In doing so, one must place oneself entirely at risk. This is the political dimension of Lynch's film: no Republican National Committee member would accept the risk that Lynch shows the mythical America requires. In the act of creating it, one finds the innermost core of one's subjectivity externalized for others to see and to mock. It is only the ability to experience this type of humiliation that allows the subject to enjoy in the real and thus to overcome the idea that a hidden enemy threatens or has stolen the subject's enjoyment. Only the authentically enjoying subject can avoid the paranoia rampant today and become an exemplar of contemporary ethics.

NINE Navigating *Mulholland Drive*, David Lynch's Panegyric to Hollywood

Beginning with Sense

When officials at ABC forced Lynch and cocreator Mark Frost to solve the mystery of Laura Palmer's murder in the middle of the second season of *Twin Peaks*, in Lynch's mind they effectively killed the show. This, along with other mistreatment, drove Lynch to swear off working in television. But he broke this vow after making *The Straight Story* (1999) and created the pilot for *Mulholland Drive*, a new series for ABC. The show met a fate worse than that of *Twin Peaks*: network executives hated the first cut they saw of the pilot and never aired it, even as a cut-down television movie. But French company Canal+ stepped in to buy the pilot and allowed Lynch to reshoot and edit the footage into a feature film.[1] Despite this strange production history, the structure of the film seems almost to suggest that Lynch imagined it from the beginning as a counterpoint to *Lost Highway* (1997).

Almost everyone who sees *Mulholland Drive* (2001) notes that the first part of the film makes a good deal of sense for a David Lynch film. In contrast to the beginning of *Twin Peaks: Fire Walk with Me* (1992) or *Lost Highway*, this film opens with a relatively straightforward, if idiosyncratic, narrative. A woman emerges from a car crash without any memory, and while hiding out in an apartment she has snuck into, she meets another woman who helps her in the quest to discover her identity. While they are together, the two fall in love. This, in brief, represents the narrative trajectory of the first part of the film, and though there are bizarre accompaniments to this trajectory, the basic narrative itself makes sense. It seems to belie entirely Stanley Kauffmann's claim, in his discussion of the film's opening, that "sense is not the point: the responses are the point."[2] While one might be tempted to agree with Kauffmann concerning the film's conclusion, its opening definitely has a high degree of coherence. Yet it also has a fantasmatic aura about it that serves to undermine this coherence and to give some credence to Kauffmann's contention that Lynch means the first part of the film to be more evocative than sensible. By combining sense with the texture of fantasy, Lynch uses the first part of *Mulholland Drive* to explore the role that fantasy has in rendering our experience coherent and meaningful.

The narrative coherence of the opening section becomes especially pronounced when we contrast it with what follows. The second part of the film is structured around the incessant dissatisfaction of desire: it denies Diane (Naomi Watts) and the spectator any experience of Camilla (Laura Harring), her love object—and it emphasizes this failure visually. The first part of the film, in contrast, produces a scenario in which Diane, appearing as Betty, can enjoy the object. As we've seen in other Lynch films, this separation between the experience of desire and that of fantasy accounts for—and is accomplished by—dramatic changes in mise-en-scène, editing, and the overall character of the shots between the first and second parts of the film.

While the first part of the film is not without strange characters and events (such as the hired killer's humorously botched murder), the mise-en-scène conforms on the whole to the conventions of the typical Hollywood film: scenes are well-lit, conversations between characters flow without awkwardness, and even the plainest décor seems to sparkle. The editing here also tends to follow the classical Hollywood style, sustaining the spectator's sense of spatial and temporal orientation. However, in the second part of the film, the lighting becomes much darker, almost every conversation includes long and uncomfortable pauses, and the sets become drab, lacking the ubiquitous brightness of those in the first part of the film. The editing also undergoes a radical shift. For example, just after Diane emerges from her fantasy (and enters the world of desire), she appears to speak to Camilla Rhodes (Laura Harring). Lynch shoots Diane speaking, followed by a reverse shot of Camilla. But after another brief shot of Diane, the subsequent reverse shot depicts Diane again, occupying the position where we had just seen Camilla. This kind of disruption of the shot/reverse-shot sequence (which does not occur in the first part of the film) indicates on the level of the editing that these worlds—the worlds of fantasy and desire—are ontologically distinct.

As we contrast the first part of the film with the second, it quickly becomes evident that the first seems more real, more in keeping with our expectations concerning reality. But this sense of reality results from the film's fantasmatic dimension rather than its realism. Where we usually contrast fantasy with reality, *Mulholland Drive* underlines the link between the two, depicting fantasy's role in providing reality with the structure that it has. The film supports Lacan's claim that "everything we are allowed to approach by way of reality remains rooted in fantasy."[3] As a category, fantasy should not be opposed to reality because it is fantasy that sustains what we experience as reality. But even this idea—that fantasy supports our sense of reality—is evident in *Lost Highway* and earlier Lynch films.

Mulholland Drive represents an advance on *Lost Highway* because it emphasizes not only that fantasy offers a solution to the deadlock of desire but also that fantasy provides a way of staging an encounter with trauma and an authentic experience of loss that would be impossible without it. The film celebrates the fantasmatic dimension of Hollywood—its commitment to the exploration of fantasy. Because of their formal similarities, one cannot come to terms with *Mulholland Drive* without looking at it in light of *Lost Highway*. The two are companion films: *Lost Highway* explores the structure of fantasy and desire for male subjectivity, and *Mulholland Drive* does so for female subjectivity. One might even claim that *Mulholland Drive* is a feminist version of *Lost Highway*.[4]

The Mystery of Desire?

If *Mulholland Drive* in fact consists of separate worlds of desire and fantasy, it would seem that the opening part of the film represents the former since it focuses on the mystery of Rita's (Laura Harring) identity. Desire involves the confrontation with a fundamental uncertainty concerning the Other's desire—and thus is consonant with a sense of mystery. The film begins with the credit sequence that superimposes the image of Betty (Naomi Watts) over an ongoing jitterbug contest, but following this initial scene, Lynch establishes an aura of mystery that seems to be in keeping with the attitude of desire. After a brief shot of a blanket covering someone lying on a bed and a red pillow, we see a close-up of the "Mulholland Dr." street sign (which also stands in as the film's title card) and a black limousine driving Rita up Mulholland Drive. The limousine suddenly stops, prompting Rita to proclaim, "What are you doing? We don't stop here." The driver doesn't answer her question but points a gun at her and says, "Get out of the car." Just after he says this, however, a car drag-racing in the other direction on the road crashes into the limousine. The crash kills the driver and injures Rita's head, producing the amnesia that will affect her throughout the first part of the film.

This scene certainly appears to create a sense of mystery and the fundamental uncertainty that we associate with desire. It produces desire in a manner very typical of Hollywood narrative with its use of darkness and threatening characters in the mise-en-scène, ominous music, and an editing sequence that merely hints at what is really transpiring. The film does nothing extraordinary but employs without irony the narratives codes of Hollywood (and especially of film noir) concerning the production of desire. As Hollywood understands well, desire always involves not knowing, being confronted with a question that doesn't have an answer. The desiring subject confronts a mysterious, enigmatic object, an object that is never isolatable as *the* object.[5] As Lacan points out about desire in *Seminar X*, "as long as I desire, I know nothing of what I desire."[6] To portray desire, a film must create a scene that situates spectators in a position of non-knowledge, and this is exactly what the opening of *Mulholland Drive* does. It does this first of all through the mise-en-scène—the near-total darkness of the setting, the isolation of the mountain road, and so on. In addition, the film employs Angelo Badalamenti's low, haunting music to contribute to the pervasive sense of a mystery. The action of the scene also works to keep us in the attitude of questioning: we see the limousine driving up a dark mountain road and have no idea where it's going. When the driver stops the limousine, the spectator is in the same position as Rita: we don't know why he has stopped, or why he pulls a gun. This moment foregrounds the essential question of desire—"What do you want?" Like Rita, the spectator has no idea what the driver wants, and it is the non-knowledge of this desire that triggers the subject's desire. By placing the spectator in the same position as the desiring subject on the screen—and by immersing both in total uncertainty—Lynch seems to set up the first part of *Mulholland Drive* as a world of desire.

This becomes even more apparent after the car crash that turns Rita into an amnesiac. Following this event, she wanders the streets of Los Angeles, uncertain about where she might go or even who she is. Again the film places the spectator in the same position as Rita—without a foundation on which one might make sense of Rita's situation or her identity. Rita's uncertainty about her own identity is at the same time uncertainty about the desire of the Other: not knowing who one is results from not knowing who one is for the Other. At this point in the film, Rita has lost any sense of where she exists relative to the Other. This complete uncertainty about what the Other wants from her places Rita even more directly in the position of desiring subjectivity. As Bruce Fink points out, the enigma of the Other's desire is unbearable for the subject, which is why the subject necessarily has recourse to fantasies about what the Other wants. He says,

> Rather than anxiously waiting to find out what you are, you may well prefer to jump to conclusions (precipitate answers) about what the Other wants of you, with you, from you, and so on. The unknown nature of the Other's desire is unbearable here; you prefer to assign it an attribute, any attribute, rather than let it remain an enigma. You prefer to tie it down, give it a name, and put an end to its angst-inducing uncertainty. Once it is named, once you conclude that *this* is what the Other wants of you—to stay out of the way, for instance—the angst abates.[7]

One eliminates the anxiety that the enigma of the Other's desire produces by fantasizing a resolution to that enigma, and this is exactly what *Mulholland Drive* indicates that Rita does. After she wanders the streets, Lynch shows Rita falling asleep on the ground outside an apartment complex, and the next morning she wakes up to a world that has become far less mysterious.

If Rita falls asleep tormented by the mystery of the Other's desire, she awakens into a world that is much friendlier. In the apartment complex, a woman is conveniently leaving her apartment for an extended trip, and Rita procures a place to stay by sneaking into the apartment. Betty, the niece of this woman, arrives in Los Angeles as a fledgling actress. Though Betty discovers Rita in the apartment and realizes that Rita doesn't even know her aunt, she befriends Rita and assists her in the quest to discover her identity. These events clearly seem to indicate that the film has entered the terrain of Rita's fantasy: the open apartment and Betty's arrival function as wish fulfillments for Rita as a desiring subject. Lynch even underlines the fantasmatic status of Betty in the way that he shoots her arrival in Los Angeles. As Betty walks through the Los Angeles airport terminal, the scene is brightly lit, and soft, comforting music plays in the background. We see a shot of Betty's smiling face, and then a reverse shot of a "Welcome to Los Angeles" sign. An old couple that Betty has presumably met on the flight accompanies her through the terminal and wishes her well as she enters a taxi. As she says good-bye to the couple, we see her looking down at her suddenly missing bags, fearing that someone has stolen them. The shot of Betty looking down—and exclaiming "My bags!"—also builds in the spectator a sense that someone has taken advantage of Betty's naïveté about the big city. In the next instant, a reverse shot shows a cabbie placing her bags in the trunk of his cab and asking her, "Where to?" This is not a Los Angeles where thieves steal the bags of unsuspecting visitors from the country but one in which everyone is eager to help. It is, as Betty says to Rita later, a "dream place." But it is Betty herself who occupies the central position in the fantasy, as she seemingly enters the film in order to help Rita solve the enigma of desire.

Throughout the first part of the film, Betty assists Rita in tracking down the details of the accident that triggered her amnesia and in following up on the memory fragments that come to her. All of Betty's efforts to help Rita—and her eventual declaration of love—suggest that she is nothing but a fantasy object for Rita, a way for Rita to put a stop to the anxiety of her own desire. But as the second part of the film unfolds, it becomes apparent that the entire first part of the film has *not* been structured around Rita's desire but rather around a fantasmatic resolution of the desire of Diane Selwyn (who is also played by Naomi Watts). Whereas it initially seems that Betty arrives as a fantasy figure for Rita, helping her to solve the enigma of her desire, the second part of the film reveals that, in fact, Rita has all along played the central role in the elaboration of Diane's fantasy and Betty is actually Diane's own ideal ego in this fantasy. As a mysterious, unknown object, Rita provides a way for Diane/Betty to escape her unbearable desire.

The fantasy relation between Betty and Rita is a reimagining of Diane's failed relation—which we see only in the second part of the film—with the movie star Camilla Rhodes (who is also played by Laura Harring). Though we usually associate mysteriousness and uncertainty with the difficulty of desire, the enigma of Rita is far more bearable for Diane than the impossibility that haunts her relationship with Camilla. Diane's fantasy transforms Camilla Rhodes, the impossible object, into Rita, the mysterious object. This transformation offers Diane an escape from the impossibility of the object-cause of desire.

This impossible object is what sticks out and cannot be smoothly integrated into the subject's world. It is, as Lacan points out, "the object that cannot be swallowed, as it were, which remains stuck in the gullet of the signifier."[8] The desiring subject must recognize the impossibility of integrating this impossible object, but a sense of mystery obscures and provides respite from desire's constitutive impossibility. This is why Diane turns from Camilla Rhodes to Rita. As Lynch shows, fantasy doesn't just resolve the mystery of desire, it creates a sense of mystery as well in order to obscure the necessary deadlock that animates all desire. With Camilla, Diane desires, and yet she knows that this desire must remain dissatisfied. Unlike Camilla, Rita offers Diane (as Betty) a mystery that she can solve; she is *not* an object that remains always out of reach, despite her enigmatic status.

By initially setting up Rita and the first part of *Mulholland Drive* as exemplary of desiring subjectivity and later revealing this as itself part of a fantasmatic scenario, Lynch creates a more complex and expansive idea of fantasy than in his earlier films. Desire confronts an impossibility, and by transforming impossibility into mystery or uncertainty, fantasy renders the impossible possible. Bruce Fink is right to claim that "the encounter with the Other's desire is anxiety producing,"[9] but what produces anxiety is not the enigma of the Other's desire; instead, the subject feels anxiety because she grasps the impossibility of this desire—that there can be no answer to the question that it asks, not that the subject simply doesn't know this answer.

Mulholland Drive leads us (through the use of mise-en-scène and editing) toward the error of seeing Rita as a figure of desire not simply to toy with our expectations but to reveal the extent to which fantasy determines our experience. It not only provides answers to our questions about our identity, but it even produces the questions themselves. The film reveals that the province of fantasy extends much further—and its power is much greater—than even Lynch's previous films had envisioned.

Fantasized Temporality

If all Lynch's films split into worlds of desire and fantasy, *Mulholland Drive* represents a major step forward in how we might conceive of the dynamics of this split. *Mulholland Drive* radicalizes the split beyond a film like *Lost Highway* because it creates a world of desire that is far less coherent and thus displays more emphatically the role that fantasy plays in rendering our experience meaningful. The world of desire in *Mulholland Drive* (the second part of the film) lacks even a sense of temporality. Events occur in this world in a random order, without a clear narrative logic. At the beginning of this part of the film, Diane's former roommate (and, it seems, lover) retrieves her belongings, including an ashtray shaped like a miniature piano, from Diane's apartment. But in a subsequent scene, the piano ashtray reappears on the coffee table, as if the roommate had not yet removed it even though we know that she had. The same thing happens with a blue key. It is lying on the coffee table as the second part of the film begins and then disappears until the end of the film, when Diane again sees it on the coffee table. The disappearance and reappearance of these objects does not indicate anything magical at work, but simply that this part of the film operates according to the atemporal logic of desire. There is no chronology in the world of pure desire because desire does not move forward; instead, it circulates around the impossible object—in this case, the impossible enjoyment in Camilla Rhodes that Diane Selwyn longs for and yet cannot access.[10] As a world of desire, the second part of the film moves according to the compulsion to repeat rather than according to the dictates of time.

In contrast, the first part of the film—the elaboration of Diane's fantasy—operates according to a standard temporal logic. Events occur in a chronological order and follow the laws of causality. This is precisely the opposite of what we might expect: we are accustomed to thinking of fantasy as an imaginative flight that allows us to violate the various exigencies—including, perhaps especially, that of temporality—that constrain our experience of reality. But the film reveals here the role that fantasy plays in constructing our sense of temporality. Though classical Hollywood films also rely on the power of fantasy to construct a sense of temporality, they take pains not to reveal this in the way that *Mulholland Drive* does. The classical Hollywood film hides fantasy's role in producing temporality by not depicting any moments bereft of fantasy—no moments of desire as such, in which neither fantasy nor temporality operates. In *Mulholland Drive*, on the other hand, we see Diane's experience of pure desire in the second part of the film. As a subject of desire without any fantasmatic supplement, Diane experiences only the repetition of the drive. As Betty, the fantasy figure who allows Diane to escape this repetition, she experiences temporality. The point here is that we do not employ fantasy to escape from the horrors of time, but that we employ fantasy to construct time as a respite from the horrors of repetition.[11] As Slavoj Žižek notes, "fantasy is the primordial form of *narrative*, [. . . and] *narrative as such* emerges in order to resolve some fundamental antagonism by rearranging its terms into a temporal succession. It is thus the very form of narrative which bears witness to some repressed antagonism."[12] By providing a narrative and temporal structure through which we can have experiences, fantasy delivers us from the timeless repetition of the drive.

Fantasy provides not just temporality, but it also constantly works to fill in the gaps that populate the fragmentary experience of desire. Without fantasy, our experience would lack a sense of coherence, just like the latter section of Lynch's film. This role of fantasy becomes apparent in the way that the first part of the film takes fragments of experience from the second part and elaborates on them. Such a process is crucial to the subject's ability to make sense of a situation: we understand and discover meaning because fantasy provides the background for our fragmentary experience. By filling in gaps, fantasy helps us to produce a seamless experience of the world. At film director Adam Kesher's (Justin Theroux) party in the second part of the film, Diane hears Adam's brief account of his recent breakup with his wife. She overhears him saying, "So I got the pool, and she got the pool man."

This sentence presumably provides all the information that Diane has about the breakup. It exists for her—and for us as spectators—as just a fragment of sense, a fragment unconnected to any coherent narrative of the relationship between Adam and his wife. But in the first part of the film, we have already seen the events that Adam's statement alludes to. Diane creates a fantasmatic scenario surrounding this fragment of knowledge that renders it completely sensible.

In the first part of the film, Diane's fantasy produces the background for Adam's statement about the "pool man." After losing his film for refusing to bow to mob pressure and hire Camilla Rhodes for the female lead, Adam returns to his home and finds his wife Lorraine in bed with the pool man. Rather than evincing guilt for her infidelity, from the moment Adam sees her Lorraine begins berating Adam for coming home at the wrong time. She says, "Now you've done it," and she asks of him, "What the hell are you even doing here?" Adam says nothing, but proceeds to douse her jewelry box (and the jewelry in it) with pink paint, which occasions a fight between Adam, Lorraine, and the pool man. Finally, Adam leaves, covered in pink paint and with a bloody nose. In light of this scene, we have a context through which to understand Adam's statement about his wife and the pool man in the second part of the film. But it is, I contend, only the elaboration of Diane's fantasy that has produced this narrative context. The fantasy takes up a fragmentary piece of experience and provides it with a coherent past that explains its emergence in the present. In this way, fantasy offers subjects respite from the incoherence that plagues their experience.

Diane's Wish Fulfillment

Not only does fantasy fill in the gaps of our experience, but it also—even more importantly—delivers us from the dissatisfaction constitutive of our status as desiring subjects. In the second part of *Mulholland Drive*, which depicts a world of desire without fantasy to supplement it, Diane feels desire's perpetual lack: she longs for Camilla Rhodes but cannot have her; she wants a career as an actress but struggles with bit parts; and she sees the opulent lifestyle of Hollywood's elites but lives in relative squalor. As we watch the second part of the film, we see the originary, dissatisfying form of the events of Diane's life, events that the first part of the film completely transformed. This occurs most obviously in the relationship between Diane and Camilla Rhodes, which becomes the relationship between Betty and Rita in Diane's fantasy.

Despite Diane's desire for Camilla Rhodes, she must constantly endure Camilla's open displays of affection with Adam Kesher and with other women as well. Camilla flaunts her enjoyment in front of Diane, but always in such a way that leaves Diane out of it. What's more, Camilla seems purposefully to stage her enjoyment for Diane, in order to sustain Diane's desire. This becomes apparent when we see Diane, whom Camilla has invited, on the set of a film that Adam is shooting with Camilla. At one point in the shoot, Adam clears the set so that he may demonstrate—privately—how he wants an actor to kiss Camilla. But Camilla asks Diane to stay while everyone else leaves the set, and as Adam passionately kisses her, she looks at Diane, who is the sole audience for this kiss. Lynch emphasizes Camilla's concern with Diane seeing her enjoyment by showing her looking at Diane during Adam's kiss. It is as if Camilla invites Diane to stay on the set and kisses Adam solely to arouse Diane's desire. Immediately before this scene, the film shows Camilla and Diane together in Diane's apartment, lying naked on the couch. As they begin to kiss, Camilla stops, and what she says makes clear the position into which she pushes Diane. She tells Diane, "You drive me wild. We shouldn't do this anymore." Camilla lures Diane toward her at the same time that she keeps Diane at a distance. Just at the moment Diane feels that she is close to Camilla's elusive enjoyment, Camilla withdraws it and bars access to it. After Diane responds, "It's him, isn't it?," Lynch immediately cuts to the scene on the film set where Diane witnesses Camilla and Adam kissing, which again forces Diane to experience her own failure to enjoy. Throughout the second part of the film, Diane remains within the deadlock of desire: she cannot attain the elusive enjoyment that her object seems to embody, and she cannot cast the object aside and begin to look elsewhere.

But when Camilla becomes Rita she is no longer inaccessible. In Diane's fantasy, Betty and Rita not only become lovers, but Betty is also able to come to Rita's rescue. Envisioning oneself as the rescuer of one's love object is, of course, the ultimate fantasy scenario; the rescue wins the love of the love object by proving that the subject deserves this love. This is what we see in the case of Betty and Rita. In the world of desire, Camilla Rhodes occupies a position of desire relative to Diane. But when Betty discovers her, Rita has no idea who she is, not even her name, and adopts the name "Rita" from a *Gilda* movie poster.[13] She is completely helpless, stripped of her mastery by Diane's fantasy. The attractiveness of fantasy stems from this ability to deliver the goods—to provide the subject with a narrative in which she can access the inaccessible object-cause of desire.

In creating access to this object, the fantasy structure removes and repositions the obstacles that block Diane's access to Camilla in the world of desire. Film director Adam Kesher, because of his romantic involvement with Camilla, represents a direct obstacle in Diane's path to Camilla. As a result, Diane's fantasy strips Adam of his position of power and forces him to succumb to various rituals of humiliation. Not only does he find his wife in bed with the pool man, but he also finds himself stripped of his film by the mob. When he tries to hide from the mob (specifically, the Castigliane brothers) at a downtown hotel, he learns that their reach extends everywhere, as Cookie, the proprietor, tells him: "Whoever you're hiding from, they know where you are." The mob has also stripped Adam of all his money. Cookie tells him, "You're maxed out at your bank, and your line of credit has been cancelled." When Adam receives this information, we see him all alone in a dingy downtown Los Angeles hotel. Lynch uses this setting to indicate further the depths to which Adam has fallen: he has lost everything, and now he exists in the midst of urban squalor rather than the luxury of the Hollywood hills (where we see him living in the second part of the film). In addition, Adam spends most of the first part of the film with pink paint splattered over his expensive black jacket. The paint constantly reminds us—and Adam himself—of his humiliation in finding his wife in bed with the pool man. Adam does recover his former station but only after he capitulates to the demand of the Castigliane brothers and hires Camilla Rhodes to star in his film. Thus, the fantasy transforms Adam from a figure of mastery into a victim and a pawn. It both punishes him for standing in the way of Diane's access to Camilla Rhodes and removes him as an obstacle. Through Adam's transformation, Lynch reveals the power of fantasy to clear the way to the object.

Through the turn to fantasy, Adam's situation changes dramatically, but his basic personality remains intact. In the case of Coco (Ann Miller), the fantasy demonstrates even more its transformative power as not just her situation but her personality undergoes a complete change. In the world of desire, Coco is Adam's mother, and in Diane's only interaction with her, she upbraids Diane in a harsh maternal tone for being late to Adam and Camilla's party. In Diane's fantasy, Coco remains a maternal figure, but she becomes wholly benevolent—an ego ideal, seeing Betty in the way that Betty wants to be seen. Coco is no longer Adam's mother, but the apartment manager where Betty's aunt has an apartment. When Betty arrives at the apartment complex for the first time, Coco greets her with hyperbolic warmth. She smiles and says, "Ten bucks says you're Betty." Coco's first words to Betty indicate the extreme transformation from her incarnation as Adam's mother in the world of desire. There, her first words to Betty are a rebuke; in the fantasy world, Coco's first words cheer Betty and let her know that she has a place in this world. Later, as she shows the aunt's apartment to Betty, Coco offers to acquaint Betty with her neighbors. She tells Betty, "If you'd like, later on, I'll introduce you around." When Betty doesn't respond right away, Coco adds, "Well, no hard feelings if you don't." Coco accommodates her completely, welcoming her to her new environment but at the same time giving Betty her own space. The fantasy produces her as the perfect maternal figure.

We can also understand the first part of the film as a fantasmatic response to the second part if we compare the look of Diane and Betty. Naomi Watts plays both characters, which initially suggests that they represent different versions of the same person. But the characters differ to such an extent that it almost appears as if a different actor is playing each part. When we first see Betty in the Los Angeles airport, not only does the film show her bathed in light, but it also shows her colorfully and attractively dressed. She wears a blue shirt, red sweater, and black pants. This outfit looks stylish, and it combines with Betty's smiling demeanor and bright blue eyes to indicate her cheery hopefulness. When he introduces Diane, Lynch stresses the contrast. We first see Diane in her underlit, cheap apartment, where she is dressed in a bathrobe. Diane's disheveled, dirty hair also contrasts with Betty's, which looks freshly styled and perfect. And whereas Betty constantly smiles and seems eager to meet the world, Diane is morose and seems defeated by life. The contrast reveals that Betty offers Diane a way of seeing herself as she wants to be seen.

Though Betty first appears as a naïve, hopeful ingénue from Deep River, Ontario, her character actually ranges widely. The extreme variations in Betty's subjectivity confirm her status as Diane's fantasmatic ideal ego. This becomes apparent when she arrives at a studio for an audition.[14] Up to this point, Betty exhibits the attractive innocence of a new arrival in Los Angeles, someone eager to make her way as an actor. But in the audition, the actor she works with, Woody Katz (Chad Everett), wants to play the scene not as it is written, but in a way that will provide him some sexual stimulation. Lynch lets us know this by showing Betty practice with Rita prior to the audition; we see Betty performing the scene well (and as written). Despite the fact that the words are the same, it almost seems as if Woody is performing an entirely different scene. Rather than rebuff Woody for distorting and sexualizing the scene, Betty follows his lead and even ratchets up the degree of sexualization: Lynch uses a close-up of Betty moving Woody's hand onto her buttocks to show this. Here, Betty completely defies the naïveté she exhibited until this point, showing herself to be a sexually experienced being. As a fantasmatic figure, she accomplishes the impossible: she is innocent, yet sexual; she is naïve, yet aware of how the world works; she is hopeful, yet not easily duped. In short, Betty occupies subject positions that are contradictory and mutually exclusive. This is only possible because she represents a fantasized version of Diane. The distortion of the fantasy allows Betty to be all things—the perfect ideal ego for Diane.

The fantasmatic distortion is most extreme in the case of Camilla Rhodes. This is because she represents the fantasy's nodal point; she contains the impossible object. As such, the fantasy separates the name "Camilla Rhodes" from her body in an effort to distinguish between the pathological, undesirable part of her and what is in her more than her, the *objet petit a*. The *objet petit a* is the remainder that the process of signification leaves behind, and as such, it always escapes the province of the signifier (and the name). In the fantasy, the name "Camilla Rhodes" comes to signify corruption and undeserved success. We first see this name attached to a picture that two members of the mob, the Castigliane brothers, show Adam Kesher. They insist that Adam cast this woman in his film, telling him repeatedly, "This is the girl." Through this gesture, the fantasy accomplishes a double move: it tarnishes the acting success of the actual Camilla Rhodes by suggesting that mob influence procured her big break, allowing her to overstep more talented actors, and it impugns the unnamed woman whom Diane sees kissing Camilla Rhodes at a party (because she is the woman in the mobster's photograph identified as "Camilla Rhodes"). At the same time, the actor who plays Camilla Rhodes in the second part of the film, Laura Harring, appears in the first part in an entirely different guise, as "Rita." As Rita, the desirable part of Camilla Rhodes—embodied by the actor Harring herself—persists in the fantasy, minus the undesirable part of her now linked to the other Camilla Rhodes. Lynch uses the same actor to play Camilla Rhodes in the second part of the film and Rita in the first part, but changes the name in order to illustrate fantasy's attempt to deliver the impossible object in a pure form, free of any pathological taint.

The first part of *Mulholland Drive*, the fantasy world, enacts a nearly complete transformation of the different aspects of Diane's life. It takes the dreariness and the dissatisfaction of that life and remakes it in a fully developed narrative. The fantasy replaces the dissatisfaction of desire with images of enjoyment. Subjects flee into fantasy precisely because it seems to cure the dissatisfaction that they cannot otherwise escape. As we have seen, fantasy works to cover over the many sources of discontent that plague the subject, but it saves the abundance of its power for producing an image of the successful sexual relationship. Through both parts of the film, Lynch shows that the failure of this relationship is the primary impetus for the turn from desire to fantasy.

The Successful Sexual Relationship

The essential quality of fantasy is not simply its ability to deliver wish fulfillment. Its fundamental function consists in its ability to address desire on the most important level, its ability to figure (the illusion of) a successful sexual relationship. According to Lacan, the sexual relationship—or more precisely, the failure of it—represents the primary stumbling block in human relations, a stumbling block that results from our insertion into language. As he puts it, "no relationship gets constituted between the sexes in the case of speaking beings."[15] "There is no sexual relationship" because the categories of male and female indicate a structural impasse: each position is structured in such a way that it looks for what the other does not have, not for what it has. The desires of the sexes are thus not complementary. This dooms the relation between the sexes to be antagonistic, and it dooms both sexes to a continual battle to overcome this antagonism. The only way out of this antagonism involves a turn to fantasy, though fantasy can only overcome it in an imaginary way. Fantasy allows the subject to discover, through creating a narrative around it, a way of creating the illusion that the sexual relation is possible. While the world of desire in *Mulholland Drive* stresses the failure of the sexual relation, the film's depiction of fantasy shows how the subject tries to overcome that failure. But an emphasis on this function of fantasy does not begin, in Lynch's body of work, with *Mulholland Drive*; it is also perhaps the salient feature of *Lost Highway*, and it again indicates the link between these two films.

Lost Highway depicts the failure of the sexual relation through Fred Madison (Bill Pullman) and his wife Renee (Patricia Arquette). Despite Fred's many efforts to approach Renee's enjoyment in the first part of that film, this enjoyment continually eludes him, leaving him haunted by his own failure to enjoy and by his failure to relate successfully to Renee. But as the fantasmatic figure of Peter Dayton (Balthazar Getty), Fred is able to construct a narrative in which he can enjoy Alice (also played by Patricia Arquette), a fantasized version of Renee. On the terrain of fantasy, within the narrative that it constructs, the impossible sexual relationship becomes possible. This is what leads Slavoj Žižek to insist that "fantasy is ultimately always the fantasy of a successful sexual relationship."[16] Fantasy allows the subject to bypass the structural impasse that constitutes the failed sexual relationship because it simply ignores the restrictions of the symbolic order. In fantasy, the law of non-contradiction no longer holds. For instance, the love object can occupy two contradictory positions simultaneously: it can be both out of the subject's reach, and the subject can have it, at the same time. In this way, fantasy makes the impossible possible. *Lost Highway* illustrates this operation of fantasy as it depicts Fred's attempt to compensate for the failure of the sexual relationship between Fred and Renee. *Mulholland Drive*, however, pushes the failure of the sexual relationship and its fantasmatic resolution one step further.

The impossibility of the sexual relation manifests not just between male and female, but between two women. In the second part of the film, Lynch depicts Diane Selwyn's failed sexual relation with Camilla Rhodes. The fantasmatic first part of the film represents Diane's effort to narrate a terrain on which this relation would succeed—and it is clear that the fantasy works: in the first part of *Mulholland Drive*, Betty and Rita (the fantasmatic counterparts of Diane and Camilla) manage a successful sexual relationship. By showing that the sexual relationship fails (and requires a fantasmatic supplement) even in the case of lesbian lovers, the film is not enforcing heteronormativity, reducing the lesbian relationship to the model of the heterosexual one. Instead, it evinces a refusal to romanticize the lesbian relationship or to imagine that such a relation escapes the exigencies of the subject's insertion into language.[17] No matter what its makeup, no sexual relation can succeed, and thus every such relation, out of the inevitability of its failure, spurs the subject in the direction of a fantasmatic resolution.[18]

If the fundamental role of fantasy consists in producing the image of a successful sexual relation, this also represents the site of fantasy's primary danger. By convincing the subject that the sexual relation can succeed, fantasy obscures the antagonism that haunts the functioning of the symbolic order. Covered over by the veil of fantasy, the symbolic order seems to operate without a hitch. It is at this point that one can see the political problems that the turn to fantasy produces. When subjects immerse themselves in fantasy, they blind themselves to the contradictions of the prevailing ideology. Lynch's films do not ignore this dimension of fantasy. *Mulholland Drive* illustrates repeatedly the way in which Diane's turn to fantasy obscures her position as a desiring subject. But for Lynch, fantasy's positive political possibilities—like its ability to take us to the point at which the ruling symbolic structure breaks down—are much more intriguing. The main emphasis in *Mulholland Drive* lies in this direction, in showing how fantasy might hold the key to experiences otherwise unthinkable.

Going All the Way in Fantasy

If *Mulholland Drive* is a critique of the fantasizing that we usually associate with Hollywood (and I would contend it is not), then it is not the usual indictment. Where most critics reprimand Hollywood for its excessive commitment to fantasy (at the cost of verisimilitude), Lynch takes Hollywood to task not for going too far in the direction of fantasy, but for not going far enough. Fantasy allows us to experience the real because it makes evident a place at which the symbolic order breaks down. As Lacan points out, "There is no other entrance for the subject into the real than the fantasy."[19] This becomes especially clear in *Mulholland Drive* as a result of the strict separation that Lynch establishes between the world of fantasy and the world of desire. Lynch uses film to create rigid boundaries, and their very rigidity allows us to see in relief what occurs at the point they come together. This structural logic manifests itself in *Mulholland Drive* as well. Because Lynch avoids blending together the levels of fantasy and desire, he is also able to join them together in a way that reveals the traumatic real that exists at their point of intersection. The intersection of fantasy and desire is always a point of trauma because it is a point at which signification breaks down. We construct fantasy to cover over a gap in the symbolic structure, a place where there is no signifier. Hence, the hinge that links fantasy to the symbolic structure (i.e., the world of desire) is the real, a traumatic moment that resists all symbolization.

The first time *Mulholland Drive* depicts the real of this intersection occurs when Betty and Rita investigate Diane Selwyn's apartment and discover Diane's dead body lying on her bed. Because they are within the fantasy and perceiving through its lens, they cannot recognize the body (nor can we as spectators). Nonetheless, the very narrative structure of the fantasy—its mystery story—leads them to the fantasy's point of origin, which is a traumatic point of non-sense that does not fit within the fantasy structure. After seeing the body, Betty and Rita quickly flee the apartment, and the film depicts their exit in a way that suggests that this encounter with the real has traumatized them and even thrown them out of joint. As we see them running out the front door of the apartment, the film not only uses slow motion, but it also blurs the image of both characters. We see several images of them on each frame, and consequently it looks as if Betty and Rita temporarily exist outside of themselves, as if the encounter with the real has disrupted their existence relative to time. The conventional filmic techniques—slow motion and multiply-exposed frames—here play a precise role within the narrative structure, suggesting a disruptive encounter with the real because of their place relative to the events of the narrative. But this disruption merely presages the more significant ones that follow the dissolution of Diane's fantasy.

Fantasy offers the possibility of such encounters with the real when we follow its logic to its end point, when we play out the fantasy completely. In this sense, as Lynch illustrates, fantasy holds the key to its own traversal because the logic of the fantasy itself pushes the subject to the point of its dissolution. As Alenka Zupančič puts it, "We cannot 'get beyond' the fantasy by giving up on the Cause that animates us but, on the contrary, only by insisting on it until the end."[20] The subject cannot escape fantasy simply by opting out of it. Attempting to do so places the subject all the more under fantasy's power because it allows fantasy to operate without any awareness. But when we commit ourselves to the fantasy without reserve, the radical potential of fantasy makes itself visible, as Lynch's film shows. Diane commits wholly to the fantasy of herself as Betty and follows it as far as embracing Rita's quest for the truth. On this quest, Betty even crawls through a window to enter Diane's locked apartment where she encounters Diane's dead body, even though she doesn't recognize it as such (and, in fact, the fantasy causes both Rita and Betty to misperceive the body and see in it a resemblance to Rita). Fully embracing her fantasy leads Betty/Diane right into the path of the real as it appears in the form of an encounter with her own dead body. As this scene suggests, *Mulholland Drive* is a panegyric to the existential and political possibilities of fantasy.

In the denouement of the fantasy, it becomes clear that *Mulholland Drive* offers us a specifically feminine structure to its fantasy, in contrast to *Lost Highway*, which employs a masculine structure. Because fantasy employs narrative, it cannot depict the successful sexual relationship as a static relation: we are either approaching it or in the process of losing it. In each of these positions, the fantasy allows us to encounter the trauma of the real in a unique way, a way indicative of either a male or a female fantasy structure. A male fantasy always comes up short; it approaches a successful sexual relation but never quite attains it. The enjoyment of a male fantasy remains a potential enjoyment, an experience never quite achieved. This is why at the moment Peter Dayton would finally connect with Alice in *Lost Highway*, Alice abruptly withdraws from the sex act and tells Peter, "You'll never have me." Peter approaches the experience of enjoyment through the fantasy structure, but he never quite arrives at it. The male fantasy holds back; it refuses to give itself over entirely to the object. A female fantasy, on the other hand, goes too far. It is a fantasy of giving oneself entirely to the love object. Thus, it does not stop short; the female fantasy depicts the achievement of the successful sexual relation.

In *Mulholland Drive*, Lynch shows Betty and Rita starting to kiss, and then, as they begin to have sex, Betty says to Rita repeatedly, "I'm in love with you." The sexual relation comes off. Afterwards, Lynch shoots them holding hands in their sleep, hinting at the bond that exists between them. But the fantasy cannot simply stop at this point. It exists within a temporal structure, and it moves forward with time. The film begins to illustrate the dilemma of the female fantasy. If male fantasy stops too quickly, female fantasy inevitably goes on too long. We experience the successful sexual relation, but also the inescapable loss that follows. In male fantasy and female fantasy, the relation to the real is fundamentally different. The male subject experiences the real as always futural while the female subject experiences it as past, an experience of loss.[21]

Lynch depicts this loss occurring just after we see the image of Betty and Rita holding hands in their sleep. Rita wakes Betty up in the middle of the night with her outbursts of the word "Silencio." Despite the late hour, she convinces Betty to go with her to Club Silencio. From the way that Lynch shoots their arrival, it is clear that at Club Silencio Betty and Rita are nearing the edge of the fantasy world. In a very long shot, we see them arrive in a cab, and as they enter the club, the camera tracks rapidly to the door of the club to enter along with them. This unusual positioning of the camera suggests that Club Silencio is dangerous (thus the camera keeps its distance) and yet alluring (which explains the fast track forward). Inside the club, Betty and Rita watch the emcee insist on the unreality of what they are about to see. He does this in a variety of languages, saying repeatedly "*No hay banda*—and yet we hear a band"; "It's all recorded"; "*Il n'y a pas d'orchestre*"; and "It is all on tape." By showing the emcee speaking in different languages, the film suggests the unimportance of the signifiers themselves relative to what they cannot capture—the absence of the impossible object. In many forms, the emcee repeatedly attests to this fundamental absence. When the emcee speaks, we see a man seeming to play a muted trumpet enter the stage. But the man moves the trumpet from his mouth, and the sound continues, indicating that, as the emcee says, "It is all on tape." The fantasy indicates overtly its central concern—the object in its absence rather than presence. This suggests that Betty and Rita have reached the end point of the fantasy, the point at which it will break down.

The film depicts this collapse occurring during a song. When the emcee leaves the stage, Rebekah Del Rio (playing herself) sings a Spanish version of Roy Orbison's song "Crying."[22] As with the emcee, the fact that she sings in Spanish indicates that the words here are not the heart of the matter: what is crucial instead is Del Rio's voice—the voice detached from her body as an object, the voice as the impossible object. Despite their knowledge that the song is not live, Betty and Rita find themselves caught up in it anyway, able to disavow this knowledge. They experience the enjoyment of the impossible object in the voice. The song moves Betty and Rita to tears because it communicates a sense of loss. Rebekah Del Rio is "crying" over the lost love object, over the lost sexual relationship, and this touches both Betty and Rita, as they feel the incipient loss of what they have experienced. This feeling of loss marks the inevitable conclusion of the female fantasy. When we experience the loss of the sexual relationship in fantasy as a result of following fantasy to its end point, we experience the loss of a relation that we have never had. Fantasy effects an identification with the lost object. As Juan-David Nasio points out, "we are, in the fantasy, that which we lose."[23] In this sense, fantasy allows us to mourn the lost object in a way that we could not do without fantasizing. Since the subject never actually has the "lost" object, the only experience of loss that the subject can have must occur through fantasy.[24] Hence, the only authentic mourning necessarily involves itself in the illusions of fantasy, which is what we see occurring at Club Silencio.

Ultimately, the subject cannot hold on to the experience of loss. Just as the male fantasy cannot sustain the moment immediately prior to the sexual relationship, the female fantasy cannot sustain the moment of its loss. The structure of fantasy breaks down when the subject confronts the total emptiness of the impossible object, which is what occurs as Rebekah Del Rio's song continues after she has fainted. At this point, the fantasy collapses: Betty—i.e., Diane—can no longer disavow the illusory nature of the experience because she confronts the pure, contentless impossible object. Betty looks down in her purse and sees a blue box, a box that represents the point of exit from the world of fantasy. When Betty and Rita return to the apartment, Rita retrieves the blue key that she had earlier found in her purse and that Betty had placed in a box in a closet. As Rita moves toward the closet, the camera follows her and leaves Betty out of the shot. But when Rita turns around from the closet and the shot should again include Betty, she isn't there. As Betty and Rita reach the point at which the fantasy world intersects the world of desire, Diane's representative in her fantasy can no longer continue to exist. After Rita uses the key to open the blue box, the camera moves into the opening in the top of the box and is subsumed by the darkness inside. The film forces us to experience briefly the void that exists between fantasy and desire, but quickly we are thrust into the world of desire in which the woman who owns this apartment—Betty's "aunt" in the fantasy—walks in the apartment by herself, with no trace of either Rita or Betty.

The camera's entry into the darkness of the blue box marks the point at which *Mulholland Drive* shifts worlds—leaving Diane's fantasy and entering a world of desire. Lynch shows Diane lying on her bed, and the shots alternate between an image of her dead body and an image of her sleeping body. At this point, the Cowboy (Monty Montgomery) walks past her bedroom and says to her, "Hey pretty girl, time to wake up." The Cowboy here represents another version of the Mystery Man (Robert Blake), who appears in *Lost Highway*. His appearance testifies once more to the link between the two films but also to a crucial difference. Like the Mystery Man, the Cowboy is on the one hand a figure of paternal authority, but on the other he is almost completely asexual. Both men have faces that look feminine, without any facial hair—even eyebrows. In addition, both have a small build and speak softly. This is especially noticeable in the case of the Cowboy (in part because of our expectations about cowboys). In *Lost Highway*, the Mystery Man functions as a superegoic presence for Fred Madison, an internal representative of the Law. He calls Fred to take up his position within the symbolic order. The Cowboy performs a similar function in *Mulholland Drive*: after the dissolution of Diane's fantasy, he pushes Diane in the direction of her symbolic position. Calling Diane back into the world of desire, the Cowboy enacts a superegoic function. But the film also reveals superfluity of the superego: he tells Diane to wake up *after* her fantasy has already broken down. Why? The presence of the Cowboy qua superego allows Diane to believe that her experience of the emptiness of the object was the result of the law's intervention rather than a revelation about the object itself. That is to say, the superegoic command—"wake up," in this case—preserves for the subject the idea that, but for this command, the sexual relationship might have succeeded.

The subject creates cowboys and mystery men in order to avoid recognizing the truth of the object.

While the superego provides an alibi for the failed sexual relation, it also pressures the subject to enjoy itself sexually. Like the Mystery Man, the Cowboy is also a superegoic figure because he represents a pressure to enjoy. As Lacan points out in his account of the superego, "Nothing forces anyone to enjoy except the superego. The superego is the imperative of jouissance—Enjoy!"[25] Hence, the superego places contradictory demands on the subject—at once requiring obedience to the law and enjoyment. This is why the Cowboy appears to Diane at Adam's party just at a moment when she helplessly looks on and envies those who are enjoying Camilla (right after Camilla kisses another woman and right before Adam announces their engagement). The superego capitalizes on the subject's sense that the other is enjoying in its stead, which is precisely what Diane feels in this situation.[26] The Mystery Man first appears to Fred Madison at a similar moment—at a party where he sees others enjoying his wife Renee. But the Cowboy is a much less terrifying figure than the Mystery Man. If the Mystery Man is a filmic manifestation of the superego, then the Cowboy is a lesser version.

The difference between the Mystery Man and the Cowboy attests to the association of *Lost Highway* with the structure of male subjectivity and *Mulholland Drive* with the structure of female subjectivity. For the female subject, the superego lacks the ferocity that it attains in the case of the male subject. As Freud infamously puts it, "I cannot evade the notion (though I hesitate to give it expression) that for women the level of what is ethically normal is different from what it is in men. Their super-ego is never so inexorable, so impersonal, so independent of its emotional origins as we require it to be in men."[27] Critics have, of course, often condemned Freud for this account of the superego's lack of development in women. But Freud's only mistake consists in his belief that attributing a lessened superego to women represents an ethical indictment. On the contrary, as Lacan emphasizes in his seminar on ethics (*Seminar VII*), the superego marks the point at which the subject abandons the ethical position and gives ground relative to her desire. If the male subject has a more developed superego, this testifies to his ethical failing, not his ethical purity. When we contrast the Cowboy with the Mystery Man, *Mulholland Drive* makes evident the relative timidity of the superego that Diane must face. And yet, this lessened superegoic pressure does not ease the burden of desire, as the second part of the film reveals.

By showing us a world of desire entirely separate from any fantasmatic resolution to that desire, Lynch illustrates just how unbearable the subject (Diane, in this case) finds the position of pure desire. The enjoyment that the impossible object contains seems to exist right before her eyes—in the figure of Camilla Rhodes—and yet it remains wholly out of reach. Unable to sustain her status as the subject of desire, Diane "gives ground relative to her desire," as she hires a killer to eliminate Camilla. She sacrifices the object because she cannot endure the inescapable dissatisfaction that it produces.[28] But as the conclusion of *Mulholland Drive* underlines, the subject cannot simply eliminate the object-cause of one's desire. This object is the subject's correlate. The ontological consistency of the subject's world depends on the existence of the impossible object, the object that resists integration into that world and yet sustains it with this resistance. As a result, Diane's world of desire finally breaks apart when she succeeds in destroying her love object. At the end of the film, a blue key appears on the coffee table of Diane's apartment, signaling to Diane that the killer whom she hired to kill Camilla has completed the job.

With the death of Camilla, the barrier between the world of desire and the world of fantasy collapses, and Diane's fantasy life begins to intrude into her life of desire. The intrusion occurs in the form of fantasy figures from the first part of the film. The smiling elderly couple who comforted Betty on her arrival in Los Angeles here returns to terrify Diane. The film shows the old man and woman literally crawling out of the fantasy, as they emerge in miniature from the blue box that connects the worlds of fantasy and desire. (The ferocious figure behind Winkie's has the blue box in a paper bag when the elderly couple emerges from it.)[29] In this miniature form, Lynch shows them sliding under the door of Diane's apartment. But in the subsequent shot, they appear in full size and pursue Diane into her bedroom, where she shoots herself in order to escape them. The elderly couple is so terrifying to Diane—she would rather die than endure their presence—because they belong to another world and are completely out of place. The film depicts them in such a way that their terror becomes fully evident: the comforting smiles of their earlier appearance here become sadistic, as if they are smiling at Diane's impending demise. Diane has fantasized about this elderly couple and clearly finds comfort in their fantasmatic presence. But this in no way means that she actually wants to encounter them. As Freud notes in his discussion of Dora's neurosis, "If what [subjects] long for the most intensely in their phantasies is presented to them in reality, they none the less flee from it."[30] This is what occurs with the arrival of the fantasmatic elderly couple into the world of desire. When Diane confronts them, she confronts the traumatic real that emerges from the heart of her fantasy and that triggers a breakdown of the very structure of her world. In the end, she opts for suicide rather than enduring the trauma of this encounter.

But for a final brief montage, Diane's death concludes *Mulholland Drive*. Through her suicide, the film suggests the intractability of the situation for the subject. The turn to fantasy, a gesture that promises respite from the tortures of desire, always comes back to haunt the subject. In providing an escape from desire, fantasy pushes the subject in the direction of the traumatic real. As Lynch's film shows, fantasy opens the subject to an otherwise impossible experience. Subjects often retreat from desire into fantasy, but just as often, they retreat from fantasy rather than experience the sense of loss—the encounter with the emptiness of the impossible object—with which it confronts them. But *Mulholland Drive* obeys completely the logic of fantasy. Hence, it is appropriate that a fantasy figure has the last word in the film. In the film's final shot, Lynch depicts a woman with blue hair sitting in the balcony at Club Silencio who utters the word "Silencio." The film's final word is not Lynch's warning to the spectator to abandon the illusions of fantasy. It is not a call for quiet after all the rumblings of Diane's fantasy. On the contrary, *Mulholland Drive* makes clear that it is only by insisting on fantasy to the end that one arrives at the experience of silence. This is the silence that exists between fantasy and desire—the traumatic silence of the real that the noise of everyday life always obscures.

Mulholland Drive is Lynch's most existential film. By concluding with the traumatic silence of the real, it allows the spectator to experience the moment of loss that generates subjectivity itself and yet which all the actions of the subject attempt to escape. The loss of the privileged object is the moment of the subject's birth and the moment that defines subjectivity as such. If we could sustain contact with this moment, we would free ourselves from the illusory promises of ideology and the blandishments of capitalist accumulation. We would see that enjoyment derives from not having the object rather than having and thus avoid the struggle to have more. Lynch takes us to this point of pure loss, and he does so, paradoxically, through the very fantasy that tries to escape it.

Most fantasies—and especially the mass-produced fantasies of Hollywood—fail to be fantasmatic enough because they refuse to follow their own logic to its end point. They thus never arrive at the experience of silence that concludes *Mulholland Drive*. This is precisely the shortcoming that drives Theodor Adorno's critique of Hollywood film. As he says in *Minima Moralia*, "It is not because they turn their back on washed-out existence that escape-films are so repugnant, but because they do not do so energetically enough, because they are themselves just as washed-out, because the satisfactions they fake coincide with the ignominy of reality, of denial."[31] For Adorno, Hollywood films do not fail—they are not ideological—because they go too far in the direction of fantasy but because they do not go far enough. As we have seen, *Mulholland Drive* functions as a kind of implicit response to Adorno's critique. It turns to fantasy completely—"energetically enough," in Adorno's idiom—and it demands such a response from its spectators. Subjects today have remained too removed from fantasy, resisting the experience toward which it compels them. But *Mulholland Drive*, like all of Lynch's films, calls us toward a full immersion into fantasy, toward abandoning ourselves to its logic. Only in this way can we achieve the impossible.

CONCLUSION The Ethics of Fantasy

If Lynch's films do, as I've suggested, present us with the ethical dimension of fantasy, this is not a common way of thinking about ethics. While psychoanalytically inclined thinkers have elaborated ethical positions based on desire or the drive, few have explicitly conceived of an ethics of fantasy.[1] The notion that fantasy has an ethical component seems absurd on the surface because fantasy represents a turn away from others rather than an attempt to engage them. How can I be acting ethically when I retreat into my own private construction in order to avoid the disappointments of the external world?

It is Immanuel Kant who provides the answer. Though it has been Hegel and psychoanalysis that have until this point provided the terms for my approach to Lynch, only Kant clarifies the direct link between fantasy and ethics that guides Lynch's filmmaking. This is because Kant creates the same divide in his thought between the realm of desire and the realm of fantasy that Lynch constructs in his films. This divide allows both Kant and Lynch to see how ethics might lie on the side of fantasy.

In the *Critique of Pure Reason*, Kant explores the incompleteness of our social reality (what I'm calling the realm of desire) through his analysis of human reason's limitations. Kant shows that reason cannot apply the concepts from our understanding beyond the limit of possible experience and that when it attempts to do so, it falls into antinomies. Antinomies are points at which reason arrives at two contradictory conclusions, and they testify to reason's failure to understand everything. But the limit is not just epistemological: the very existence of the antinomies indicates an incompleteness in our very reality itself that no effort of thought could remedy. As Kant argues in his discussion of the third antinomy, if we try to reason about freedom, we will inevitably fall into contradiction, proving that we are free *and*, at the same time, that causality governs all our actions. Both causality and freedom are true, but they can't both be true (which indicates that reason here oversteps its bounds, speculating beyond the field of possible experience into ultimate questions).[2] Just as Lynch's films reveal the impossible bind of a desiring subject like Diane (Naomi Watts) in *Mulholland Drive* (2001), Kant's antinomies show the powerlessness of reason to solve the most important questions. As long as we remain within the field of our social reality—on the plane of desire—we have questions without answers.

One of Kant's chief aims in writing the *Critique of Pure Reason* is to convince us to accept the limitations of reason and abandon our speculative, philosophical fantasies concerning the impossible questions that reason cannot answer. The first *Critique* is thus an anti-fantasmatic text par excellence, as Kant's language often indicates. For instance, as he argues at one point, "The Pillars of Hercules . . . were erected by nature itself in order that we pursue reason's voyage only as far as the steadily continuing coasts of experience extend; for we cannot leave these coasts of experience without venturing upon a shoreless ocean that, after offering to us outlooks forever deceptive, compels us in the end to give up, as hopeless, all our burdensome and tedious endeavor."[3] This anti-fantasmatic ethic belongs to a long tradition within philosophy, from Plato through Descartes, Spinoza, and Leibniz. According to this line of thought, eliminating fantasy allows us to avoid deceiving ourselves about the existence of a beyond; it allows us to grasp the limitations that govern our thought and our lives in order that we might fully think through our situation within those limitations. Though he never had an anti-fantasmatic attitude, Lynch began his filmmaking career with more ambivalence concerning fantasy, as we saw in the discussion of *Eraserhead* (1977), than he would have subsequently. Lynch's first feature ends with an emphasis on the destructiveness that a commitment to fantasy engenders. Like the Kant of the *Critique of Pure Reason*, the early Lynch focuses on the dangers of fantasy.

But Kant does not stop writing with the first *Critique*, just as Lynch does not stop making films with *Eraserhead*. When he composes the *Critique of Practical Reason*, Kant explores the sphere of fantasy (though he doesn't use this term) that goes beyond the limitations he outlined in the first *Critique*. In the second *Critique*, Kant locates the moral law at precisely the point of a fantasmatic beyond. Kantian ethics as it is articulated in this work marks a fundamental break from the implicit, antifantasmatic ethic of the first *Critique*. For Kant, our very ability to give laws to ourselves sticks out excessively from the phenomenal world of representation. If causality governed all events without a hitch, Kant wonders, why would a being construct laws, when their very form— you must obey regardless of what natural causes are leading you to do—suggests a freedom that defies causality?[4] Kant's great insight reverses our usual way of thinking about the relationship between law and freedom: we don't have laws because we are free; we are free because we have laws. Or, as Kant puts it, the subject recognizes "that he can do something because he is aware that he ought to do it and cognizes freedom within him, which, without the moral law, would have remained unknown to him."[5] Our ability to give ourselves laws does not fit within the world of causality and proves that another realm—a realm of freedom—necessarily exists.

Because the moral law has this excessive relation to the phenomenal world, one cannot simply see Kant as proffering two alternate and parallel modalities of subjectivity—one theoretical and one practical.[6] It is not just that we are either determined or free depending on the perspective that one takes. Instead, the two modalities exist in a dialectical relation: practical reason (fantasy) emerges in response to the failure of theoretical reason (desire). Practical reason is fantasmatic because it permits us to know the impossible—the fact of our freedom, which is precisely what theoretical reason leaves constitutively unknowable. Through the use of our practical reason, we can identify with a fantasmatic beyond—that is, embrace the moral law—and thereby transcend the limits of theoretical reason, limits which are consonant with those established by the symbolic law. It is only through fantasy that we discover freedom—or, in Kant's terms, autonomy rather than heteronomy.[7]

This is the freedom that we see Laura Palmer (Sheryl Lee) discover at the end of *Twin Peaks: Fire Walk with Me* (1992), when she acts against all pathological motivations and puts on the ring in order to defy BOB. It is the freedom that allows Alvin Straight (Richard Farnsworth) to endure multiple humiliations in order to see his brother a final time in *The Straight Story* (1999). These acts occur when subjects transcend their everyday social reality through their absolute commitment to fantasy.

There is something fundamentally liberatory in the structure of fantasy. Because fantasy stages a scene rather than providing an answer on the level of thought alone, it is able to show us what necessarily remains invisible within the symbolic structure.[8] Fantasy takes the subject beyond the rules that govern possible experience—beyond the limits of the understanding—and thereby envisions the impossible, as we have seen in each of Lynch's films. On the one hand, this image of the beyond deceives the subject into thinking that it has access to an object that it doesn't in actuality have; but on the other hand, the fantasmatic scenario allows the subject to enter a place where the ordinary rules no longer apply. By immersing ourselves in this beyond and remaining faithful to fantasy's logic, we inject, as it were, a different order of causality into the phenomenal world. It is in this sense that complete identification with the fantasy's detour has the status of an ethical act, an act in which we disregard the entire field of representation and the dictates of symbolic law.

Fantasy allows us to discover our freedom only when we cease regarding it as an escape from our reality and begin to see it as more real than our reality. The real becomes visible in the obvious fakery of the fantasy. By identifying fully with one's fantasy as what is real, one values the fantasmatic distortion in being over being itself—and thereby privileges the gap in the structure of ideology and the breach in the reign of causality. By embracing one's own fantasy publicly and giving up the idea of one's own fantasy as a private retreat from the world, one accomplishes the ethical act.[9]

Cinema is the privileged site for facilitating such acts because its very form involves the public screening of private fantasy. But in order to realize the ethics of fantasy, cinema must find a way to take fantasy to its end point. This is what David Lynch accomplishes by isolating the world of fantasy as a distinct realm within the filmic experience. He enables us to see how the insistent devotion to one's fantasy thrusts the subject into the realm of freedom. Rather than being an imaginary retreat from an unpleasant reality, fantasy becomes for Lynch the path that takes us beyond the false limitations that make up our everyday reality. Through an absolute commitment to our fantasies, we change the nature of reality itself.

NOTES

Introduction: The Bizarre Nature of Normality

1. See Rainer Maria Rilke, "The Archaic Torso of Apollo," *The Selected Poetry of Rainer Maria Rilke*, trans. Stephen Mitchell (New York: Vintage, 1989), 61–62.

2. Orson Welles and Peter Bogdanovich, *This Is Orson Welles*, ed. Jonathan Rosenbaum (New York: HarperCollins, 1992), 217.

3. For an elaboration of this idea, see Christian Metz, *The Imaginary Signifier: Psychoanalysis and Cinema*, trans. Celia Britton, Annwyl Williams, Ben Brewster, and Alfred Guzzetti (Bloomington: Indiana UP, 1982).

4. Metz, *Imaginary Signifier*, 48.

5. Laura Mulvey, "Visual Pleasure and Narrative Cinema," in Bill Nichols, ed., *Movies and Methods*, vol. 2 (Berkeley: U of California P, 1985), 307.

6. This is a point that Jean-Paul Sartre stresses in his chapter on "The Look" in *Being and Nothingness*. For Sartre, the subject cannot avoid its fundamental situatedness, which means that it cannot avoid the Other's look, which follows the subject everywhere. As Sartre puts it, "The Other is present to me everywhere as the one through whom I become an object." Jean-Paul Sartre, *Being and Nothingness*, trans. Hazel E. Barnes (New York: Washington Square Press, 1956), 373.

7. Wittgenstein makes a similar point when he insists that there is no private language. For Wittgenstein, language, with its basis in rules, depends on the existence of multiple speakers. To give a rule to oneself alone would be

nonsensical because no one could say whether one violates the rule or not. As Saul Kripke puts it in his groundbreaking work on Wittgenstein's private language argument, "all talk of an individual following rules has reference to him as a member of a community" (Saul Kripke, *Wittgenstein on Rules and Private Language: An Elementary Exposition* [Cambridge: Harvard UP, 1982], 109). Though we can use language privately, language originates as a public activity, and this public dimension continues to inform every private use.

8. Even the filmmaker who makes films just for her/himself, films never to be screened for a single spectator, nonetheless posits the nonexistent spectator in the making of the film. As is the case with the diarist, this filmmaker makes reference to the spectator or audience through the very act of turning to an inherently public medium. If one were simply making a film for oneself or writing for oneself, there would be no need for the detour through a form that others are able to comprehend. This detour testifies to the presence of the public at the heart of the most private production.

9. The test screening is the objective correlative of this dynamic; it reveals explicitly that the studios shape films according to the spectator's look. But even films that studios don't submit to a test screening (like the majority of Lynch's films) still anticipate the spectator's look in the way that they are structured. A director creates a film in order that the spectator will see it in a specific way, even if, perversely, the ultimate hope is that the spectator will despise it. Though it is structurally impossible to make a film *not* organized around the spectator's look, it is very difficult to make the spectator aware of this fact.

10. Joel Black, *The Reality Effect: Film Culture and the Graphic Imperative* (New York: Routledge, 2002), 61.

11. Bertolt Brecht, "The Epic Theatre and Its Difficulties" in *Brecht on Theater*, ed. and trans. John Willett (New York: Hill and Wang, 1964), 23.

12. Mulvey, "Visual Pleasure and Narrative Cinema," 315. Mulvey was not content simply to theorize this alternative. She also made a film, *Riddles of the Sphinx* (1977), codirected with Peter Wollen, which attempts to place the spectator in the position of "passionate detachment."

13. Metz, *Imaginary Signifier*, 3.

14. Constance Penley, "The Avant-Garde and Its Imaginary," in Nichols, ed., *Movies and Methods* 2:596 (her emphasis).

15. Instead of Godard, one might equally focus on Agnès Varda, Chris Marker, Stan Brakhage, or Chantal Ackerman, just to name a few.

16. Pascal Bonitzer, *Le champ aveugle: Essais sur le réalisme au cinéma* (Paris: Cahiers du cinéma, 1999), 91 (my translation).

17. Karl Marx, *Capital*, vol. 1: *A Critical Analysis of Capitalist Production*, trans. Samuel Moore and Edward Aveling (New York: International Publishers, 1967), 77.

18. It was Herbert Marcuse who first noticed the disconnection between belief and obedience in advanced capitalist society—an idea developed more fully by Peter Sloterdijk and Slavoj Žižek. In *One-Dimensional Man*, Marcuse laments, "The new touch of the magic-ritual language rather is that people don't believe it, or don't care, and yet act accordingly." Herbert Marcuse, *One-Dimensional Man* (Boston: Beacon Press, 1964), 103.

19. Chion's book, while full of outstanding insights into Lynch's films, never tries to bring these insights together into a coherent vision of Lynch as a filmmaker. In fact, Chion actively resists such a vision and would undoubtedly see it as a violation of the fragmented nature of Lynch's project. Žižek's book, in contrast, grasps a central idea behind Lynch's filmmaking and links it to psychoanalytic theory, but he does not extend this connection beyond *Lost Highway*.

20. Martha Nochimson, *The Passion of David Lynch: Wild at Heart in Hollywood* (Austin: U of Texas P, 1997), 13.

21. The relationship between the deconstructive attitude and sustaining distance is evident in the thought of Jacques Derrida. Deconstruction enables Derrida to avoid being pinned down to a specific philosophical position. Whenever a critic attempts to say straightforwardly what deconstruction is, the critic always gets it wrong because deconstruction has no essence; it is instead the force that undermines essence. One necessarily deconstructs from a safe distance.

22. Paul A. Woods, *Weirdsville, USA: The Obsessive Universe of David Lynch* (London: Plexus, 1997), 7.

23. The division between the worlds of desire and fantasy in Lynch's films takes place within the larger fantasy structure that is the film itself. Because he presents the world of desire within the fantasmatic medium of film, this world is necessarily a fantasized image of the world of desire.

24. Joan Copjec, *Read My Desire: Lacan Against the Historicists* (Cambridge: MIT Press, 1994), 54 (her emphasis).

25. Sigmund Freud, "Negation" (1925), trans. James Strachey, in *The Standard Edition of the Complete Psychological Works of Sigmund Freud* (hereafter, *SE*), vol. 19 (London: Hogarth Press, 1961), 237 (Freud's emphasis). The conception of a psychoanalytic normality has no direct root in Freud's own thought. Freud never upholds a certain idea of normality, even one in contrast to bourgeois normality, for fear that psychoanalysis might become a normalizing practice (as it largely became in the United States). Nonetheless, one can

construct the idea negatively on the basis of what Freud says about neurosis and psychosis. This idea of normality cannot serve as anything but a way of understanding the direction that psychoanalysis takes the subject.

26. This idea figures prominently in phenomenological film theory. As Frank Tomasulo has pointed out in his essay on the Rodney King videotape, "Human beings rarely enter a situation, historical or otherwise, with a fresh, untainted perspective. In other words, people generally do not come to believe things *after* seeing them; they see things only when they *already* believe them—based on their prior *Lebenswelt* and media exposure." Frank Tomasulo, "'I'll See It When I Believe It': Rodney King and the Prison-house of Video," in Vivian Sobchack, ed., *The Persistence of History: Cinema, Television, and the Modern Event* (New York: Routledge, 1996), 82 (Tomasulo's emphasis).

27. As Freud puts it, "both in neurosis and psychosis there comes into consideration the question not only of a *loss of reality* but also of a *substitute for reality*." Sigmund Freud, "The Loss of Reality in Neurosis and Psychosis" (1924), trans. James Strachey, in *SE*, vol. 19 (1961): 187 (Freud's emphasis).

28. For more on the cinematic deployment of desire and fantasy, see Todd McGowan, *The Real Gaze: Film Theory After Lacan* (Albany: State U of New York P, 2007).

29. To put it in the terms of Russian Formalism, *Memento* gives us a *syuzhet* (plot) without a *fabula* (story): it is impossible to construct a coherent fabula from the details that the syuzhet gives us. If one does attempt to construct a fabula (as is perhaps inevitable), the fantasmatic dimension of the exercise becomes obvious because one must clearly rely on one's own assumptions rather than on conclusive indications from the syuzhet. This suggests that the construction of a fabula as such is a fantasmatic gesture and that films which allow the spectator to decipher a coherent fabula betray an investment in fantasy.

30. This is not to say, of course, that the films contain pure representations of fantasy and pure representations of worlds wholly lacking in fantasmatic elements. Instead, in one we see the general structure of fantasy and in the other the general structure of desire. One cannot entirely separate fantasy and desire, but by establishing clear differences in the style between the two parts of the film, Lynch is able to reveal the distinct logic of each.

31. Slavoj Žižek, *Looking Awry: An Introduction to Jacques Lacan Through Popular Culture* (Cambridge: MIT Press, 1991), 6 (Žižek's emphasis). Marx makes a similar point about the relationship between desire and fantasy when he points out that, "Mankind thus inevitably sets itself only such

tasks as it is able to solve, since closer examination will always show that the problem itself arises only when the material conditions for its solution are already present or at least in the course of formation." Karl Marx, *A Contribution to the Critique of Political Economy*, trans. S. W. Ryazanskaya (New York: International Publishers, 1970), 21.

32. There have been directors who have followed Fleming's division more exactly. Both Andrei Tarkovsky in *Stalker* (1979) and Wim Wenders in *Wings of Desire* (1987) use the difference between black-and-white and color photography in the same way that Fleming does in *The Wizard of Oz*.

33. Chris Rodley, ed., *Lynch on Lynch* (London: Faber and Faber, 1997), 194.

34. In the *Introductory Lectures*, Freud says, "neurotics merely exhibit to us in a magnified and coarsened form what the analysis of dreams reveals to us in healthy people as well." Sigmund Freud, *Introductory Lectures on Psycho-Analysis* (1916–17), trans. James Strachey, in *SE*, vol. 16 (London: Hogarth Press, 1963), 338.

35. For an elaboration of this idea of the spectator conceived in terms of the theater rather than the cinema, see Walter A. Davis, *Get the Guests: Psychoanalysis, Modern American Drama, and the Audience* (Madison: U of Wisconsin P, 1994).

36. Freud defines the experience of the uncanny as the recognition of the familiar within the strange, and, according to this definition, one must count Lynch as one of the premiere filmmakers of the uncanny. See Sigmund Freud, "The Uncanny" (1919), trans. Alix Strachey, in *SE*, vol. 17 (London: Hogarth Press, 1955), 218–56.

37. One could also count Alfred Hitchcock, Andrei Tarkovsky, Alain Resnais, Wim Wenders, and Jane Campion among the filmmakers with a Hegelian orientation. Each creates distance in relation to the spectator in order subsequently to break it down. But Lynch has made this aesthetic more central and taken it further than anyone else.

38. G. W. F. Hegel, *The Phenomenology of Spirit*, trans. A. V. Miller (Oxford: Oxford UP, 1977), 14 (Hegel's emphasis).

39. Hegel, *Phenomenology of Spirit*, 200 (Hegel's emphasis).

40. Ibid., 492.

41. Just as Lynch insists on a cinematic commitment to fantasy without respite, the chapters that follow evince a similar commitment to the theoretical fantasy that makes sense of Lynch's cinema in terms of its relationship to fantasy. That is to say, at no point do I note how Lynch's films might *not* fit within this theoretical approach. I have constructed the book in this way—creating an absolute interpretation, to put it in Hegel's terms—out of the belief that only such an interpretation takes the inexplicable dimen-

sion of Lynch's work seriously by showing how it functions rather than by simply pointing it out.

42. Jacques Lacan, *Le Séminaire, livre XVII: L'Envers de la psychanalyse*, ed. Jacques-Alain Miller (Paris: Seuil, 1991), 143 (my translation).

43. By eliminating distance, Lynch's films also eliminate any sense of an objective relationship between spectator and screen. As Christèle Couleau puts it, "What is important is often less what one sees (many details remain undecidable, even image by image) than what one *believes* one sees, what one *wants* to see." Christèle Couleau, "Éloge et pouvoir de l'Absent: Sur *Lost Highway* et *Mulholland Drive* de David Lynch," *Recherches et travaux* 64 (2004): 241 (Couleau's emphasis; my translation).

1. Sacrificing One's Head for an Eraser

1. Christian Metz, *The Imaginary Signifier: Psychoanalysis and Cinema*, trans. Celia Britton, Annwyl Williams, Ben Brewster, and Alfred Guzzetti (Bloomington: Indiana UP, 1982), 91.

2. Daniel Dayan, "The Tudor-Code of Classical Cinema," in Bill Nichols, ed., *Movies and Methods*, vol. 1 (Berkeley: U of California P, 1976), 451.

3. Infinite regress is not, of course, the end of the story for Kant. The use of reason to address transcendent questions like that of the origin of the world results in dynamical antinomies where both possible answers are wrong. Reason can prove both that the world cannot have had a definite origin and that it must have originated at some point. The question of origin is thus one of the key questions for its ability to reveal the limitations of reason.

4. As Joan Copjec points out, "we are born not into an already constituted world that impinges on our senses to form perceptions, but in the wake of a primordial loss." Joan Copjec, *Imagine There's No Woman: Ethics and Sublimation* (Cambridge: MIT Press, 2002), 192.

5. Jacques Lacan, *The Four Fundamental Concepts of Psycho-Analysis*, trans. Alan Sheridan (New York: Norton, 1978), 197.

6. Lacan, *Four Fundamental Concepts*, 198.

7. Michel Chion, *David Lynch*, trans. Robert Julian (London: BFI, 1995), 35.

8. Aaron Taylor points out that Lynch's use of lighting produces partial bodies on screen. According to Taylor, "the viewer's complete attention is focussed on the bodies of the characters and how they operate in space and time. These are bodies that may be thought of as rarely complete or whole, especially considering their fragmentation by the very select pools of light which only illuminate parts of their anatomy, while blending the rest into the surrounding darkness" (Aaron Taylor, "'Rough Beasts Slouch toward Bethlehem to Be Born': *Eraserhead* and the Grotesque Infant [Whose Hour

Has Come Round at Last]," *Canadian Journal of Film Studies* 9.2 [2000]: 68). By fragmenting the body with light, Lynch creates a body of desire, a body visibly burdened by lack.

9. David Lynch, *Lynch on Lynch*, ed. Chris Rodley (London: Faber and Faber, 1977), 56.

10. Paul A. Woods, *Weirdsville, USA: The Obsessive Universe of David Lynch* (London, Plexus, 1997), 34.

11. Greg Hainge, "Weird or Loopy? Specular Spaces, Feedback, and Artifice in *Lost Highway*'s Aesthetics of Sensation," in Erica Sheen and Annette Davison, eds., *The Cinema of David Lynch: American Dreams, Nightmare Visions* (London: Wallflower, 2004), 138.

12. There is a direct parallel between the worker's sacrifice of enjoyment for the sake of the machine and the parent's sacrifice of enjoyment for the sake of the child. The machine and the child enjoy in the place of the worker and the parent. *Eraserhead* implicitly acknowledges this parallel through the link between its mise-en-scène (which provides the background of the enjoying machine) and its narrative (which highlights the presence of the enjoying baby). In each case, one sacrifices enjoyment in hopes of gaining more than one has sacrificed—in the form of either future riches or the vicarious enjoyment of the child who will have opportunities that the parent did not. As *Eraserhead* shows throughout, capitalism capitalizes on the structure of human reproduction in order to convince subjects to invest themselves in it.

13. Lacan notes that it is Marx's conception of surplus value that allows him to discover the existence of surplus enjoyment, the enjoyment that emerges in the subject after an initial sacrifice of enjoyment. See Jacques Lacan, *Le Séminaire, livre XVII: L'Envers de la psychanalyse*, ed. Jacques-Alain Miller (Paris: Seuil, 1991).

14. Sigmund Freud, *Five Lectures on Psycho-Analysis* (1910), trans. James Strachey, in *SE*, vol. 11 (London: Hogarth Press, 1957), 50.

15. Of course, the depiction of the moment when fantasy emerges in *Eraserhead* is entirely mythical. As I pointed out earlier, fantasy accompanies the experience of desire from the beginning; there is no desire without its fantasmatic supplement. But Lynch's separation of these realms has the virtue of allowing us to see more precisely what strengthens and furthers the subject's attachment to fantasy.

16. Jacques Lacan, *Le Séminaire, livre X: L'Angoisse,* 1962–1963, ed. Jacques-Alain Miller (Paris: Seuil, 2004), 89 (my translation).

17. Chion, *David Lynch*, 46.

18. Given the link between sexed reproduction and castration, it is not surprising that Lynch locates the genesis of the idea for *Eraserhead* at the time when he found out he was going to be a father.

19. G. W. F. Hegel, *First Philosophy of Spirit*, trans. H. S. Harris, in *"System of Ethical Life" and "First Philosophy of Spirit"* (Albany: State U of New York P, 1979), 233.

20. Judith Butler gives this position its most elaborate expression. See Judith Butler, "Competing Universalities," in Judith Butler, Slavoj Žižek, and Ernesto Laclau, *Contingency, Hegemony, Universality: Contemporary Dialogues on the Left* (New York: Verso, 2000), 136–81.

21. Few have probably fantasized about their heads being used as material for the production of erasers, but the structure of fantasy requires at least some type of masochistic dimension, even if it transposes this masochism into sadism. In order to access the lost object, fantasy must revisit the experience of loss, though it may do so by imposing loss on someone else.

22. Karl Marx, *The Economic and Philosophic Manuscripts of 1844*, trans. Martin Milligan (New York: International Publishers, 1964), 150 (Marx's emphasis).

23. For more on the continued presence of the demand for sacrifice amidst contemporary capitalist society and its demands that we enjoy ourselves, see Todd McGowan, *The End of Dissatisfaction? Jacques Lacan and the Emerging Society of Enjoyment* (Albany: State U of New York P, 2004).

24. When the subject makes the initial choice to enter the social order, she/he does not experience it as a free choice. It is, in Lacan's way of putting things, a forced choice, like the one that the thieves present to their victims when they ask, "Your money or your life?" The forced choice offers the subject a no-win situation in which one must choose life (the social order) in order to have anything at all. Before entering the social order, the subject is nothing, not even a subject, and thus must agree to the act of sacrifice. This sacrifice constitutes the subject as such. But the initial forced choice is not the end of the story. Because the subject continually upholds this choice by a sustained commitment to the social order, she/he can always revisit it and choose otherwise.

25. Jacques Lacan, *The Seminar of Jacques Lacan, Book XX: Encore, 1972–1973*, trans. Bruce Fink (New York: Norton, 1998), 42.

26. Lacan, *Seminar XX*, 42.

2. The Integration of the Impossible Object in *The Elephant Man*

1. Lynch and the film lost the Oscar race to Robert Redford and his first feature film, *Ordinary People*. Lynch, Christopher de Vore, and Eric Bergren also lost in the adapted screenplay race to Alvin Sargent, who wrote *Ordinary People*. Their screenplay for *The Elephant Man* was based in large part on the account of John Merrick's life written by Frederick Treves, the doc-

tor who rescued Merrick from carnival life. It was not based on the Bernard Pomerance play, which was adapted into a television movie in 1982.

2. Martha P. Nochimson, *The Passion of David Lynch: Wild at Heart in Hollywood* (Austin: U of Texas P, 1997), 141–42.

3. Lynch's focus on the warning "No Entry" echoes the opening shot of the paradigmatic film devoted to the impossible object—*Citizen Kane* (Orson Welles, 1941). Welles begins the film with a shot of a "No Trespassing" sign on the gate to the Kane estate, and the film subsequently revolves around the absent object attached to the signifier "Rosebud." In each case, the sign assists in situating the object as impossible.

4. Enjoyment is not confined to moments to when one exceeds a symbolic limit, when one transgresses, as we might expect. It is much more common for subjects to enjoy respecting the limit, even though this leaves them within the confines of the symbolic law. Enjoyment exceeds the law, but it is also the point at which the law exceeds itself, which is why one can enjoy driving 55 miles per hour every bit as much as one can enjoy driving 155 miles per hour. When one enjoys driving 55, one enjoys this excess that is internal to the law. This is what Lacan did not yet see in *Seminar VII*, where he sees transgression as the sole path to enjoyment. As he puts it there, "We are, in fact, led to the point where we accept the formula that without a transgression there is no access to *jouissance*, and, to return to Saint Paul, that that is precisely the function of the Law. Transgression in the direction of *jouissance* only takes place if it is supported by the oppositional principle, by the forms of the Law." Jacques Lacan, *The Seminar of Jacques Lacan, Book VII: The Ethics of Psychoanalysis*, 1959–1960, trans. Dennis Porter (New York: Norton, 1992), 177.

   The problem with this formulation stems from the external opposition that Lacan posits between law and enjoyment, as if one could not enjoy one's obedience. By 1972, Lacan himself senses the problem with this formulation of law and enjoyment, which prompts him to begin his *Seminar XX* with a self-critique focused on *Seminar VII*, a work that he subsequently finds rife with "stupidity."

5. In *Seminar XX*, Lacan conceives of the superego in terms of the command to enjoy. He says, "Nothing forces anyone to enjoy except the superego. The superego is the imperative of jouissance—Enjoy!" Jacques Lacan, *The Seminar of Jacques Lacan, Book XX: Encore*, 1972–1973, trans. Bruce Fink (New York: Norton, 1998), 3.

6. William E. Holladay and Stephen Watt contend that "Lynch not only thwarts Treves's desire to view Merrick but also delays satisfying the audience's similar curiosity. The film thus promises a very special gaze and then withholds fulfillment of the promise, piquing viewers' interest in the

spectacle" (William E. Holladay and Stephen Watt, "Viewing the Elephant Man," *PMLA* 104 [1989]: 874). This statement does not go far enough in its grasp of Lynch's strategy. Lynch does not delay the introduction of Merrick's body in order simply to enhance our interest in seeing it; he uses the film's form to construct this body as an impossible object that we cannot see. When we do later see it repeatedly, it is no longer *the* body.

7. Jacques Lacan, *The Four Fundamental Concepts of Psycho-Analysis*, trans. Alan Sheridan (New York: Norton, 1978), 182.

8. The initial encounter with Merrick's body is an encounter with the gaze in Lacan's strict sense of the term. The gaze, for Lacan, is not the all-seeing look of a subject that masters or controls all that it sees, as the infamous "male gaze" has been thought to do. Instead, the gaze indicates the viewing subject's failure of mastery, the moment at which the subject encounters an object in the visual field that testifies to the subject's involvement in that field through her/his desire. Encountering the gaze, the subject ceases to have a sense of safe distance from what she/he sees and the sense of invulnerability that comes from distance.

9. The two ways that Merrick appears in the film—as inaccessible object and as ordinary object assimilated into the visual field—suggest that he does not function as a figure of the sublime, though this is what we might expect given his extreme disfigurement. For Lynch, unlike a sublime figure, Merrick does not shatter the field of representation. To put it in Lacan's terms, he is not *das Ding*, the Thing embodying the ultimate enjoyment. The sublime Thing is an inescapable presence in the visual field, whereas the *objet petit a* is a constitutive absence that cannot be reduced to the visual field without becoming an ordinary object. For a contrasting reading of Merrick as the sublime Thing, see Slavoj Žižek, *Enjoy Your Symptom! Jacques Lacan in Hollywood and Out* (New York: Routledge, 1992).

10. Holladay and Watt, "Viewing the Elephant Man," 875.

11. For Martha Nochimson, the film is simply a condemnation of this fantasy for the destructive effect that it has on "Merrick's tenuous grasp on reality" (Nochimson, *Passion of David Lynch*, 143). All the characters who contribute to this fantasy are, in Nochimson's view, just as guilty as Bytes himself for exploiting and using Merrick. Merrick falls victim to these characters and the fantasy they purvey because he suffers from false consciousness. As Nochimson describes it, "suffocated by sweetness, Merrick does not even know enough about this form of abuse to protest it" (*Passion of David Lynch*, 143). The problem with this standard false consciousness thesis is that it fails to acknowledge the role that fantasy plays in structuring our very sense of reality. Fantasy does not simply prompt us to loosen our grip on reality through its inducements to enjoy, but it actually creates our sense

of reality in the first place. As a result, we cannot criticize the falseness of fantasy as if there were a true reality unadorned by it.

12. It is not enough to say that no one has a pure relation to Merrick, that everyone—both within the film and viewing it—feels at once kindly and abusively toward him. Perhaps every spectator would readily admit this compromise position. But the speculative identity of Kendal and the night porter—of Treves and Bytes—means that one must see the fundamental link between the noblest attitude toward Merrick and the basest. One must see the base within the noble and vice versa rather than seeing them as indistinctly melding into each other. In short, one must see oneself in every evil that one condemns.

13. In the *Phenomenology of Spirit*, Hegel calls the compassionate subject the beautiful soul. According to Hegel, what the beautiful soul fails to recognize about itself is that it belongs to the vicious world that it condemns. There is no condemnation that comes entirely from the outside. The beautiful soul does act, though its action takes the form of flight. Hegel claims, "It lives in dread of besmirching the splendour of its inner being by action and an existence; and, in order to preserve the purity of its heart, it flees from contact with the actual world." G. W. F. Hegel, *The Phenomenology of Spirit*, trans. A. V. Miller (Oxford: Oxford UP, 1977), 400.

14. Jacques Lacan, "Le Séminaire XIV: La logique du fantasme, 1966–1967," unpublished manuscript, session of January 11, 1967 (my translation).

15. *The Elephant Man* shows us that both castration and the fantasmatic resolution of it require some form of sacrifice. We turn to fantasy thinking that it provides a way of eluding a necessary sacrifice, but then its logic leads us ineluctably toward another sacrifice—the sacrifice of all pathological concerns for the sake of our enjoyment.

16. James R. Keller, "'Like to a Chaos': Deformity and Depravity in Contemporary Film," *Journal of Popular Film and Television* 23.1 (1995): 9.

17. One can easily imagine a Foucaultian critique of the film that attacks the reduction of Merrick's difference to the terrain of the normal. Lynch creates an image of normal subjectivity from which no one escapes. While this is undoubtedly the case, the fundamental (Hegelian) contention of the film is that there is, in the last instance, no difference between identity and difference. Thus, insisting on difference is a disguised way of insisting on identity.

18. In *The Elephant Man* and elsewhere, Lynch shows himself to be one of the great anti-Deleuzean filmmakers. Deleuze inveighs against the reduction of difference to sameness and against the attempt to see an underlying identity in difference. As he describes his project, "We propose to think difference in itself independently of the forms of representation which re-

duce it to the Same." Gilles Deleuze, *Difference and Repetition*, trans. Paul Patton (New York: Columbia UP, 1994), xix.

3. *Dune* and the Path to Salvation

1. The one voice who clearly breaks from the prevailing critical view of *Dune* is Slavoj Žižek, who, in a survey conducted by *Sight and Sound*, places the film—and no other Lynch film—on his top ten list of the greatest achievements in the history of cinema. Though many of the 253 critics, theorists, and filmmakers polled list Lynch films, no one else includes *Dune* among the best ten films ever made.

2. Erica Sheen, "Going into Strange Worlds: David Lynch, *Dune*, and New Hollywood," in Erica Sheen and Annette Davison, eds., *The Cinema of David Lynch: American Dreams, Nightmare Visions* (London: Wallflower, 2004), 35.

3. Sheen, "Going into Strange Worlds," 36.

4. Chris Rodley, ed, *Lynch on Lynch* (London: Faber and Faber, 1997), 119.

5. David Bordwell, *Narration in the Fiction Film* (Madison: U of Wisconsin P, 1985), 157.

6. For Lacan, the sexual antagonism (which has nothing to do with biology) is the primary social antagonism because it manifests the two opposed, though noncomplementary, modes of entering into language. One comes into language either as a man or as a woman, and one's sexed being attests to one's lack of completeness. But these two lacking beings cannot come together to form a harmonious one. All other social antagonisms—class, race, etc.—follow from this fundamental disjunction between the sexes.

7. Typically, the classical Hollywood narrative focuses on particular instances of the sexual and social antagonisms rather than on these antagonisms as such. But in the act of showing the possibility of overcoming particular instances of them, the narratives imply that antagonism—a constitutive split *of* the social order—is nothing but a problem to be addressed *within* this order, not a division that undermines its very coherence. This is the primary ideological function of Hollywood cinema. For instance, films often emphasize how class antagonism can be overcome through a relationship between people from opposed classes, as we see in the conclusion of a film like Frank Capra's *It Happened One Night* (1934).

8. Chani's status in the film, in contrast to her status in Frank Herbert's novel, underlines Lynch's commitment to the classical Hollywood narrative pattern in *Dune*. In the novel, Chani is a concubine, and Paul marries Princess Irulan rather than her. By eliminating Paul's relationship with Irulan,

Lynch transforms the triangular romance of the novel for the standard Hollywood coupling and concluding heterosexual union. Rather than view this as a compromise on Lynch's part, we should see how he uses it to emphasize the overcoming of antagonism.

9. The stabilizing effect of most voice-over narration becomes clear when one views the theatrical version of Ridley Scott's *Blade Runner* (1982) alongside the director's cut. Scott removes the voice-over narration in the director's cut precisely in order to undermine the stable position of the spectator that the theatrical version supports.

10. One might argue that Lynch's subversion of the mastery typically associated with voice-over narration has ties to cinema's historically patriarchal attitude toward the female voice. According to this reading, Lynch undermines the authority of the female voice-over rather than the voice-over as such. But the problem with this purportedly feminist critique is its own (patriarchal) investment in the illusory authority of the voice-over. The stability that the voice-over provides for the spectator is always false: it obscures the gaps that haunt every narrative structure and thus works to dupe the spectator concerning the truth of the narrative. The evident gaps in Irulan's voice-over testify above all to its truthfulness.

11. Slavoj Žižek, "The Lamella of David Lynch," in Richard Feldstein, Bruce Fink, and Maire Jaanus, eds., *Reading Seminar XI: Lacan's Four Fundamental Concepts of Psychoanalysis* (Albany: State U of New York P, 1995), 209.

12. Michel Chion, *David Lynch*, trans. Robert Julian (London: BFI, 1995), 70.

13. The weirding module that Paul gives to the Fremen to aid in their revolution also partakes of the fantasmatic collapse of internal and external. The weapon uses the sound created by a thought. As Paul describes it, "Some thoughts have a certain sound, that being equivalent to a form. Through sound and motion, you will be able to paralyze nerves, shatter bones, set fires, suffocate an enemy, or burst his organs."

14. When the Emperor (José Ferrer) derisively refers to the Baron as a "flying fat man," this indicates that others in the film find his flying offensive, and they do so because it acts as a public display of his private enjoyment.

15. The most telling aspect of life of Giedi Prime is the existence of the heart plug. The heart plug, installed in every citizen of the Harkonnen society, suggests the proximity between inside and outside. With one tug, all of a sudden the inside of one's body will rush out.

16. Ordinarily, unlike Baron Harkonnen, we guard carefully the private status of our fantasies so that no one else will see us enjoying. To become visible in the act of enjoying oneself is to become vulnerable. This is not a problem for the Baron, however, because enjoyment proliferates everywhere in the fantasmatic world of *Dune*.

17. The only place in *Dune* where prohibition seems to exist is on Caladan, where enjoyment appears relatively contained within stable social relations.

18. Jacques Lacan, *The Seminar of Jacques Lacan, Book VII: The Ethics of Psychoanalysis,* 1959–1960, trans. Dennis Porter (New York: Norton, 1992), 71.

19. In *Civilization and Its Discontents*, Freud ties the oceanic feeling to fantasy: he claims, "we are perfectly willing to acknowledge that the 'oceanic' feeling exists in many people, and we are inclined to trace it back to an early phase of ego-feeling." Sigmund Freud, *Civilization and Its Discontents* (1930), trans. James Strachey, in *SE*, vol. 21 (London: Hogarth Press, 1961), 72.

20. Jacques Lacan, *The Seminar of Jacques Lacan, Book XX: Encore,* 1972–1973, trans. Bruce Fink (New York: Norton, 1998), 74.

21. This is why Lacan identifies mysticism with feminine enjoyment. Mysticism, like feminine enjoyment, allows subjects to transcend their own finite subjectivity and access the infinite directly. Lacan does not make this comparison in order to impugn mysticism, to bring it down to the level of feminine enjoyment, but, on the contrary, to elevate feminine enjoyment to the level of mysticism—an authentic connection with the infinite.

4. Fantasizing the Father in *Blue Velvet*

1. Betsy Berry, "Forever, in My Dreams: Generic Conventions and the Subversive Imagination in *Blue Velvet*," *Literature/Film Quarterly* 16.2 (1988): 82.

2. Laura Mulvey, *Fetishism and Curiosity* (London: BFI, 1996), 151.

3. Slavoj Žižek, *The Art of the Ridiculous Sublime: On David Lynch's "Lost Highway"* (Seattle: U of Washington P, 2000), 45.

4. For Fred Pfeil, the idealized nature of the film's images (especially those in the opening sequence) force the spectator into a "recognition and admission of the obvious artifice" that accompanies the viewing experience (Fred Pfeil, "Home Fires Burning: Family Noir in *Blue Velvet* and *Terminator 2*," in Joan Copjec, ed., *Shades of Noir* [New York: Verso, 1993], 237). As a result, one can recognize the falsity of social convention and even of one's own desire. The film leads to the insight that "what most of us consider our deepest and strongest desires are not our own" (ibid., 238). This reading of the film focuses on the deceptive dimension of fantasy (and how *Blue Velvet* brings this deception to light), but it overlooks fantasy's revelatory power. Rather than exploring the revelations that fantasy provides, *Blue Velvet* becomes, for Pfeil, a warning about its dangers. The film thus promotes spectator distance instead of collapsing it.

5. C. Kenneth Pellow, "*Blue Velvet* Once More," *Literature/Film Quarterly* 16.2 (1988): 173. Though Pellow's attack focuses on the film's narrative inconsistencies, it is clear from his essay that the motivation for the attack lies elsewhere. Though he claims that this is not his reason for disliking the film, he does note, "The film is obscene, it does shock and disturb and revolt almost any viewer, and it does want to posit a view of humankind that most of humankind desires to reprobate" (ibid.).

6. Pellow, "*Blue Velvet* Once More," 174.

7. Slavoj Žižek, "'I Hear You with My Eyes'; Or, the Invisible Master," in Renata Salecl and Slavoj Žižek, eds., *Gaze and Voice as Love Objects* (Durham: Duke UP, 1996), 116 (Žižek's emphasis).

8. David Cronenberg's masterful *A History of Violence* (2005) is very similar to *Blue Velvet* in its structure. It depicts a fantasmatic small American town and a violent underside that threatens its idyllic space. But Cronenberg's aim is quite different than Lynch's: rather than showing the parallel between the dream world and the nightmarish underside, he wants to reveal how the dream world relies on the violence of the nightmare—specifically the violent acts of Tom Stall (Viggo Mortensen)—in order to sustain itself.

9. Jane M. Shattuc, "Postmodern Misogyny in *Blue Velvet*," *Genders* 13 (1992): 79. Adopting a slightly different position, Lynne Layton contends that Dorothy is the key figure in the film, but that on an emotional level the men have the privileged position. She says, "The dream at the center of the film is one of total possession of the mother. But here, as elsewhere in male popular culture, the emotional intensity of the film seems less focused on women, or on the relationship between women and men, than on men and their relations with each other." Lynne Layton, *Who's That Girl? Who's That Boy?: Clinical Practice Meets Postmodern Gender Theory* (Northvale, N.J.: Jason Aronson, 1998), 149.

While it is certainly true that the men in the film evince *more* emotions than Dorothy, it is not the case that their emotions are thus the central focus of the film. Dorothy is the character whose central affect—anxiety—permeates among both the other characters and among spectators. Dorothy's anxiety is more powerful than the series of emotions that Jeffrey and Frank display, and it defines the film.

10. Fredric Jameson, "Nostalgia for the Present," in *Postmodernism; Or, the Logic of Late Capitalism* (Durham: Duke UP, 1991), 294. Jameson criticizes the film for its depiction of the American small town as a bulwark under siege from a threatened nature. The problem, for Jameson, is not so much that Lynch believes in the ideal of the small town but that he cannot successfully imagine an outside. The only outside is the blind horror of nature.

11. Though the Law of the Father, for Lacan, provides the prohibition that inaugurates the subject's desire, we should not confuse Tom Beaumont with this structural function. Any actual father who attempts to take up the position of the Law of the Father will fall short, but Lynch's film gives no indication that Jeffrey's father even tries.

12. David Lynch, *Lynch on Lynch*, ed. Chris Rodley (London: Faber and Faber, 1977), 136.

13. Janet L. Preston, "Dantean Imagery in *Blue Velvet*," *Literature/Film Quarterly* 18.3 (1990): 169.

14. Lynch often lights his films leaving spaces of darkness within the image in order to convey the absence that characterizes a world of desire. The technique becomes most pronounced, as we'll see, in *Lost Highway* (1997).

15. Michel Chion, *David Lynch*, trans. Robert Julian (London: BFI, 1995), 94. Chion adds that the fantasy here is not confined to the character of Jeffrey. Even Frank Booth, seemingly a character in Jeffrey's fantasy, is enacting a fantasy scenario *for himself* in order to make sense of Dorothy's desire.

16. Berry, "Forever, in My Dreams," 84.

17. Sam Ishii-Gonzales, "Mysteries of Love: Lynch's *Blue Velvet*/Freud's Wolf-Man," in Erica Sheen and Annette Davison, eds., *The Cinema of David Lynch: American Dreams, Nightmare Visions* (London: Wallflower Press, 2004), 52.

18. Jacques-Alain Miller, "On Semblances in the Relation Between the Sexes," in Renata Salecl, ed., *Sexuation* (Durham: Duke UP, 2000), 22.

19. Chion, *David Lynch*, 94. My analysis of Dorothy and the film as a whole owes a great debt to Chion, who was the first to see the importance of Dorothy's desire for what occurs in the film. It is difficult to imagine another interpreter of the film ever surpassing the originality of Chion's insights.

20. Chion, *David Lynch*, 95.

21. Miller, "On Semblances in the Relation Between the Sexes," 17.

22. When Linda Bundtzen claims that "Lynch has erected a film that ultimately privileges the maternal over the paternal" (Linda K. Bundtzen, "'Don't look at me!': Woman's Body, Woman's Voice in *Blue Velvet*," *Western Humanities Review* 42.3 [1998]: 201), she rightly sees that Dorothy is the central figure around which *Blue Velvet* revolves, but she too quickly associates Dorothy with maternity. Maternity is not a position that Dorothy inhabits; it marks for her, as the idea of her as a mother does for others in the film, a retreat from the trauma of her desire for nothing. That the role of mother is a fantasmatic position Dorothy adopts becomes clear when we recognize, as Marcia Smith Marzec points out, that she uses the same words with Frank—"Mommy loves you"—that she uses with her

son Donny to calm him down. See Marcia Smith Marzec, "*Blue Velvet* as Psychomachia," *Journal of Evolutionary Psychology* 15.1–2 (1994): 87–92.

23. The popularity of *Blue Velvet* among Lynch's films stems almost entirely from the character of Frank Booth. Devotees of the film quote his lines— "Heineken? Fuck that shit! Pabst Blue Ribbon!" or "Don't you fucking look at me!"—rather than those of Jeffrey or even Dorothy. This indicates, as Hitchcock insists, that the villain makes the film, but it also shows that Frank's presence in the film provides pleasure rather than fear. Frank pleases us not least of all because he offers us a humorous relief from Dorothy.

24. Most fantasies distort the object through the agency of the father, who demands that this object fit smoothly within the fantasy structure. This is especially visible in the films of Steven Spielberg. In *Jurassic Park* (1993), for instance, the paternal figure Alan Grant (Sam Neill) domesticates the trauma of the encounter with the dinosaurs—and their desire—through his knowledge and courage. He makes the encounter bearable and at times pleasurable for the other characters in the film and the spectator. As long as the father remains the central figure in the fantasy, the impossible object never appears in its actual traumatic form. But *Blue Velvet* shows us what happens when the father is absent and the object appears. In this case, the emergence of the object creates a rift within the fantasy and exposes the desire of the subject.

25. Jacques Lacan, *The Four Fundamental Concepts of Psycho-Analysis*, trans. Alan Sheridan (New York: Norton, 1978), 105 (Lacan's emphasis).

5. The Absence of Desire in *Wild at Heart*

1. These are just a few of the allusions that the film makes to *The Wizard of Oz*. David Hughes counts no fewer than thirteen. See David Hughes, *The Complete Lynch* (London: Virgin, 2001), 146–47.

2. The structure of *Wild at Heart* is closest to that of *Dune* (1984): in both films, we witness enjoyment proliferating throughout the filmic world. But whereas *Dune* shows a world of desire menaced by proliferating enjoyment, this world exists in *Wild at Heart* only as a present absence. This allows the latter film to serve, in a way *Dune* does not, as a commentary on the contemporary abundance of images of enjoyment.

3. Jeff Johnson, *Pervert in the Pulpit: Morality in the Works of David Lynch* (Jefferson, N.C.: MacFarland, 2004), 104.

4. The excessive form of *Wild at Heart* bears an ultimately misleading resemblance to that of Oliver Stone's *Natural Born Killers* (1994). Though both

films criticize the contemporary proliferation of open displays of enjoyment, they do so from opposite directions. For Stone, the intrusions of private enjoyment on public space result from too much fantasy, too much engagement with media representations; for Lynch, the intrusions stem from a failure to commit fully to fantasy and to follow the logic of fantasy far enough. In this sense, any attempt to see the two films as part of a similar cinematic project would be inapt.

5. Michael Dunne notices that excess characterizes the language in the film as well. Not only do the characters use profanity excessively, but they also often speak in ways that transcend their typical modes of speech. This type of speech, according to Dunne, "serves to signal its nature as language more than as an element of character" (Michael Dunne, "*Wild at Heart* Three Ways: Gifford, Lynch, and Bakhtin," *Literature/Film Quarterly* 23.1 [1995]: 10). As a result, language itself becomes conspicuous as an excess.

6. Jana Evans Braziel, "'In Dreams . . . ': Gender, Sexuality, and Violence in the Cinema of David Lynch," in Erica Sheen and Annette Davison, eds., *The Cinema of David Lynch: American Dreams, Nightmare Visions* (London: Wallflower, 2004), 114.

7. For a complete analysis of the importance of this scene, see Slavoj Žižek, *The Plague of Fantasies* (New York: Verso, 1997), 185–89.

8. For a discussion of this change in the status of authority, see Todd McGowan, *The End of Dissatisfaction? Jacques Lacan and the Emerging Society of Enjoyment* (Albany: State U of New York P, 2004).

9. Michel Chion, *David Lynch*, trans. Robert Julian (London: BFI, 1995), 140.

10. Kenneth C. Kaleta, *David Lynch* (New York: Twayne, 1993), 166.

11. Martha P. Nochimson, *The Passion of David Lynch: Wild at Heart in Hollywood* (Austin: U of Texas P, 1997), 55.

12. Sharon Willis, *High Contrast: Race and Gender in Contemporary Hollywood Film* (Durham: Duke UP, 1997.), 143.

13. Annette Davison, "'Up in Flames': Love, Control, and Collaboration in the Soundtrack to *Wild at Heart*," in Sheen and Davison, eds., *The Cinema of David Lynch*, 121.

14. Davison, "'Up in Flames,'" 121.

15. Sharon Willis sees this scene as the ultimate instance of Lynch's racist and sexist filmic vision. She laments that because "a white man is forced to kill the black male agent of 'Mama's' murderous sexual lust . . . the brutal murder of a black man by a white man is surreptitiously charged to the white *woman*'s account" (Willis, *High Contrast*, 138; Willis's emphasis). Two aspects of the scene bother Willis most: that Lemon is the only black character and that Marietta's look controls both Lemon and the scene itself. In her analysis, Willis necessarily diminishes the importance of Sailor's over-

reaction (the brutality of the murder) and his subsequent posing (and looking at Marietta). These actions indicate the extent to which Sailor is acting out his private drama. It is from this perspective that Lemon is especially threatening as a black man and that Marietta controls everything.

16. David Lynch, *Lynch on Lynch*, ed. Chris Rodley (London: Faber and Faber, 1977), 194.

17. Lynch, *Lynch on Lynch*, 205.

18. Both Sailor and Lula are instructive for what they indicate about the appearance of lawlessness and freedom. It is always tempting to see absolute freedom in the wanton violence of the criminal or the open sexuality of the libertine, but one must interpret these guises. The examples of Sailor and Lula show how the appearance of freedom is not equal to freedom but to its opposite. Because the subject has to express itself through the signifier, it cannot simply be identical to itself. The signifier transforms appearances into their opposites, so that necessity appears as freedom and freedom appears as necessity. The subject becomes freest at the point where it recognizes the extent to which it is caught within the web of necessity.

19. Joan Copjec, *Imagine There's No Woman: Ethics and Sublimation* (Cambridge: MIT Press, 2002), 167 (Copjec's emphasis).

20. Jacques Lacan, *Le Séminaire, livre V: Les Formations de l'inconscient, 1957–1958*, ed. Jacques-Alain Miller (Paris: Seuil, 1998), 286 (my translation).

21. *Wild at Heart* has many more tangential moments than the typical Lynch film, but in each case these moments, though tangential to the narrative, fit within the film thematically. In fact, the lack of narrative coherence in a world filled with public displays of enjoyment *is* the film's central idea.

22. It might seem as if Jingle Dell is one character in the film who insists fully on his fantasy even to the point where it no longer provides pleasure. But Jingle Dell's image of Christmas lasting all year is not yet fantasy proper. Fantasy produces enjoyment by narrating the loss of the impossible object and promising access to it, but its structure is predicated on the initial loss of the object. This is what Jingle Dell refuses, and this refusal never allows the space for fantasy to develop. It is in this sense that he is the representative figure in the film. The subsequent development of a perversion is a response to a failure to enjoy, not an indication of a commitment to fantasy.

23. Lynch, *Lynch on Lynch*, 198.

24. Hughes, *The Complete David Lynch*, 142.

25. Of course, no one would say that all the threats in the contemporary world are the result of a paranoid attitude that perceives threats everywhere. There are real threats. But for the subject who is "truly wild at heart" or fully committed to its fantasy, these threats cease to matter and cease to be ubiquitous.

26. Jacques Lacan, *Le Séminaire, livre XVII: L'Envers de la psychanalyse*, ed. Jacques-Alain Miller (Paris: Seuil, 1991), 89 (my translation).

6. *Twin Peaks: Fire Walk with Me* and Identification with the Object

1. Because the show featured Laura and her murder as its structuring absence, the network's demand that Lynch and cocreator Mark Frost provide a solution to Laura's death midway through the second season effectively killed the show, according to Lynch himself.

2. Michel Chion, *David Lynch*, trans. Robert Julian (London: BFI, 1995), 155.

3. Chion, *David Lynch*, 156.

4. One should resist the idea that the many roles Laura occupies testify to Lynch's status as an ironic or postmodern filmmaker who sees identity as variable and constructed. The point is not that Laura's identity is multiple but that none of these roles capture her. Her identity cannot find adequate expression because there is nothing to express.

5. Surely one of the main reasons for the popular failure of the film rests in the way that the film treats fans of the series. By sustaining Laura as an absence, the series encourages viewers to fantasize without restraint about Laura, but the film explodes these fantasies by confronting viewers with the presence of the fantasy, forcing viewers to abandon their former ideas about Laura. The trauma for viewers is something akin to that which accompanies seeing radio personalities for the first time after a lifetime of just hearing their voices.

6. Whereas Lynch's other films confront the spectator with the speculative identity of the social reality with its fantasmatic alternative, *Fire Walk with Me* depicts speculative identity within fantasy itself, showing how the difference between our ideal fantasies and our nightmare fantasies conceals an underlying identity. By doing so, the film forces the spectator to experience the lack of an alternative within the fantasmatic alternative.

7. One famous example is Jonathan Demme's *Silence of the Lambs* (1991), in which the discovery of each victim of the serial killer Buffalo Bill is accompanied by a caption identifying the location.

8. David Hughes, *The Complete Lynch* (London: Virgin, 2001), 166.

9. Cate Racek, "Lacking Language in David Lynch's *Twin Peaks: Fire Walk with Me*" (unpublished paper).

10. Jacques Lacan, *The Seminar of Jacques Lacan, Book XX: Encore, 1972–1973*, trans. Bruce Fink (New York: Norton, 1998), 24.

11. Jeff Johnson, *Pervert in the Pulpit: Morality in the Works of David Lynch* (Jefferson, N.C.: MacFarland, 2004), 117.

12. Chion, *David Lynch*, 152.

13. Jacques Lacan, "The Signification of the Phallus," in *Écrits: The First Complete Edition in English*, trans. Bruce Fink (New York: Norton, 2006), 581. For Lacan, the phallus is not a body part, not the penis, but a signifier. But it is not just any signifier: it occupies an exceptional position among all signifiers—a position outside the signifying field where meaning derives from how each signifier relates to all other signifiers. As a signifier of exception, the phallus does not depend on its relation to any other signifier, but this means that it is a meaningless signifier, a signifier-without-signified that signifies only itself. Thus, if one reproaches Lacan for his phallocentrism (for retaining the phallic signifier at the center of the symbolic order), one must at the same time recall that the phallus stands out, according to Lacan's vision of things, for its stupidity and for its impotence.

14. When Mrs. Tremond's son appears after Leland flees from the motel where he sees Laura, we see him not only wearing the phallic mask but also jumping repeatedly as he walks in circles, mimicking the nonsensical and excessive activity that the phallus uses to disguise its impotence.

15. Diane Hume George, "Lynching Women: A Feminist Reading of *Twin Peaks*," in David Lavery, ed., *Full of Secrets: Critical Approaches to "Twin Peaks"* (Detroit: Wayne State UP, 1995), 117–18.

16. Even if one insists on the supernatural status of BOB, this in no way renders Leland free from all guilt. Through the character of Laura (who never allows BOB to inhabit her completely), the film makes it clear that human subjects have the capacity to resist BOB.

17. Fantasy does not just provide a signified for nonsensical terms like "garmonbozia." One might say that the signified itself is fantasmatic. Though we tend to identify signifiers with a specific signified, they actually acquire their signification through their interaction with other signifiers—through a system of difference. The fantasy of the signified allows us to treat concepts and things as independent of the entire system that constitutes them.

18. Jacques Lacan, *The Four Fundamental Concepts of Psycho-Analysis*, trans. Alan Sheridan (New York: Norton, 1978).

19. Lacan, *Four Fundamental Concepts*, 205.

20. Slavoj Žižek, *The Indivisible Remainder: An Essay on Schelling and Related Matters* (New York: Verso, 1996), 157 (Žižek's emphasis).

21. Žižek, *Indivisible Remainder*, 158.

22. Serge André, *What Does a Woman Want?*, trans. Susan Fairfield (New York: The Other Press, 1999), 248 (André's emphasis).

23. André, *What Does a Woman Want?*, 248.

24. Chion, *David Lynch*, 152.

25. It seems odd to say that Laura views Donna as a non-lacking Other when Laura also dismisses Donna as utterly naïve. But these two attitudes are

not at all contradictory: for Laura, Donna can avoid lack through her innocence, an innocence that would attest to the fact that she is not yet subject to castration.

26. Laura Plummer, " 'I'm not Laura Palmer': David Lynch's Fractured Fairy Tale," *Literature/Film Quarterly* 25.4 (1997): 309.

7. Finding Ourselves on a *Lost Highway*

1. Anne Jerslev, "Beyond Boundaries: David Lynch's *Lost Highway*," in Erica Sheen and Annette Davison, eds., *The Cinema of David Lynch: American Dreams, Nightmare Visions* (London: Wallflower, 2004), 155.

2. David Foster Wallace, in his discussion of *Lost Highway*, considers this possibility: "the movie's plot could . . . simply be incoherent and make no rational sense and not be conventionally interpretable at all" (David Foster Wallace, *A Supposedly Fun Thing I'll Never Do Again: Essays and Ruminations* [New York: Little, Brown, 1997], 160). According to Wallace, this is not necessarily a problem with the film. As he says, "Lynch seems to run into trouble only when his movies seem to the viewer to *want* to have a point—i.e., when they set the viewer up to expect some kind of coherent connection between plot elements—and then fail to deliver any such point" (ibid., 161; Wallace's emphasis).

3. The negative critical response to *Lost Highway* necessitated what will probably be remembered as one of the strangest advertising campaigns in the history of film advertising. Promoters of the film used *negative* comments from popular critics ("two thumbs down") in their advertisements, in an effort to transform the film's lack of acceptance among popular critics into a reason for seeing it. The fact that such advertisements appeared only a month after *Lost Highway* opened suggests that they were not part of a preconceived advertising strategy, but a response to a lukewarm and even hostile critical—and popular—reception.

4. Lynch's use of two actors playing the same role works to different ends than Buñuel's in *That Obscure Object of Desire* (1977). By having different actresses playing the same character, Buñuel emphasizes the ultimately ineffable quality of the object of desire, our inability to grasp it definitively, rather than a sharp distinction between desire and fantasy.

5. The obvious question here is "if Peter Dayton is constructed as a part of Fred Madison's fantasy, then why can everyone else see him?" The easy answer would be that what follows simply occurs within Fred's fantasy until the second transformation near the end of the film. Such an answer misses, I think, Lynch's insight here. Lynch gives Fred's fantasy a seeming reality in the film to emphasize the extent to which our everyday sense of

reality is molded by fantasy. It even shapes the way one sees one's own body—and hence the way in which that body is presented to and perceived by others. This is why the other characters in the film see a different person when Fred enters into his own fantasy.

6. Jacques Lacan, "Kant with Sade," in *Écrits: The First Complete Edition in English*, trans. Bruce Fink (New York: Norton, 2006), 652–53.

7. Martha P. Nochimson, *The Passion of David Lynch: Wild at Heart in Hollywood* (Austin: U of Texas P, 1997), 209 (Nochimson's emphasis).

8. This is why giving in to the superego is always a no-win situation. The more you give, the more it wants. The superego is, in this sense, insatiable: no sacrifice of desire is ever enough to quench its thirst. One can see this dynamic of the superego is someone like Jonathan Edwards, who never ceases upbraiding himself for the depths of his sinfulness, even though to the outside observer he is an exemplar of virtue and piety. This is not just a rhetorical flourish on his part. Edwards does feel more sinful than the average person insofar as he has given in to the superego more than the average person.

9. Slavoj Žižek, *The Metastases of Enjoyment: Six Essays on Woman and Causality* (New York: Verso, 1994), 68.

10. This is why Lacan insists that "law and repressed desire are one and the same thing" (Lacan, "Kant with Sade," 660).

11. It is only at the end of the film that the association between the Mystery Man and the videotapes becomes completely clear: we see him armed with a video camera. However, the scene at Andy's party, in which the Mystery Man shows Fred that he is inside Fred's house, gives us our first clue of the link.

12. The name "Mystery Man"—a name given only in the credits, not within the film itself—is certainly an appropriate name for the superego. It is mysterious because its prohibitions are excessive and irrational, and can never be made to make sense. Something about the superego always remains irreducible to meaning. This kernel irreducible to meaning is the enjoyment that it receives from the renunciation of desire that it commands in the subject.

13. Sigmund Freud, *New Introductory Lectures on Psycho-Analysis* (1933), trans. James Strachey, in *SE*, vol. 22 (London: Hogarth Press, 1964), 62.

14. Freud, *New Introductory Lectures*, 62. Freud, like Lynch in *Lost Highway*, gives this internalization a temporal dimension that it doesn't have to make it clear structurally. As soon as one enters into the social order and encounters the law as an "external restraint," there is always already an internalized counterpart to this external law, the superego.

15. Which is not to say that the erecting of the superego could somehow be avoided. It is the necessary accompaniment of our entrance into the do-

main of the social order and the symbolic law. However, in *Lost Highway*, the superego seems avoidable because we can see its introjection as part of a process, rather than as something that has always already occurred.

16. Jacques Lacan, *The Four Fundamental Concepts of Psycho-Analysis*, trans. Alan Sheridan (New York: Norton, 1978), 275–76.

17. By quickly passing over the trial and sentencing, Lynch makes clear that the strength of the external powers-that-be pale in comparison with the intra-psychical voice of authority. Unlike external authorities, the superego never allows the subject a moment of respite, no time when it relaxes its power.

18. Tim Lucas, "Kiss Me Doubly: Notes on David Lynch's *Lost Highway*," *Video Watchdog* 43 (1998): 31.

19. Reni Celeste, "*Lost Highway*: Unveiling Cinema's Yellow Brick Road," *Cineaction* 43 (Summer 1997): 34.

20. Though one might read (incorrectly, I think) *Lost Highway* as a critique of the turn to fantasy, it is certainly not a panegyric to "reality." Given the film's grasp of the fantasmatic basis of reality, this would be incongruous. This is the impression, however, that Marina Warner has of the film: "Lynch . . . certainly mounts an attack on film narrative's mendacity, show-ing deep alarm at its hallucinatory powers of creating alternative realities. Simultaneously, it also calls into question film's capacities to document and record: everything filmed is fabrication, but that fabrication has *the dis-turbing power to supplant reality*" (Marina Warner, "Voodoo Road," *Sight and Sound* 7.8 [August 1997]: 10; my emphasis). What Warner misses here is that *Lost Highway* is also a celebration of the way in which film sup-plants reality because in doing so, as an effect of this doubling, it provides access to an otherwise obscured real.

21. Though he is clearly an obscene, primal father, Mr. Eddy nonetheless func-tions as a symbolic authority in the film, echoing the role that Frank Booth plays in *Blue Velvet* (1986). There is a multitude of other evidence to suggest this: for instance, the scene in which he runs a motorist off the road for tail-gating and then proceeds to lecture him on the danger of not maintaining a proper distance between cars. After lecturing (and beating) the man, Mr. Eddy demands, "Tell me you're going to get a manual." Though clearly an underworld figure, Mr. Eddy functions here like a symbolic authority, an extreme version of the police. The behavior of the actual police in the film further reveals Mr. Eddy's status as symbolic authority. The police, unlike Mr. Eddy, rarely display any of the characteristics of symbolic authority. They are, instead, a parody of that authority. At one point, the police even confess their haplessness. When two detectives come to the Madison's home to investigate the appearance of the videotape depicting the inside of the home, they show themselves to be incapable of discovering anything. As

they leave, Fred thanks them (though they haven't done anything), and one detective responds, "It's what we do." Clearly, "what they do" is nothing much, in contrast to Mr. Eddy, who does *do* the only effective police work in the film (when he gives his warning about tailgating). The fact that an underworld figure is the symbolic authority in *Lost Highway* is not merely a contingent aspect of the film, but one related to the historical situation in which it appears. When the film appears, symbolic authority has gone underground, as the status of "legitimate" symbolic authorities—the police, political leaders, etc.—has eroded. *Lost Highway* is the attempt to depict how this movement of symbolic authority underground exacerbates paranoia about the Other's excessive enjoyment.

22. Jaques Lacan, *Le Séminaire, livre XXIII: Le Sinthome,* 1975–1976, ed. Jacques-Alain Miller (Paris: Seuil, 2005), 19 (my translation).

23. The nonsensical voice is a voice of pure enjoyment, because it is a voice completely stripped of meaning and thus resounds beyond the confines of the symbolic order. The voice is what remains of the signifier once meaning is subtracted from it. The type of voice Peter hears at Andy's furthers his perception of enjoyment in it. It is no coincidence that Peter Dayton, a fairly typical white male American subject, would posit this enjoyment of the voice in the exotic and foreign chants he hears upon entering Andy's house. Peter wants this enjoyment for himself, and yet posits himself culturally excluded from it. Fred Madison also has a similar relation to this "exotic" enjoyment, which explains why he plays tenor saxophone in a jazz band. Through his playing, Fred tries to approach the enjoyment of the Other which he has posited in jazz (and specifically in the jazz solo) and which he feels himself excluded from. The night when he calls home and Renee doesn't answer, he feels this exclusion from enjoyment most poignantly, and so he launches into a wild solo, attempting to capture in another direction, as it were, the enjoyment he feels he is missing with Renee.

24. This picture ends up providing additional support for the idea that Alice is a fantasy object: when, near the end of the film, the police look at the picture, they see only Andy, Mr. Eddy, and Renee—not Alice.

25. Lynch quotes himself here: as we saw, in *Eraserhead* (1977), Henry Spencer occasions a similar bright flash when he tries to touch his fantasy object, the Radiator Lady. But the car headlights shining directly into the camera in *Lost Highway* are even brighter than the vision of Henry's union with the Radiator Lady in *Eraserhead*.

26. Slavoj Žižek, *The Art of the Ridiculous Sublime: On David Lynch's "Lost Highway"* (Seattle: U of Washington P, 2000), 15.

27. The relationship between Mr. Eddy/Dick Laurent (the Father) and the Mystery Man (the representative of the superego) is made apparent at two

different points in the film. They jointly make a threatening phone call to Peter after he begins his relationship with Alice, and when Fred Madison, at Andy's party, asks Andy the identity of the Mystery Man, Andy tells Fred that he is a friend of Dick Laurent.

28. Jacques Lacan, *The Seminar of Jacques Lacan, Book I: Freud's Papers on Technique,* 1953–1954, trans. John Forrester (New York: Norton, 1988), 102.

29. Jacques Lacan, *The Seminar of Jacques Lacan, Book VII: The Ethics of Psychoanalysis,* 1959–1960, trans. Dennis Porter (New York: Norton, 1992), 177.

30. For Hegel, both art and philosophy have a clear political task: they reconcile subjects to the existing order. Despite how this sounds, such a task is fundamentally radical rather than conservative. By reconciling subjects to the existing order, art and philosophy expose the way in which all alternatives exist in the here and now rather than in a possible or imaginary future. They are implicit in the current order, already written into it and awaiting realization, though they remain hidden in the guise of possible futures. Once one recognizes this, one becomes a politicized subject. Rather than dreaming about a fantasmatic alternative, the reconciled subject works to bring it to light.

8. The Ethics of Fantasizing in *The Straight Story*

1. Many Lynch fans regarded the film as a stunt rather than as an integral part of Lynch's body of work. This was the sentiment expressed by one of the anonymous reviewers of this book, who admitted that she/he even avoided seeing the film because of its apparent lack of seriousness.

2. It is undoubtedly due to its seeming lack of fantasmatic distortion that *The Straight Story* has occasioned so little critical commentary relative to Lynch's other work, especially films such as *Blue Velvet* (1986) or *Mulholland Drive* (2001). Critics seem to have taken the title literally and accepted that the film tells a simple story that requires little to no interpretive effort.

3. Nicholas Rombes, "*Blue Velvet* Underground: David Lynch's Post-Punk Poetics," in Erica Sheen and Annette Davison, eds., *The Cinema of David Lynch: American Dreams, Nightmare Visions* (London: Wallflower, 2004), 72.

4. Jeff Johnson, *Pervert in the Pulpit: Morality in the Works of David Lynch* (Jefferson, N.C.: MacFarland, 2004), 138.

5. Johnson, *Pervert in the Pulpit,* 138.

6. The visual emphasis on Alvin's disability parallels the treatment of John Merrick (John Hurt) in *The Elephant Man* (1980). But in the case of *The Straight Story*, Lynch depicts Alvin as a lacking subject within the image

rather than, as with Merrick, depicting him as an absence irreducible to the image.

7. In the figure of Alvin, we see a subject experience the suffering that comes from being alive and from aging. Lynch shoots Alvin in a way that registers the difficulty of even simple movements, and this difficulty marks the way in which desire in its pure form appears. In *Seminar V*, Lacan claims, "Desire has an eccentricity in relation to every satisfaction. It permits us to understand what is in general its profound affinity with pain. At the limit, it is to this that desire is confined, not so much in its developed and masked forms, but in its pure and simple form, it is the pain of existing" (Jacques Lacan, *Le Séminaire, livre V: Les Formations de l'inconscient, 1957–1958*, ed. Jacques-Alain Miller [Paris: Seuil, 1998], 338; my translation). The depiction of the "pain of existing" in the beginning of *The Straight Story* demands that the spectator confront the fundamental dissatisfaction that is desire.

8. Much speculation among Lynch fans centers on the question of why the true story of Alvin Straight appealed to Lynch as a filmmaker, given how little the story itself resembles that of his other films. But what locates it firmly within Lynch's universe is the seeming impossibility of Alvin's achievement.

9. Joe Kember, "David Lynch and the Mug Shot: Facework in *The Elephant Man* and *The Straight Story*," in Sheen and Davison, eds., *The Cinema of David Lynch*, 33.

10. Fantasy renders the subject vulnerable for the same reason that it functions ideologically: while fantasizing, the subject becomes like one of the prisoners in Plato's cave, unable to turn her/his head to see what *produces* the fascinating images on the wall. One cannot see the Other as the source of what one sees, but neither can one see the Other as looking.

11. Immersing oneself in fantasy and thereby exposing oneself to possible humiliation is the ethical position that figures prominently in the films of Wim Wenders. It represents the key moment in *Paris, Texas* (1984), *Wings of Desire* (1987), and *The End of Violence* (1997), among others.

12. What makes a great political revolutionary is precisely the public insistence on a private fantasy. Such figures refuse to accept the limitations designated by the prevailing symbolic structure and insist on the impossible.

13. G. W. F. Hegel, *The Phenomenology of Spirit*, trans. A. V. Miller (Oxford: Oxford UP, 1977), 226.

14. In *Entre ses mains* (*Between His Hands*, 2005), Anne Fontaine nicely captures visually the relationship between the disposition of the subject and the degree of enjoyment she/he sees in others. On two occasions in the film,

we see women overtaken with excessive enjoyment while dancing at a club. The shots emphasize this enjoyment through wild gyrations, extreme colors, pulsating sound, and the women's eyes closed in seeming ecstasy. But after each shot depicting excessive enjoyment, Fontaine cuts to a shot of serial killer Laurent Kessler (Benoît Poelvoorde) looking at the dancers. As spectators, we initially experience the display of enjoyment in its immediacy, but the subsequent shot undermines this experience and allows us to see the mediation at work. The shot of the serial killer looking reveals that the excess resides in the look itself, not in what that look sees.

15. Typically, fantasy *produces* rather than eliminates paranoia. By narrating our loss of the impossible object, fantasy attributes this loss to an external cause that we can imagine as the thief of our proper enjoyment. Alvin's fantasy doesn't create paranoia for quantitative rather than qualitative reasons. That is, the fantasy isn't different in structure from paranoid fantasies; it is different because he commits himself to it fully, even to the point at which it becomes traumatic.

9. Navigating *Mulholland Drive*, David Lynch's Panegyric to Hollywood

1. For a detailed contrast between the film and the television pilot, see Warren Buckland, "'A Sad, Bad Traffic Accident': The Televisual Prehistory of David Lynch's Film *Mulholland Dr.*," *New Review of Film and Television Studies* 1.1 (2003): 131–47.

2. Stanley Kauffmann, "Sense and Sensibility," *New Republic* (October 29, 2001): 28.

3. Jacques Lacan, *The Seminar of Jacques Lacan, Book XX: Encore*, 1972–1973, trans. Bruce Fink (New York: Norton, 1998), 95. This idea finds an echo in the film theory of Stanley Cavell, who claims, "It is a poor idea of fantasy which takes it to be a world apart from reality, a world clearly showing its unreality. Fantasy is precisely what reality can be confused with. It is through fantasy that our conviction of the worth of reality is established; to forgo our fantasies would be to forgo our touch with the world." Stanley Cavell, *The World Viewed* (Cambridge: Harvard UP, 1979), 85.

4. For a discussion of the specifically lesbian dimension of the fantasy presented in *Mulholland Drive*, see Heather Love's excellent "Spectacular Failure: The Figure of the Lesbian in *Mulholland Drive*," *New Literary History* 35.1 (2004): 117–32.

5. The subject cannot isolate its object because this object is not the goal of desire but the cause. Desire does not come into being in response to an identifiable object; instead, it emerges as lack. As Joan Copjec points out, "Desire is produced not as a striving for something but only as a striving for something

else or something more. It stems from the feeling of our having been duped by language, cheated of something, not from our having been presented with a determinate object or goal for which we can aim. Desire has no content—it is for nothing—because language can deliver to us no incontrovertible truth, no positive goal." Joan Copjec, *Read My Desire: Lacan Against the Historicists* (Cambridge: MIT Press, 1994), 55.

6. Jacques Lacan, *Le Séminaire, livre X: L'Angoisse,* 1962–1963, ed. Jacques-Alain Miller (Paris: Seuil, 2004), 98 (my translation).

7. Bruce Fink, *A Clinical Introduction to Lacanian Psychoanalysis: Theory and Technique* (Cambridge: Harvard UP, 1997), 61.

8. Jacques Lacan, *The Four Fundamental Concepts of Psycho-Analysis,* trans. Alan Sheridan (New York: Norton, 1978), 270.

9. Fink, *Clinical Introduction,* 60.

10. In *Seminar XI,* Lacan draws attention to this movement around the object that desire performs, a movement he associates with desire's manifesting itself in the drive. He says, "It is not that desire clings to the object of the drive—desire moves around it, in so far as it is agitated in the drive." Lacan, *Four Fundamental Concepts,* 243.

11. At this point, we might read Lynch's revelation of the fantasmatic dimension of temporality as a gloss on Kant's *Critique of Pure Reason.* According to Kant, the foundation for all experience lies in the subject's grasp of events in temporal succession, as necessarily linked with one another. Experience as such thus depends on the subject existing in a unified time. But *Mulholland Drive* suggests that the temporality of the subject is not primary—not inherent to subjectivity as such—but the result of the subject's turn to fantasy. The subject experiences temporality as it chooses to immerse itself in fantasy. In this sense, the film doesn't disprove Kant, but it does indicate that temporality is not constitutive for the human subject but the result of a fantasmatic retreat from repetition.

12. Slavoj Žižek, *The Plague of Fantasies* (New York: Verso, 1997), 10–11 (Žižek's emphasis).

13. It is not at all coincidental that Rita takes her name from a *Gilda* movie poster. As Gilda, Rita Hayworth was clearly a fantasy object, testified to by her famous declaration that in her relations with men they go to bed with Gilda and wake up with Rita Hayworth.

14. The structure of the audition itself is highly fantasmatic: the producer welcomes Betty warmly to the audition, asks her if she wants something to drink, and works hard to make her feel comfortable. There are eight people in the room during the audition, including an agent who immediately takes Betty under her wing. In actuality, of course, auditions for new actors trying out for their first part are rarely so accommodating.

15. Lacan, *Seminar XX*, 66.

16. Slavoj Žižek, *Tarrying with the Negative: Kant, Hegel, and the Critique of Ideology* (Durham: Duke UP, 1994), 117.

17. On this point, one should contrast *Mulholland Drive* with Andy and Larry Wachowski's neo-noir *Bound* (1996). *Bound* places a woman in the position of the traditional noir hero and transforms the heterosexual noir relationship into a lesbian one. The result is that the sexual relationship between the noir hero, Corky (Gina Gershon), and the femme fatale, Violet (Jennifer Tilly), succeeds, whereas in traditional film noir it always runs aground (or succeeds through the hero's taming the femme fatale, as in Robert Montgomery's *Lady in the Lake* [1947]). That the film is conscious of this becomes evident in the final lines exchanged between the women: Corky asks Violet, "You know what the difference is between you and me, Violet?" Violet says, "No." Corky responds, "Me neither." At this point, the two drive away together in a shiny new pickup truck, and the film ends. The concluding dialogue suggests that, unlike the relationship between the *male* noir hero and the femme fatale, the relationship between the female noir hero and the femme fatale encounters no structural stumbling block. The problem with this characterization is that it dooms the lesbian relationship to lovelessness. We only love in response to the failure of the sexual relationship. As Lacan puts it, "What makes up for the sexual relationship is, quite precisely, love" (Lacan, *Seminar XX*, 45). If this relationship comes off successfully (as *Bound* insists that it does), then no love can emerge.

18. One of the key political features of every Lynch film is the insistence on the failure of the sexual relation. When it does seem to succeed, as in *Blue Velvet* or *Wild at Heart*, the film clearly designates the relation as fantasmatic. This rejection of the successful sexual relation stands out because, as Raymond Bellour points out, the fundamental ideological function of cinema is the production of this relation in the form of the diegetic couple. According to Bellour, "The configuration determined by the image of the diegetic couple remains absolutely central to the fiction of a cinema powerfully obsessed by the ideology of the family and of marriage, which constitutes its imaginary and symbolic base." Raymond Bellour, "A Bit of History," trans. Mary Quaintance, in Constance Penley, ed., *The Analysis of Film* (Bloomington: Indiana UP, 2000), 14.

19. Jacques Lacan, "La Logique du Fantasme," *Autres Écrits* (Paris: Seuil, 2001), 326, my translation.

20. Alenka Zupančič, *Ethics of the Real: Kant, Lacan* (New York: Verso, 2000), 232.

21. The difference between male and female fantasy structure echoes the difference between Kantian and Hegelian epistemology. For Kant, the thing

in itself—the real—remains always outside of the subject's grasp and beyond the field of its knowledge. That is to say, the thing in itself is always and necessarily futural. Hegel, on the other hand, sees the thing in itself as part of the subject's experience that the subject has yet to recognize as its own. As in male fantasy, Kant theorizes the subject approaching the experience of the real but never arriving at it, while Hegel, following the logic of female fantasy, theorizes the subject as having always already had the experience of the real.

22. This is the second time that a character lip-syncs a Roy Orbison song in a Lynch film, the first being, of course, Dean Stockwell's famous rendition of "In Dreams" in *Blue Velvet*. Both performances occur at the heart of a fantasy space, at the edge of an encounter with a disturbing real. It is almost as if Orbison's music combines perfectly, for Lynch, the nostalgic bliss of the fantasy world *and* its underlying horror.

23. Juan-David Nasio, *Five Lessons on the Psychoanalytic Theory of Jacques Lacan*, trans. David Pettigrew and François Raffoul (Albany: State U of New York P, 1998), 103.

24. Elizabeth Cowie suggests this double role of fantasy when she points out, "Fantasy, in imagining enjoyment without loss, always posits a loss already enacted to which it answers." Elizabeth Cowie, *Representing the Woman: Cinema and Psychoanalysis* (Minneapolis: U of Minnesota P, 1997), 299.

25. Lacan, *Seminar XX*, 3.

26. In her fantasy, Diane compounds Adam's difficulties by burdening him with the demands of this superegoic figure, who pressures him to submit to the dictates of the mob and to hire Camilla Rhodes for his film, in order that he might reap the benefits of this capitulation. Here, we see the traditional role of the superego, offering enjoyment in exchange for submission.

27. Sigmund Freud, "Some Psychical Consequences of the Anatomical Distinction Between the Sexes" (1925), trans. James Strachey, in *SE*, vol. 19 (London: Hogarth Press, 1961), 257.

28. If, as I am suggesting, *Mulholland Drive* represents Lynch's most overtly feminist film, it also represents, at the same time, his least romanticized vision of femininity. In this way, the film challenges Martha Nochimson's characterization of the feminine in Lynch's work. According to Nochimson, Lynch identifies femininity with receptivity and the ability to cede control, and, in contrast to most filmmakers, he embraces these qualities. She claims, "The imbalance of value on force to the exclusion of receptivity—often equated with weakness—biases the culture and the movies against much that is associated with women's wisdom. Lynch's belief that the real requires a balance between force and receptivity suspends the usual exclusion of women from centers of cultural and narrative im-

portance. In his films, the hero must get in touch with—or be—what has been excluded when the conventional Hollywood hero 'takes control'" (Martha P. Nochimson, *The Passion of David Lynch: Wild at Heart in Hollywood* [Austin: U of Texas P, 1997], 11). But in *Mulholland Drive*, it is clear that the feminine is not "receptivity" but a desire every bit as horrific and destructive as its male counterpart (such as that of Fred Madison).

29. At the point of intersection between the worlds of fantasy and desire, we see a figure of unrestrained and horrifying enjoyment, whom Lynch shows existing behind the diner Winkie's. This figure embodies the real, and as such, one cannot endure his presence even for an instant, as we see when a man coming out of Winkie's collapses immediately upon seeing him.

30. Sigmund Freud, *Fragment of an Analysis of a Case of Hysteria* (1905), trans. James Strachey, in *SE*, vol. 7 (London: Hogarth Press, 1953), 110.

31. Theodor W. Adorno, *Minima Moralia: Reflections from Damaged Life*, trans. E. F. N. Jephcott (New York: Verso, 1978), 202.

Conclusion: The Ethics of Fantasy

1. In *Seminar VII*, Lacan conceives of ethics in terms of the relation that one adopts toward one's desire. As Lacan sees it, by refusing to give ground relative to one's desire, one sustains an ethical position because one does not give in to the demands of an oppressive social law. Slavoj Žižek, on the other hand, attempts to align ethics with the drive and its incessant repetition of a failed encounter. Because of its devotion to the lost cause, to what the social order has repressed, he claims that *"the status of the drive itself is inherently ethical."* Slavoj Žižek, *For They Know Not What They Do: Enjoyment as a Political Factor* (London: Verso, 1991), 272 (Žižek's emphasis).

2. Kant enumerates four antinomies of pure reason and divides them into two distinct forms—mathematical and dynamic. In the case of the former, reason fails because both solutions are false, and in the case of the latter, reason fails because both solutions are truth.

3. Immanuel Kant, *Critique of Pure Reason*, trans. Werner S. Pluhar (Indianapolis: Hackett, 1996), 418.

4. One might contend, of course, that laws are simply illusions that we construct in order to convince ourselves that we are free and that they prove nothing about our actual freedom. But this response to Kant still can't explain why laws emerge in the first place, why the deception would ever come into being. The very emergence of the law itself testifies to something that disrupts the order of causality from within.

5. Immanuel Kant, *Critique of Practical Reason*, in *Practical Philosophy*, trans. and ed. Mary J. Gregor (New York: Cambridge UP, 1996), 163–64.

6. The idea that Kant presents two competing modalities of subjectivity is the dominant understanding of the relation between the first and second *Critique*. For a compelling elaboration of this conception, see Christine M. Korsgaard, *Creating the Kingdom of Ends* (Cambridge: Cambridge UP, 1996).

7. Unlike Lynch, after discovering the link between fantasy and freedom through the separation of the realms of desire and fantasy, Kant fails to see the ultimate identity of these realms. He fails, in other words, to grasp the speculative identity of theoretical and practical reason. This is the step that Fichte and Hegel accomplish: they understand that the fantasy world of practical reason is the truth of theoretical reason rather than simply being an alternative to it. The solution that practical reason provides for the impasses of theoretical reason is already written into the structure of theoretical reason, which means that we never engage the world as purely theoretical subjects but always through the distorting influence of practical reason. This is an insight that Lynch brings to each of his films, and it allows him to use the Kantian separation into opposing realms of desire and fantasy to illustrate the Hegelian identity within opposition.

8. It is not coincidental that the *Critique of Pure Reason* relies almost entirely on argumentation alone, while the crucial points in the *Critique of Practical Reason* involve the use of fanciful examples. In order to prove that we are free in the latter text, Kant constructs two scenarios in which the subject breaks from the natural causality of self-interest through the intervention of law.

9. Kant identifies freedom and the ethical act. It is our capacity for ethical acts that proves to us that we are free, and it is only in ethical acts that we truly affirm our autonomy. Even though the free subject could choose not to act ethically, the decision not to do so would actually attest to the influence of pathological factors and thus to a lack of freedom.

INDEX

Brecht, Bertolt, 5–6, 8–10
Brooks, Mel, 49
Buckland, Warren, 252n
Bundtzen, Linda, 240n
Buñuel, Luis: *That Obscure Object of Desire*, 246n

Cameron, James: *Titanic*, 21
Campion, Jane, 229n
Canal+, 194
Cannes Film Festival, 11, 110, 129
Capra, Frank: *It Happened One Night*, 236n
Les Carabiniers. See Godard, Jean-Luc
Cavell, Stanley, 252n
castration, 27, 40–45, 96, 98, 120, 126, 170, 185–86, 231n , 235n, 246n
Celeste, Reni, 167
Chion, Michel, 11, 33, 40, 78, 98, 100–101, 116, 130–31, 140, 150, 227n, 240n
Christianity, 153
Citizen Kane. See Welles, Orson
commodity fetishism, 9, 28
Contempt. See Godard, Jean-Luc
Copjec, Joan, 14, 122, 230n, 252–53n
Cowie, Elizabeth, 255n
Couleau, Christèle, 230n
Cronenberg, David: *A History of Violence*, 239n

Davis, Walter, 229n
Davison, Annette, 117
Dayan, Daniel, 28
death drive, 123, 202, 220, 253n, 256n. *See also* Lynch, David (*Twin Peaks: Fire Walk with Me*)
deconstruction, 12, 30, 227n
De Laurentiis, Dino, 68
Deleuze, Gilles, 235–36n

Del Rio, Rebekah, 214
Demme, Jonathan: *Silence of the Lambs*, 244n
Derrida, Jacques, 227n
Descartes, René, 221
desire, 2, 4, 9, 13–18, 220, 228n. *See also* Lynch, David
De Vore, Christopher, 232–33n
Double Indemnity. See Wilder, Billy
drive. *See* death drive
Dune (film). *See* Lynch, David
Dune (novel). *See* Herbert, Frank
Dunne, Michael, 242n

Edwards, Jonathan, 247n
ego ideal, 4, 206
The Elephant Man. See Lynch, David
The End of Violence. See Wenders, Wim
Entre ses mains. See Fontaine, Anne
Eraserhead. See Lynch, David
Extreme Makeover (television series), 22

fantasy, 6, 8–10, 15–18, 228n. *See also* Lynch, David
feminine enjoyment. *See Dune*; Lacan, Jacques; *Twin Peaks: Fire Walk with Me*
femme fatale, 17–18, 254n
Fichte, Johann, 257n
Fink, Bruce, 198, 200
film noir, 17, 75, 254n
Fleming, Victor: *The Wizard of Oz*, 18–19, 110–11, 118–19, 126, 229n, 241n
Fontaine, Anne: *Entre ses mains* (*Between His Hands*), 251–52n
Ford, John: *Stagecoach*, 70–71
Foucault, Michel, 235n
Freud, Sigmund, 4, 15, 20, 25, 38, 83,

98, 123, 148, 162, 174, 216, 218,
227–28n, 229n, 238n, 247n
Frost, Mark, 194, 244n

Garden of Eden, 15
George, Diane Hume, 143–44
Gifford, Barry: *Night Moves*, 154; *Wild at Heart* (novel), 125, 154
Gilda, 205, 253n
Godard, Jean-Luc, 5, 7–9, 11–12; *À Bout de soufflé* (*Breathless*), 8; *Les Carabiniers* (*The Riflemen*), 8; *Le Mépris* (*Contempt*), 8; *Pierrot le fou*, 8; *Vivre sa vie* (*My Life to Live*), 8; *Week End*, 8
The Grandmother. See Lynch, David

Hainge, Greg, 35
Hayworth, Rita, 253n
Hegel, G. W. F., 41, 153, 220, 229n, 235n, 250n, 254–55n; and the beautiful soul, 235n; and the law of the heart, 190; and speculative identity, 23–24, 257n
Heidegger, Martin, 32
Herbert, Frank: *Dune* (novel), 68
A History of Violence. See Cronenberg, David
Hitchcock, Alfred, 94, 229n, 241n
Holladay, William, 233–34n
Hollywood film, 2, 4, 5, 8, 11–12, 20–21, 27, 28, 46, 49, 64, 68–72, 81, 86, 125, 167, 191, 195–97, 202, 210, 219
Hughes, David, 125, 137, 241n

ideal ego, 166, 200, 207
identification, 2, 5–7, 166, 214
imaginary, 2, 5–7, 15, 16, 107, 121–22, 125, 160, 166, 168, 174, 209, 224, 254n
"In Dreams." *See* Orbison, Roy

Ishii-Gonzales, Sam, 98–99
The Island. See Bay, Michael
It Happened One Night. See Capra, Frank

Jameson, Fredric, 95, 239n
Jenkins, Patty: *Monster*, 5
Jerslev, Anne, 155
Johnson, Jeff, 113, 140, 178, 193
Jurassic Park. See Spielberg, Steven

Kaleta, Kenneth, 116
Kansas, 13, 18, 111
Kant, Immanuel, 29, 220–22, 230n, 253n, 254–55n, 256–57n
Kauffmann, Stanley, 195
Keller, James, 66
Kember, Joe, 184
King, Rodney, 228n
Korsgaard, Christine, 257n
Kripke, Saul, 226n
Kubrick, Stanley, 49

Lacan, Jacques, 6, 48, 101, 174, 232n; and antagonism, 236n; and *das Ding*, 82–84, 234n; and death drive, 146; and the gaze, 107, 234n; and feminine enjoyment, 86, 238n; and the lamella, 31–32; and the Law of the Father, 240n; and the *objet petit a*, 51; and the phallus, 142, 245n; and the real, 9, 25, 211; and the sexual relationship, 208, 254n; and the superego, 173, 216, 233n; and surplus enjoyment, 231n; and the theory of desire, 14, 54, 123, 159, 163, 170, 197, 200, 247n, 251n, 253n, 256n; and the theory of enjoyment, 127, 140, 233n; and the theory of fantasy, 39, 66, 196, 211

New York City, 13, 49

Night Moves. See Gifford, Barry

Nochimson, Martha, 11, 50, 116, 118, 160, 234–35*n*, 254–55*n*

Nolan, Christopher: *Memento*, 16–17, 228*n*

normality, 13–16, 227–28*n*. *See also* Lynch, David

objet petit a, 53, 55–56, 64, 104, 107, 130, 139, 207. *See also* Lacan, Jacques

Oedipus, 72

Orbison, Roy: "Crying," 214; "In Dreams," 104, 255*n*

Ordinary People. See Redford, Robert

Paramount, 49

paranoia, 41, 124, 190, 243*n*, 252*n*. *See also The Straight Story*

Paris, Texas. See Wenders, Wim

Pellow, C. Kenneth, 92, 239*n*

Penley, Constance, 7

Pfeil, Fred, 238*n*

phallus, 85–86, 142–43, 147–50, 153, 169–70. *See also* Lacan, Jacques

phenomenology, 228*n*

phrenology, 23–24

Pierrot le fou. See Godard, Jean-Luc

Plato, 221, 251*n*

Plummer, Laura, 152

Pomerance, Bernard, 233*n*

Powermad: "Slaughterhouse," 117–19

Preston, Janet, 96–97

Pretty Woman. See Marshall, Garry

psychoanalytic film theory, 3

psychosis, 16, 228*n*

Racek, Cate, 139–40

Redford, Robert: *Ordinary People*, 232–33*n*

Republican National Committee, 178, 193

Resnais, Alain, 229*n*

Riddles of the Sphinx. See Mulvey, Laura

The Riflemen. See Godard, Jean-Luc

Rilke, Rainer Maria: "The Archaic Torso of Apollo," 1

Rombes, Nicholas, 178

Romeo and Juliet. See Shakespeare, William

Russian formalism, 228*n*

sadism, 232*n*

Sargent, Alvin, 232–33*n*

Sartre, Jean-Paul, 225*n*

Saturday Night Fever. See Badham, John

Schindler's List. See Spielberg, Steven

Scott, Ridley: *Blade Runner*, 237*n*

Shakespeare, William, 1; *Romeo and Juliet*, 57

Sheen, Erica, 69

Silence of the Lambs. See Demme, Jonathan

Six Figures Getting Sick. See Lynch, David

"Slaughterhouse." *See* Powermad

Sloterdijk, Peter, 227*n*

speculative identity, 61, 67, 89, 128, 175–76, 235*n*, 244*n*. *See also* Hegel, G. W. F.

Spheeris, Penelope: *Wayne's World*, 10

Spielberg, Steven: *Jurassic Park*, 241*n*; *Schindler's List*, 5

Spinoza, Baruch, 221

Stagecoach. See Ford, John

Star Trek, 68

Star Wars. See Lucas, George

The Straight Story. See Lynch, David

Stalker. See Tarkovsky, Andrei

Stone, Oliver: *Natural Born Killers*, 241–42*n*
Stockwell, Dean, 255*n*
superego, 52, 76, 115, 247–48*n*, 255*n*. *See also* Lacan, Jacques; *Lost Highway*; *Mulholland Drive*
surplus enjoyment, 4. *See also* Lacan, Jacques
surplus value, 36
Sweeney, Mary, 177
symbolic law, 81, 103, 121, 143, 223
symbolic order, 6–7, 25, 86, 122, 210, 215, 249*n*

Tarkovsky, Andrei, 229*n*; *Stalker*, 229n
Taylor, Aaron, 230–31*n*
That Obscure Object of Desire. See Buñuel, Luis
Titanic. See Cameron, James
Tomasulo, Frank, 228*n*
Total Recall. See Verhoeven, Paul
Travolta, John, 13
Treves, Frederick, 232–33*n*
Twin Peaks (television series). *See* Lynch, David
Twin Peaks: Fire Walk with Me. See Lynch, David
"Twin Peaks Theme." *See* Badalamenti, Angelo

Varda, Agnès, 226*n*
Verhoeven, Paul: *Total Recall*, 88
Virgil, 29, 75

Vivre sa vie. See Godard, Jean-Luc
"the voice." *See Dune*; *Lost Highway*
voyeurism, 3–4, 6

Wachowski, Andy: *Bound*, 254*n*
Wachowski, Larry: *Bound*, 254*n*
Wallace, David Foster, 246*n*
Wall Street Journal, 13
Warner, Marina, 248*n*
Waters, John, 49
Watt, Stephen, 233–34*n*
Wayne's World. See Spheeris, Penelope
Week End. See Godard-Jean-Luc
Welles, Orson, 1; *Citizen Kane*, 233*n*
Wenders, Wim, 229*n*; *Paris, Texas*, 251*n*; *Wings of Desire*, 229*n*, 251*n*; *The End of Violence*, 251*n*
Willis, Sharon, 117, 242–43*n*
Wild at Heart. See Lynch, David
Wild at Heart (novel). *See* Gifford, Barry
Wilder, Billy: *Double Indemnity*, 17–18
Wings of Desire. See Wenders, Wim
The Winslow Boy. See Mamet, David
Wittgenstein, Ludwig, 225–26*n*
The Wizard of Oz. See Fleming, Victor
Wollen, Peter: *Riddles of the Sphinx*, 226*n*
Woods, Paul, 13, 34

Žižek, Slavoj, 11, 76, 91, 92, 147–148, 161, 202, 209, 227*n*, 236*n*, 242*n*, 256*n*